Revisiting Sol Plaatje's Mafeking Diary
Reconsideration and Restoration

First published by Jacana Media Pty (Ltd) in 2023

10 Orange Street
Sunnyside
Auckland Park 2092
South Africa
+2711 628 3200
www.jacana.co.za

© Individual contributors, 2023

All rights reserved.

ISBN 978-1-4314-3429-9

Cover design by publicide
Cover image: Molema/Plaatje Papers, Wits University Historical Papers, UW A979-Fca2
Editing by Russell Martin
Proofreading by Adam Potterton
Set in Ehrhardt 11.5/15.5pt
Printed by Creda Communications, Cape Town
Job no. 004085

See a complete list of Jacana titles at www.jacana.co.za

Revisiting Sol Plaatje's Mafeking Diary
Reconsideration and Restoration

Edited by

Sabata-mpho Mokae
and
Brian Willan

Contents

	Contributors	vii
	Introduction	1
1.	Re(dis)covering the Extraordinary: A Reflection, 50 Years On *John Comaroff*	17
2.	Sol Plaatje's Mafeking Pen and a New Imagining of the Anglo-Boer War *Bill Nasson*	31
3.	Writing under Siege: Reading Plaatje's Mafeking Diary 120 Years Later *Kevin Davie*	43
4.	The Missing Pages *Siphiwo Mahala*	57
5.	The Music of 'Au Sanna' *Laurence Wright*	67
6.	The Personal Thoughts of Two Black Britons? Comparing Sol Plaatje's Diary with Tiyo Soga's Journal *Vivian Bickford-Smith*	87
7.	'Part of a Longer Story': The Sieges of Mafeking 1882 and 1899–1900 Compared *Andrew Manson*	101

8.	The Interpreter	
	Andries Walter Oliphant	117
9.	Sol Plaatje's Diary and African Views of the Pax Britannica	
	Stephen Volz	133
10.	Past and Present in Sol Plaatje's Mafeking Diary: The Making of a Diarist	
	Brian Willan	145
11.	The Mafeking Diary of Sol Plaatje and the History of Literary Journalism in South Africa	
	Lesley Mofokeng	159
12.	The Heart Goes After Whom It Loves	
	Sabata-mpho Mokae	175
	Acknowledgements	185
	Notes	187
	Index	211

Contributors

Vivian Bickford-Smith is Extraordinary Professor in the History Department at Stellenbosch University and Emeritus Professor in Historical Studies at the University of Cape Town. Much of his work has been on modern South African history, especially urban history, racial and ethnic identity, and the relationship between film and history. His publications include *Ethnic Pride and Racial Prejudice in Victorian Cape Town*; *Cape Town: The Making of a City*; *Cape Town in the Twentieth Century*; *Black and White in Colour: The African Past on Screen*; *The Emergence of the South African Metropolis: Cities and Identities in Twentieth Century South Africa*; and *Illuminating Lives*.

John Comaroff is Hugh K. Foster Professor of African and African American Studies and of Anthropology, and an Oppenheimer Research Fellow, at Harvard University. His authored and edited books include, with Jean Comaroff, *Of Revelation and Revolution* (two vols.); *Ethnography and the Historical Imagination*; *Modernity and its Malcontents*; *Civil Society and the Political Imagination in Africa*; *Millennial Capitalism and the Culture of Neoliberalism*; *Law and Disorder in the Postcolony*; *Ethnicity, Inc.*; *Theory from the South: or, How Euro-America Is Evolving toward Africa*; *The Truth about Crime*; and *The Politics of Custom: Chiefship, Capital, and the State in Contemporary Africa*.

Kevin Davie has been a journalist for 40 years, mostly in financial journalism, for leading South African newspapers. A Nieman Fellow at Harvard, he co-founded South Africa's first online stockbroker and online-only news portal Woza. Davie taught economics journalism for 12 years at the University of the Witwatersrand, where he is now a research associate. He co-led a narrative non-fiction stream where 25 students completed long-form theses as part of their MA requirements. Davie has published numerous such pieces himself, sometimes written from the seat of a bicycle.

Siphiwo Mahala is an author, playwright and academic. His debut novel, *When a Man Cries*, was published in 2007. He is the author of two short-story collections, *African Delights* and *Red Apple Dreams and Other Stories*, and two critically acclaimed plays, *The House of Truth* and *Bloke and His American Bantu*. His latest book, *Can Themba: The Making and Breaking of the Intellectual Tsotsi*, offers the most definitive study of Can Themba's life history. He is a Senior Lecturer at the University of Johannesburg, Senior Fellow at the Johannesburg Institute for Advanced Study, and editor of *Imbiza Journal for African Writing*.

Andy Manson is a Research Fellow at the University of South Africa (Unisa). Formerly he was Professor of History at North-West University (Mafikeng Campus), a position he held until 2005. Subsequently he taught at the universities of Rhodes and Fort Hare before returning to North-West University in Mafikeng as a Research Professor. He has published extensively on Batswana societies in the western Highveld (today's North West province). His significant publications include *'People of the Dew': A History of the Bafokeng of the Rustenburg District of South Africa, from Early Times to 2020*, and *Land, Chiefs, Mining: South Africa's North West Province since 1840*, both with B. Mbenga.

Lesley Mofokeng is an Associate Lecturer in the Journalism Department of the University of the Witwatersrand, where he is also a PhD candidate. His thesis is on the contribution Sol Plaatje made to South African journalism, studying the newspapers Plaatje edited from 1901 to 1915, namely *Koranta ea Becoana*, *Tsala ea Becoana* and *Tsala ea Batho*. Mofokeng has presented papers on Plaatje twice at the International Association of Literary Journalism Studies. He is a former journalist who worked for the titles *Sunday Times*, *City Press* and *Sowetan*. He has authored several biographies and his latest book, *The Man Who Shook Mountains*, is an adaptation of his master's dissertation.

Sabata-mpho Mokae teaches Creative Writing in African Languages at Sol Plaatje University in Kimberley. He is the author of a biography, *The Story of Sol T. Plaatje* (2010), and the novels *Ga ke Modisa*, *Dikeledi* and *Moletlo wa Manong*. He is a co-editor, alongside Professor Brian Willan, of two academic books, *Sol T. Plaatje: A Life in Letters* and *Sol Plaatje's Mhudi: History, Criticism, Celebration*. He is the recipient of the M-Net Literary Award for Best Setswana Novel (2013), M-Net Film Award (2013), Humanities and Social Sciences Award (2021), the South African Literary Award (2011, 2019 and 2021) and PanSALB Multilingualism Award (2022). In 2014 he was a Writer-in-Residence at the University of Iowa in the United States, where he was subsequently awarded a fellowship. He is an affiliate of the Tsikinya-Chaka Centre at Wits University.

Bill Nasson was born in Cape Town in 1952, where he survived schooling before being educated in England at the universities of Hull, York and Cambridge. He lectured in economic history and in history at the University of Cape Town for many years before a twilight stint at Stellenbosch University, where he is Emeritus Professor of History and a Fellow of the Stellenbosch Institute of Advanced Study (STIAS). He has held several visiting fellowships at universities in England, the United States, Australia and Ireland. His books include *Abraham Esau's War*; *Britannia's Empire*; *The War for South Africa*; *Springboks on the Somme*; and *History Matters*.

Andries Walter Oliphant is a former Fulbright Scholar in Comparative Literature, a writer, critic and cultural policy developer. He chaired the Ministerial Arts and Culture Task Team and co-wrote the 1996 White Paper on Arts, Culture and Heritage and its 2020 revision. He is the Founding Chair of the Arts Culture Trust (ACT). Former editor of *Staffrider Magazine* and the *Journal of Literary Studies*, he served on the editorial boards of the *English Academy Review*, *Alternation*, *Scrutiny2* and *De Arte*. A co-founder of Congress of SA Writers Publishing, he formulated the criteria for the Sunday Times Fiction Award and chaired its adjudication panel. He writes on South African literature, art and photography. He is a recipient of the Thomas Pringle Award for Short Stories (1992), the Sunday Independent Book Journalist of the Year Award (1997) and an ACT Lifetime Achievement Award (2019).

Stephen Volz received a PhD in history from the University of Wisconsin–Madison, and he is an Associate Professor in the Department of History at Kenyon College in the United States. Among his other publications are *Words of Batswana: Letters to 'Mahoko a Becwana', 1883–1896*, edited and translated in partnership with Part T. Mgadla; and *African Teachers on the Colonial Frontier: Tswana Evangelists and Their Communities during the Nineteenth Century*.

A former publisher, *Brian Willan* is an Extraordinary Professor at Sol Plaatje University and Senior Research Associate at the Institute for the Study of Englishes of South Africa, Rhodes University. He has a doctorate from the School of Oriental and African Studies, London University, and has written extensively on nineteenth- and twentieth-century South African history and literature. His book *Sol Plaatje: A Life of Solomon Tshekisho Plaatje, 1876–1932* won an award for non-fiction (biography) from the National Institute for Humanities and Social Sciences, as did *Sol Plaatje's Mhudi*, which he co-edited with Sabata-mpho Mokae. *Sol T. Plaatje: A Life in Letters*, also co-edited with Mokae, won the 2021 South African Literary Award.

Laurence Wright is an Extraordinary Professor at North-West University. He was formerly H.A. Molteno Professor of English and Director of the Institute for the Study of English in Africa at Rhodes University. He was accorded the Vice-Chancellor's Distinguished Research Medal and elected to the Academy of Science of South Africa in 2009. He is a Fellow of the English Academy of Southern Africa (FEASA) and holds the Academy's Gold Medal. He is also Honorary Life-President of the Shakespeare Society of Southern Africa. He has published widely on Shakespeare, on the future of the humanities, and on South African education and language policy. Currently he is working on unpublished manuscripts by the pioneering South African psychoanalyst Wulf Sachs.

Introduction

Sol Plaatje's *Mafeking Diary* is one of South Africa's most remarkable and original pieces of writing. Written – in English – during the famous siege, surrounded by Boer forces, it is perceptive, beautifully written, often very funny and among the best of the multitude of diaries written during the South African War of 1899–1902. It is the only one, however, to have been written by a black South African – or at least the only one to have survived – and it has a unique importance in South African history and its literature.

It could easily have disappeared – the fate of a number of Plaatje's other manuscripts and papers. Plaatje wrote his diary as a private journal and he seems to have had no thought of trying to get it published. In the aftermath of the siege he once referred to it when giving evidence in a court case (it helped to date the incident in question) but thereafter nothing more was heard of it during his lifetime. There were times when he might have mentioned it – for example, in his chapter about the siege in his book *Native Life in South Africa* (1916), or in a newspaper article in 1930 recalling his memories of the siege – but he didn't.[1]

The notebook in which Plaatje wrote his diary passed – either before or after his death – to his daughter Violet. Along with some of Plaatje's other papers, it returned to Mahikeng, because this is where Violet went to live after she married Rex Molema, a member of a prominent local family. It remained unknown to the wider world until the late 1960s when John Comaroff, carrying out anthropological fieldwork in the Mahikeng district, appealed to local people for any written documents they could show him. Violet Molema had died a few years before this, but her son Barolong Molema delved into a back room and retrieved the diary, buried beneath a number of other documents and papers. Recognising its importance, Comaroff set about editing the diary and prepared it for publication, achieving this in 1973. Subsequent editions, incorporating the results of further research and information supplied by Brian Willan, the late Professor Tim Couzens, Andrew Reed and the late Solomon Molema (a younger brother of Barolong Molema), were published in 1989, 1999 and 2023.

Fifty years on from the diary's first publication, this is a good moment not only to celebrate its publication, and its miraculous survival, but to reassess and to reconsider. Such a celebration is all the more necessary because Plaatje's *Diary*, it is fair to say, has never received the attention and acclaim it deserves.[2]

It is worth questioning why this has been so. Historians, for example, have drawn upon the diary as a source of information, containing as it does unambiguous evidence of the extent of black involvement in the defence of Mafeking – something that Colonel Baden-Powell, adhering to the fiction that he was fighting a 'white man's war' in which blacks were not involved, had wilfully misrepresented. Thus, Plaatje's diary is often cited by historians as part of a larger project to reclaim the South African War as a conflict that involved all the people of the region. Plaatje makes it very clear that far from being bystanders in a war fought by whites, black South Africans in Mafeking (and some on the Boer side too) were very much involved, and he describes many actions in which his people fought against the Boer besiegers.

What has largely been missing, however, is any substantive engagement with Plaatje's diary in its own right. This is true of literary scholars and critics too. They have been far more interested in Plaatje's other writings – particularly his novel *Mhudi* (1930), his political book *Native Life in South Africa* (1916), and his engagement with Shakespeare, evident in his translations of *Comedy of Errors* (1930) and *Julius Caesar* (1937).

Why, then, has his diary been largely overlooked? One reason is that the genre of the diary has always had a somewhat indeterminate status, falling at times between fiction and non-fiction and of undeniably lesser status than the novel (compare the sheer volume of what has been written about Plaatje's novel *Mhudi* with the paucity of what there is on Plaatje's *Mafeking Diary*). Related to this, we believe, is that the diary's subject matter – the drama of the siege – has rather predominated over the form, discouraging a proper consideration of the ways which the story of the siege was represented and mediated through Plaatje's experiences and perceptions.

And if the genre of the diary has posed problems, another is that it is sometimes perceived as an alien literary form, even 'un-African' in character. If the diary was 'rarely or ever', as John Comaroff has pointed out, 'a literary genre of choice among black South Africans', and if it 'belonged culturally and ideologically to a European bourgeois sensibility',[3] is there a need to engage with something that might be viewed as no more than an instance of post-colonial 'mimicry'? Such a perception, however, fundamentally misunderstands the nature of what Plaatje was doing in his diary, and fails to recognise the creativity and originality that he brought to his task.

Related to this, and perhaps the main reason for the diary's critical neglect, is that its content does not fit in very readily with what one might call a grand narrative of nationalism, the notion that black writing is to be judged by its contribution to the struggle for freedom. Such a paradigm, it might be argued, fits more comfortably with some of Plaatje's other writings, particularly *Native Life in South Africa* and *Mhudi*. In both these books Plaatje speaks to a wider audience, he is concerned with larger narratives of politics and history, and in *Native Life in South Africa* in particular he is acting quite consciously as a spokesman for a wider cause. He wrote it, indeed, at a time when he was general secretary of the South African

Native National Congress, and a member of its delegation to Britain during the First World War.

But Plaatje's *Mafeking Diary* is different. It is a private rather than a public document, and the historical context in which it was written is very different from that of a decade and a half later. In 1899 and 1900 South Africa was not yet defined by the binaries of the segregationist grand project, nor did Plaatje carry the burden of representation – as public leader and spokesman – which was to determine the course of much of his later life. The Cape Colony in which he grew up provided space and opportunities for the mission-educated African community of which he was a part. Their ethos, reflected in Plaatje's diary, was one of optimism and hope that their world would be secured by British victory in the war of 1899–1902. To understand Plaatje's diary we therefore need to engage a little more closely with the context in which he wrote it, and the ideas and experiences that he brought to this task.

How, then, did Plaatje come to write his diary, and how had his experiences and life to date made such a thing possible?

Sol Plaatje was born on 9 October 1876 at Doornfontein, a farm in the Boshof district of the Orange Free State.[4] He was of Barolong origin, his family being *Barolong ba ga Modiboa* (the Barolong of Modiboa), and distinct from the four main Barolong groupings of Tshidi, Ratlou, Rapulana and Seleka. His parents were adherents of the Berlin Mission Society, and shortly after his birth they moved from the Society's mission at Bethanie, in the Orange Free State, to another of its missions at Pniel, near Barkly West, at that time part of the British Colony of Griqualand West but soon to be incorporated into the Cape Colony.

It was at Pniel that Plaatje received most of his formal education, attending the mission school run by the Rev. Ernst Westphal, a young missionary recently arrived from Germany. His education would be supplemented by further instruction – in English – at the Church of England mission in Beaconsfield, part of Kimberley, from the Rev.

Herbert Crossthwaite and then some further tuition, outside the classroom, from Ernst Westphal and his wife Marie.

Plaatje left Pniel in 1894 to take up a job with the Post Office in Kimberley, an institution well known for its willingness to take on African employees. Here, on the diamond fields, he found himself part of a well-established mission-educated community, attracted to the town by the jobs that were on offer, and drawn from all over southern Africa, but particularly from the Eastern Cape, the earliest field of missionary endeavour in southern Africa. The members of this community created a distinctive life for themselves, rich in social, musical and cultural clubs and societies, and took full advantage of the opportunities that were on offer. Many of them qualified for the franchise, the right to vote, and they took a keen interest in the affairs of the Cape Colony, seeking out and working with whites who were sympathetic to their interests (these included the novelist Olive Schreiner and her husband Cronwright Schreiner when they lived in Kimberley in the 1890s). They were pro-British in their outlook, believing that the imperial government provided the best guarantor of their rights, in contrast to many of the local colonists who thought that their rights and aspirations should be strictly curtailed. They looked to the law too, and to the Cape Colony's non-racial constitution, as they sought out the means to defend themselves.

An ethos of improvement and progress, individually and collectively, was very much in evidence, none more so than in the person of the young Solomon Plaatje. He took part in an organisation known as the South Africans Improvement Society, which was devoted to helping its members improve their command of English, essential if they were to secure the best jobs that were going. At one of their fortnightly meetings in 1895 he was reported to have read a chapter from a book called *John Bull and Co.*, by Max O'Rell, but it was not an unqualified success: 'his style of reading and pronunciation', it was reported, 'was fairly criticised'. A month later, however, he read a paper on 'The History of the Bechuana', when he 'showed great mastery over his subject'.[5]

Plaatje was also a diligent reader in private, for enjoyment as well as for furthering his education and improving his job prospects. He developed a fascination for Shakespeare and went to see his plays in the Kimberley Theatre. In the relatively liberal Cape Colony racial boundaries were more fluid than in other parts of southern Africa, he and his friends were not excluded from what were predominantly white forms of recreation and entertainment, and they were free to hire municipal halls themselves when the need arose.

After four years with the Post Office in Kimberley, Plaatje was on the lookout for a job as a court interpreter, one of the best and most prestigious jobs open to Africans at this time. He had long been fascinated by the law, and he was inspired by the example of his close friend Isaiah Bud-M'belle, an Mfengu, with whom he shared lodgings for a while. Bud-M'belle was clerk and translator for the Griqualand West High Court, fluent in a variety of different languages and a leading figure in the social and cultural life of Kimberley's black mission-educated community. He was secretary of no less than eight local clubs and societies.

Plaatje met Isaiah Bud-M'belle's sister Elizabeth on a visit to the diamond fields, and fell in love. Despite the objections of their respective families, they were married in January 1898. Later that year came the career opportunity he had been looking for. The position of clerk and court interpreter to the magistrate and civil commissioner in Mafeking, some 200 miles to the north of Kimberley, fell vacant, and he applied. By now fluent in English, Dutch, isiXhosa, German and Sesotho, as well as Setswana, he made a good impression in his interview with Charles Bell, the magistrate and civil commissioner, and he was offered the job. He also had the advantage of a recommendation from Silas Molema, a prominent local chief, whom he had met on some earlier visits to Mafeking. Plaatje accepted the job offer and commenced his duties in Mafeking on 14 October 1898.

Plaatje had a year in Mafeking before the outbreak of war. As in Kimberley, it is clear that he made the most of his opportunities and he was keen to get on. He soon became a proficient interpreter, impressing Bell with his work, and planned to take some Civil Service examinations to help further his career and improve his prospects of promotion. In August 1899 he wrote off to register for papers in Dutch, German and Typewriting, expecting to travel to Cape Town in December to sit the examinations. War, however, intervened. Mafeking was surrounded by Boer forces on 13 October 1899, and the inhabitants of Mafeking, black and white, prepared for a siege.

Plaatje never stated explicitly why he decided to start writing a diary. Nobody around him was in any doubt as to their likely significance. F. Geyer, the senior clerk and assistant resident magistrate, and the magistrate and civil commissioner, Charles Bell, his boss, were among his fellow diarists. Bell started his diary on 1 October 1899, two weeks before the beginning of the siege, and Plaatje soon had the job of typing it out for him, referring to this in his own diary entry for 26 November 1899.

Even without the example of Charles Bell and others around him, Plaatje had little need of encouragement, for a culture of writing and self-expression were already central to his being. Growing up at Pniel, he would have become familiar with the lengthy handwritten *Tagebücher* of the Rev. Ernst Westphal and the other missionaries, which were sent back to Berlin as a detailed record of their activities; indeed, members of his family, prominent in the life of the mission, were often mentioned in them. In Kimberley, improving his English was a constant preoccupation, and he was known to have kept a notebook in which he wrote details of transactions made and money spent – he mentions this in evidence he gave in a court case, arising from a dispute with his landlord over rent, and the details it contained helped him to win the case. He may well have used the notebook to practise his English as well as to record details of the rent he paid to his landlord.

Given this background, and the popularity of diary writing in the English-speaking world in the late-Victorian period, starting a diary was a natural thing to do. It just needed a trigger, and this was provided by the outbreak of the war and the start of the siege. Nobody around him was in any doubt as to the likely significance of the events that were about to unfold.

The first entry of Plaatje's diary was on 29 October 1899, the third Sunday after the declaration of war. He had decided to write it in English. This must have seemed the appropriate medium for him to write about the public spectacle about to unfold, and it also afforded an ideal opportunity to practise and improve his fluency – and in a rather different register from the formal, legal language required in his daily routine in court and office. But writing it in English also meant that it could be read, in due course and God willing, by his wife Elizabeth. She was of Mfengu origin, and although he spoke some isiXhosa, and she some Setswana, English was for them the most convenient form of written communication. She had left Mahikeng in August 1899 with their young son, Frederick St Leger ('Sainty'), and had not returned.

Plaatje maintained his diary for five and a half months, recording the events of the siege as he witnessed them, drawing upon his own memories and experiences to help frame what he saw and described. We hear not only about the major events of the siege which preoccupied the many other diarists – the constant shelling and sniping, the disastrous British attack on a Boer fort on 26 December 1899, the shortages of food and arrangements for rationing – but of the part played by blacks in the siege: the role of the Barolong contingent in defending the *stadt* (their township), the situation of the black refugees and their desperate attempts to escape from Mafeking, the dispatch runners making their way through the Boer lines, the exploits of Mathakgong and his band of cattle raiders. And of his own role in liaising between civil and military authorities, in collecting intelligence from returning cattle raiders and spies, and in interpreting in the Court of Summary Jurisdiction and the challenges this work presented.

Plaatje was concerned with individuals and their stories as much as the events that shaped their lives. We hear about his friend David

Phooko and his foibles, and how David wrote down some of his entries after he dictated them to him; about Miss Ngono, left destitute after the death of her lover; about Emily Murumolwa, the 14-year-old daughter of Chief Lekoko who worked for a while as his housekeeper; or the seven-year-old Phalaetsile, who escaped from the Boer laager and made a model of one of their forts for Colonel Baden-Powell to come and examine personally.

Plaatje's diary is revealing of his own sensibilities, and he often draws upon his own past experiences to help describe what he saw going on around him. He was adept at representing different aspects of his being: the family man, missing his wife and young son over Christmas, and marking their anniversaries; the conscientious, privileged servant of the colonial government, identifying with Charles Bell in his efforts to deal humanely with the black refugees – but well aware, as he wrote on 13 January 1900, that 'there is a very great difference between white and black even in a besieged town' when it came to food rationing. At other times he speaks as a loyal British subject, upholding the cause of the Imperial government, sharing the sufferings of his white fellow citizens, wondering like them whether they are to be relieved or abandoned to their fate. 'Surely these Transvaal Boers are abominable', he wrote on 21 March 1900.

The last entry of Plaatje's diary was on 30 March 1900, some six weeks before Mafeking was relieved by British forces. He ended his final entry in mid-sentence, his last words some three-quarters of the way down the foolscap page. Most likely pressure of work lay behind this. On 20 March he had written that he was 'very busy officially', and it is clear from other evidence – such as the number of intelligence reports he had written – that this was indeed the case. Moreover, he was now required to prepare an 'official diary, all the doings in connection with Native Affairs',[6] as he described it, in addition to the intelligence reports he composed after extracting information from returning dispatch riders and cattle raiders. As food shortages worsened, he was also busier than ever with arrangements for rationing. As circumstances grew increasingly difficult, and as he was rushed off his feet with his 'official duties', maintaining his private diary simply became too much.

In this book we have drawn together a distinguished cast of contributors to celebrate the 50th anniversary of Plaatje's *Mafeking Diary*, to subject it to the scrutiny it deserves, to tease out its wider significance, and to better understand the context in which it was written. And, in the case of the three short stories that form part of this collection too, from three of South Africa's leading writers, to show how they and we can be inspired by it.

John Comaroff, editor of the original edition of the diary in 1973, sets the scene by reviewing the remarkable transformation in Plaatje's reputation – and that of the diary – in the 50 years since it was first published. By the late 1960s Plaatje was 'all but forgotten beyond the world of his descendants', but since then his rehabilitation has been as 'remarkable and as rapid as his earlier demise'. Alongside this, Comaroff shows, his diary has been rehabilitated too, although not at quite the same rate: 'No longer should it be regarded merely as a historical curiosity, the accidental product of a colonised black South African writing in a genre hitherto associated with bourgeois Eurocentric culture'. And while Plaatje may have chosen to write his diary in English, his simultaneous rootedness in Tswana culture is plainly evident in its pages, his 'maturing selfhood played out in relation to others in a manner inspired by a Tswana as much as an English world view'.

Bill Nasson, in chapter 2, recounts his own personal odyssey of discovery of Plaatje's diary and its impact upon him, beginning from the moment he happened upon the 1975 paperback edition when he was a student at Hull University. He found it 'absolutely revelatory, a highly educative lesson which pricked unthinking assumptions about who the war affected, how it was fought, and what it encompassed'. He goes on to assess the importance of the diary 'in stretching the historical universe of the Anglo-Boer conflict, in restoring to that world of war an assortment of lives and experiences which had been all but lost to posterity'. He concludes with a look at the ways in which the diary's impact is being felt today, making the case that it has a wider significance as a civilian record of an episode in the war, that in its 'ironic sensibility' it foreshadows many First World War diaries, and that it should be located 'within the developing canon of a contemporary war imagination'.

Kevin Davie's chapter comes next, combining an account of a visit to Mahikeng ('largely conformed to a frontier town: busy, bustling, even though coronavirus restrictions had not been completely lifted') with an exploration of Plaatje's style of writing in his diary. Past and present are thus linked. His special concern is to see how Plaatje's diary measures up against the tenets of what some scholars call literary journalism or narrative non-fiction, 'a style of storytelling which presents factual stories using techniques more usually associated with fiction writing'. He introduces us to the journalist George Steevens, besieged in Ladysmith at the same time as Plaatje was in Mafeking, and a proponent of such a style. Plaatje's diary measures up rather well, he concludes, and has stood the test of time rather better than has Steevens, who 'appears as a protagonist for a dated imperial project', his writing marred by racist language and attitudes.

In chapter 5 Laurence Wright explores what he identifies as one of the diary's most striking characteristics, 'the extraordinary buoyancy and emotional lightness – the *jouissance* – we encounter in Plaatje's writing', especially noticeable during the early days of the siege. The tone of his writing is quite distinct from that of other siege diarists. None share the linguistic exuberance and musicality of language which Plaatje displays. This has poetic meaning, Wright argues, and is explicable in terms of Plaatje's own experiences and memories, and the connectedness he felt with the cultural and social worlds of which he was a part. Here was somebody for whom a late-nineteenth-century world had provided opportunities eagerly grasped, his thoughts expressed with flair and exuberance.

In chapter 6 Vivian Bickford-Smith offers an illuminating comparative perspective, comparing the lives and diaries of two black South Africans, Tiyo Soga and Sol Plaatje. Both kept diaries (Soga's was kept intermittently between 1857 and 1870) but both have been neglected, in part, Bickford-Smith argues, because they do not conform to how later generations might have wished them to be. Both have been considered too pro-British in their outlook, perhaps for this reason too compromised, and in Soga's case overly concerned with a missionary zeal for converting the heathen and recording the details as he did so. The key to an understanding of both diaries, Bickford-Smith shows, is to set aside the burden of subsequent history and to seek to understand both diaries – and to recognise their achievement – in the context of the times in which they lived.

Andrew Manson, in chapter 7, tells the story of the little-known siege of Mahikeng of January to October 1882. Unlike the siege of 1899–1900, which has been minutely documented and has become part of imperial mythology, its predecessor of 1882 – when Barolong were likewise besieged by Boers – has been almost entirely forgotten. And yet it figured prominently in the memories of Barolong in 1899–1900, as Plaatje himself testifies in his diary, and it speaks to a local historical context that was central to the actions and perceptions of the Barolong. The famous siege of 1899–1900, in other words, is part of a much longer story – and helps explain why the Tshidi Barolong, Plaatje included, were so strongly pro-British in their allegiance.

If an understanding of the local historical context helps explain the actions and experiences of the Barolong in Mahikeng, as recorded in Plaatje's diary, there is also a wider African context to consider. Steven Volz, in chapter 9, explores the notion of Pax Britannica and how this was viewed by both black South Africans like Plaatje and Africans from other parts of the continent, and how this conditioned the way they viewed the South African War. 'In general,' Volz says, 'West Africans supported the British effort and hoped for a British victory, but, like Plaatje, they were also concerned about British motives and methods, questioning whether they really had the best interests of Africans at heart.'

In chapter 10 Brian Willan sets out to explain how Plaatje's previous life and experiences had led to him working for the magistrate in Mafeking, and had at the same time equipped him to write such a remarkable diary. The diary itself provides plenty of clues since he often refers back to earlier episodes in his life and mentions people and places he knew. But there are plenty of gaps. This chapter aims to fill some of them, looking at the history of his family, at his years growing up on a German mission station, and then at the time he spent in Kimberley in the 1890s. This left a huge mark. Here he learnt much from friends and colleagues, and they contributed greatly to nurturing his talents and abilities. Given this context, it is clear that he should be viewed not so much as a lonely genius but as the product of a generation of mission-educated Africans who sought to make a place for themselves in the particular circumstances of the late-nineteenth-century Cape Colony. In a way Plaatje's diary can be seen as their testament, for these memories permeate his diary as much as his observations of what he witnessed going on around him in Mafeking during the siege.

And in chapter 11, Lesley Mofokeng explores Plaatje's introduction to the world of journalism during the siege, in particular his relationship with the journalists Angus Hamilton and Vere Stent. He considers the contribution of Plaatje's diary to his subsequent career as a journalist himself, identifying in it many of the characteristics of literary journalism. In his diary Plaatje 'delivered a master class in storytelling, taking the mundane work of recording daily occurrences and turning the task into a magnificent and well-crafted narrative'. In *Native Life in South Africa* (1916), his devastating indictment of the infamous Natives Land Act of 1913, the skills and techniques developed in his Mafeking diary reached their full expression.

In addition to these chapters that explore different aspects of Plaatje's diary, we are very fortunate to be able to include in this book three short stories by three acclaimed South African writers and academics: Andries Walter Oliphant (University of South Africa), Siphiwo Mahala (University of Johannesburg) and Sabata-mpho Mokae (Sol Plaatje University).

Perhaps it is the title of Mahala's story (chapter 4) that captures the role of historical fiction in correcting the wrongs created by omissions in historical sources such as war diaries. Mahala's story is titled 'The Missing Pages', and in the case of South Africa, where history has been told from the vantage point of the victor, pages are also missing. Mahala's story reimagines black people being fed horsemeat in Mahikeng while, owing to food rationing, only the white residents could still eat beef, albeit in smaller amounts than usual. 'As I turned around the corner, a horse's head was placed next to the fire. The long face with a white blaze looked too familiar. I looked at the long queue, and realised that before I cry over Motsamai, the story of how these people ended up feasting on horsemeat needed to be told,' Mahala concludes his story, also inadvertently emphasising the role of a fiction writer as a chronicler of feelings as well as a historian when history is told selectively.

In 'The Interpreter' (chapter 8), Andries Walter Oliphant reimagines and re-creates Sol Plaatje's daily routine, which includes performing his duties as a court interpreter, being a typist, and overseeing the dispatch runners and spies, who played a major role in how the war ended. He also brings us closer to the conversations between Plaatje and Magistrate Charles Bell as well as between Plaatje and the villagers. In the story, the author also re-creates the local black population's roles in the war. These included cattle raiding, which was very important as it was a major attempt to keep the residents fed while their town was besieged.

Sabata-mpho Mokae's story in chapter 12 focuses on the aftermath of the war: the destruction of towns and villages as well as the attempt of people to rebuild their lives. The story is titled 'The Heart Goes After Whom It Loves', which is a direct translation of a Setswana idiom 'pelo e ja serati'. This makes it a love story as well. Elizabeth and Sol Plaatje were newlyweds when the latter got appointed to the position of court interpreter in Mafeking, and they could not see each other as the war limited and, in some cases, curtailed human movement. During the siege, Plaatje spent his first-born son's first birthday away from both his son and wife. 'The Heart Goes After Whom It Loves' is about reunion, and the rebuilding of a ravaged country and its people's lives.

One

Re(dis)covering the Extraordinary: A Reflection, 50 Years On

John Comaroff

PROLOGUE

August 1996, Mahikeng, evening.

A motley clutch of history students at the apartheid-era University of Bophuthatswana (aka Unibo), soon to be renamed the University of the North-West, gather in our sitting room. 'Our', here, refers to my wife and colleague, Jean Comaroff, and myself. It is a bitterly cold winter night. The chatter before we begin the class rumbles out a cacophony of questions: What was the Enlightenment? Does history have a future in South Africa? What is an archive? Many more, but it is questions about the future of history and the archive that detain us. We are scheduled to teach a lesson in Tswana history. An inescapable irony this, two ageing white South Africans, living abroad, coming 'home' to teach nine or ten young Tswana men and women about *their* history. This in a notorious former bantustan.

Where even to begin?

A time check here. Remember, in the mid-1990s, obsessive talk of decoloniality was not yet a part of everyday life in the academies of the Global North or South. In South Africa, decolonisation had been lived very recently as a visceral struggle, one with a serious body count, not as a loosely defined abstraction clothed in Afropessimist-speak. The country was living through a moment of national optimism. History, it seemed, was no longer necessary; as Jean Comaroff and I have written elsewhere, it had migrated into popular entertainment, monumentalisation and memory, and away from its older scholarly forms.[1] Now that the *ancien régime* had fallen – or, at least, appeared to have fallen – the future seemed assured; with apologies to Nietzsche, history-as-learned had become redundant. But, as time passed, there was a dawning realisation, especially in non-metropolitan South Africa, that the end of the struggle did not necessarily usher in the promised 'better life for all'. In the countryside, it was soon to bring with it a bitter harvest of immiseration. A few of those Unibo students were history teachers who had not been paid in months. Some could not afford the paper and pens needed to take class notes or write essays. The question of whether history had a future at that moment was, therefore, a non-trivial one for them, a question as much material as it was epistemic. Even more pressing for them was whether the future itself had any sort of future.

It was in this context that we began our class on Tswana history. But, again, where to begin that history, a history from and for a 'new' South Africa? The answer to which we came, in a feverish conversation that went on long into the night, was the archive. If Tswana history was going to be repossessed, to be learned, valorised and claimed for a future yet unmade, it required its own vernacular documentary sources. Which is where Solomon Tshekisho Plaatje entered the room, a shadow, an intellectual ancestor, a ghost who walked, and wrote, this landscape just less than a century earlier. Nor did he walk alone. He walked it with Silas Modiri Molema, another giant of black South African historiography, author of, among other works, *The Bantu, Past and Present*.[2] Brian Willan's magisterial biography of Sol Plaatje traces the relationship between the two men. Both had left behind them copious unpublished papers. This, then, is where we began, by imagining how, where and with what to build an archive: with the papers of these literati, and with those of others yet to be disinterred, ordinary voices yet to be rediscovered, to invoke Njabulo Ndebele's apt phrase.[3] The most notable, of course, was Sol Plaatje's *Mafeking Diary* itself, although it was far from the first historically significant document to be written by Tswana people; many, some of them public intellectuals, had penned letters, newspaper articles and the like for many decades. Never intended for publication, Plaatje's journal entries provided an iconic example of what an archive of the future history of South Africa, told from one Tswana perspective – needless to say, there are many – might look like. It is where we began our history classes all those years ago.

At the time, we did not realise that the *Diary* would enter into the new, and newly decolonised, South African canon, celebrated in its own right as a *literary* work. Over the past half-century, it has become recognised for two things in addition to its significance as a historical archive; as an account, that is, of an imperial war told from a hitherto silenced perspective, one attuned to the vantage of the colonised as well as that of the colonisers. The first of those two things is that it is a brilliant example of the diary form recommissioned by African literati from its Euromodernist 'home', vernacularised and laced with quite different culturally nuanced sensibilities – thereby producing an entirely new kind of writing. The second is that it is a distinguished work in the genre of prose non-fiction – even of auto-ethnography, recently emerged as a popular form of rapportage in anthropology – despite never having been intended for publication. It is with these two things in mind that I offer this reflection on Sol Plaatje's *Mafeking Diary*.

FIFTY YEARS ON

The *Diary*, variously titled in its different published editions, has turned 50 years old. It is an especially auspicious anniversary. The document itself, obviously, is much older, having begun its life in

October 1899, in a town whose designation has also changed over the past decades. It is now officially rendered as Mahikeng, closer to its Setswana vernacular. The translation, however, remains the same, 'Place of Rocks'. But its place in the rocky political and economic history of southern Africa has morphed dramatically. So has its place in the narrative cartography of the country; in the telling, that is, of its geographical relevance over time. Once the far-flung chiefly capital of an autonomous African polity – the Barolong boo Ratshidi, a Tswana nation – it is now the administrative centre of the North West province in post-apartheid South Africa. Since its founding in the mid-nineteenth century, it has witnessed many turbulent, troubled turns in a *longue durée* of conflict and sovereign struggle over land, people, rights and resources; even over the telling of its history, past and present.

Sol T. Plaatje, as a historical figure, has also undergone radical transformation – actually, transformations, more than one – since his early Mafeking/Mahikeng days, the Days of the Diarist as a Young Man. Indeed, ever since the first publication of the *Diary*, in 1973, he has been reinscribed on the literary and political landscape of South Africa, attracting a substantial scholarly literature. Some of those transformations echo, and have occurred in counterpoint with, the history of the country at large. To wit, Plaatje, the largely unknown bit player during the Siege of Mafeking, stands in sharp contrast to his later emergence as a public intellectual, cultural producer, newspaper editor and political activist, which began in 1902 with his editorship of *Koranta ea Becoana* and ended with his death in 1932. Thereafter, he suffered almost total eclipse for several decades, until his recuperation began during the years when revisionist Africanist historiography documented the anti-apartheid struggle. It came to full fruition, finally, with his establishment as a significant ancestral presence in post-apartheid South Africa, thus bringing to conclusion a trajectory brilliantly told by Brian Willan in *Sol Plaatje: A Biography* (1984) and *Sol Plaatje: A Life of Solomon Tshekisho Plaatje, 1876–1932* (2018).

There is no need to recount that story here, except to remind ourselves quite how remarkable Sol Plaatje's rise was, in 13 years, from a 23-year-old court translator with limited education – and a willing subaltern in the British colonial regime at Mafeking – to the first general secretary of the South African Native National Congress (SANNC, later the ANC), of which he was a co-founder. As a leading player in black public life, he travelled to the United Kingdom, the United States and Canada representing the struggle for liberation, enfranchisement and land rights – which he did with celebrated eloquence and unflagging energy. His activism abroad put him in touch with the likes of W.E.B. Du Bois, Marcus Garvey and others, bringing him, and his writings, to the attention of the Pan-African movement. This was a complex moment in black political history, a moment in which African leaders sustained the sanguine hope that they could bring about racial emancipation by persuading the world at large of the merits of their cause, of their right to equality, of the oppressive conditions under which black South Africans lived; and that telling their story on world stages might produce an effect at home.

For his own part, Sol Plaatje came to embody a one-man African Renaissance. Alongside his unrelenting political activism, he pursued what can only be described as a hyperbolic modernism, of which he was a prime living instance: vide his copious, often critical, self-consciously cosmopolitan journalism; his translations of Shakespeare into Setswana and his accomplished sociolinguistic scholarship; his prose fiction, epitomised in *Mhudi*, the first full-length novel in English by a black South African; and his extraordinary *Native Life in South Africa*, itself part organic anthropology, part political argument, part forensic journalism, part elegy to a changing countryside. Also, his easy fluency in a number of African and European languages, both spoken and written; his stage performances as actor and singer; and his devout Christianity and devotion to the life of his embourgeoised family.

Plaatje, in sum, exemplified the Modern African Person, at least as he and the emerging black elite of the time envisaged that figure – both as an aspiration, a civilising mission for their people at large, and as a political argument for their claim to equality as citizens of South Africa. It was an emphatically male-centric, middle-class vision, one clearly influenced by mission Protestantism and the politesse of British colonial society. But it coexisted, as Plaatje made plain in his preface to the first edition of *Mhudi*, with an explicit effort to retain the values intrinsic to African vernacular cultures, *mentalité*, lifeways. Regarded retrospectively, with the faux certainty of 20/20 vision, the diarist appears to have been a man of irreconcilable contradictions. As Peter Limb, among others, has pointed out, he was a 'British Empire enthusiast' who admired the ways and means of its Establishment. Yet he was often quick to criticise those ways and means, sometimes with sharply barbed irony. He was 'staunchly opposed to radical working class forces' yet he repeatedly espoused black rights, expressing a heartfelt aversion to the 'terrible conditions of African workers and the plight of African women, including working women'.[4] And, while he was a prolific author in the English language, entirely fluent in its stylistic conventions and universalist pretensions, he devoted a great deal of effort to the sustenance of Setswana, Tswana language and culture, its performative genres and its oral literature.

To Plaatje himself, however, these were not contradictions at all. Nor were they irreconcilable, as critical ('decolonial') twenty-first-century scholars and commentators would almost certainly argue, looking backwards into history through a glass darkly.[5] They were the partible, principled responses of an obviously thoughtful black activist-intellectual seeking his own way, as subject *and* citizen, through the labyrinthine challenges of life under colonialism. He was also seeking ways to meliorate the 'terrible conditions' wrought upon the mass of his contemporaries by what is now broadly referred to as racial capitalism. But, most of all, it was this very capacity to speak and act in multiple, often countervailing directions that made Sol Plaatje a public figure whose voice breached the so-called colour bar, itself not a common accomplishment for black South Africans back then. 'Our Great Leader', the Rev. John Langalibalele Dube, first president of the South African Native National Congress, called him in his obituary in

1932.[6] As one Edison Malebe Bokako put it, in verse, on the occasion of Plaatje's death, 'Self-schooled by small degrees he rose, / Till fame her own declared him far, / A leader of men and high in prose, / He'd hitched his wagon to a star'.[7] Some white notables, among them academics and journalists, spoke in similar terms. *The Times* of London, which did not accord obituaries to many Africans, published a highly laudatory one for Plaatje, the politician, polymath, public figure and praise poet for Africa. Some distinctly racist colonial tropes bled through, too. For example, the Catholic missionary Father Bernard Huss described him, patronisingly, as 'an example of what Africans can become under the influence of European culture';[8] testimony, this, to a wilful misunderstanding of everything Plaatje embodied and stood for, from a cleric who sought to extend 'paternalistic influence over rural African communities and resist more radicalizing political influences'.[9]

No wonder, then, that at the time of his death Solomon Tshekisho Plaatje was a figure of considerable public heft in black South Africa – and among the few whites who paid attention to the lives and times of the vast majority of those who peopled the country in which they lived.

Soon, however, as noted earlier, Plaatje slipped into oblivion. It happened rather quickly, given his erstwhile prominence. Brian Willan observes in *Sol Plaatje: A Biography* that, for all the talk of his greatness at his large funeral in Kimberley in June 1932, an occasion marked by some memorable oratory, 'much of what he strove for came to naught, his political career was largely forgotten, his manuscripts were lost or destroyed, his published books largely unread. His novel *Mhudi* formed part of no literary tradition, and was long regarded as little more than a curiosity.'[10] Apartheid killed off not just 'what he strove for' but much of the memory of the man.

To be sure, in 1969–70, at the time I happened upon the *Diary*, the 'Great Leader', as public personage, was all but forgotten beyond the world of his own descendants – and, presumably, the relatively small circle of scholars, intellectuals and activists for whom the struggle history of the SANNC/ANC was a matter of concern. I do not recall having heard him mentioned in the innumerable conversations about South African political history in which I participated as a college student during the middle apartheid years. Nor did I come across any of his writings. None were referred to, not even, as far as I was aware, by historians then at the University of Cape Town. Black South Africans with whom I interacted spoke of many prominent political figures, past as well as present, but not of him. His trace had largely disappeared. In truth, I have no memory of how I first became aware, even dimly, of his name before I started working in Mahikeng. It was only there that I came to realise how important he had once been. Prior to that, he was no more than a sketchy echo in my consciousness, a spectral figure about whom I could not have offered much detail even at a push. The return of Sol T. Plaatje in the years thereafter, however, was to be as rapid, and as remarkable, as his earlier demise. It began, as I said a moment ago, even before the *ancien régime* gave way formally in 1994 and has accelerated dazzlingly since then – roughly at the rate that old South African history-as-written has been decolonised by more recent South African history-as-lived and, in tandem, rewritten. Perhaps the publication of the *Diary* even had a little to do with it all.

Sol Plaatje's recuperation is, by now, the stuff of legend: of biography, of scholarship, theatre, art and architecture, of documentary TV, even of music – the earliest recording of the national anthem, 'Nkosi Sikelel' iAfrika', sung by him in 1923 in London, can be heard on YouTube.[11] He has joined the Pantheon of Past Black Luminaries, political and cultural. The signs are almost everywhere. Usually mentioned are the naming of a municipality and a university for him in the Northern Cape province; the founding of the Sol Plaatje Educational Trust and Museum at his former home in Kimberley, which is now a national monument and a heritage site, as is his grave; and the creation of several literary, educational and other awards that bear his name. Also named for him are the Department of Education building in Pretoria, a dam and power station, a university library and at least two schools. A somewhat awkward statue of him writing at his desk is to be found in the Ernest Oppenheimer Memorial Gardens, Kimberley. Another, by Egon Tania and Guy du Toit, has been on display in a public garden in Bloemfontein and at the National Heritage Museum in Pretoria; more life-like, it pictures him with the bicycle – replete with typewriter strapped to its rear – that he is said to have ridden around the country doing his research for *Native Life in South Africa*.[12] Nor is this list exhaustive.[13] It does not include the growing literature about his writings, which fall beyond our purview here. Except, of course, for the *Diary*.

At the time of its first publication, I had no idea that Plaatje would emerge as a historical figure of such memorial heft. Or that his writings might become the object of literary criticism, part of a newly rejuvenated post-colonial canon in which black authors would at last be given their long-deferred due; in other words, that their erasure itself would finally be erased. Brian Willan has noted that, compared with Plaatje's other publications – especially *Native Life in South Africa* and *Mhudi,* which have received a great deal of attention over the past few decades – the *Diary* has been relatively neglected; beyond its frequent citation, that is, by historians intent on decolonising the view that the war in South Africa in 1899–1902 was a 'white man's war', a claim entirely discounted by the diarist's eyewitness account.[14] This is not to slight its value as a historical source, however. Quite the opposite. As its reviewers have often observed, the *Diary* shed sharp new light on the siege as a military, political and cultural encounter – which is hardly surprising, given the unique perspective of its author, a man placed both at the centre of administration of the town and at the seams that joined black and white, military and civilian, citizen and subject. But Plaatje's journal is much more than an event history. It is more, even, than a chronicle of the inequalities of suffering borne along lines of race in a war among colonisers; or of the unspoken reliance of white belligerents on indigenous populations; or of promises made by the British to their black allies and then casually, callously broken. It captures the zeitgeist of its time in an altogether singular manner, a point to which I shall return.

Beyond being plumbed as an archival resource, Willan goes on to insist, the *Diary* ought, at this moment in South African literary history, to be read for what it is in its own right: a piece of prose nonfiction. No longer should it be regarded merely as a historical curiosity, the accidental product of a colonised black African writing in a genre hitherto associated with bourgeois Euromodernist culture – a view that, implicitly, has Plaatje as mimic-man, which is a grotesque, not to mention racist, misreading of both the man and his work.

As it happens, the *Diary* has begun of late to show signs of drawing critical attention in its own literary right. A review of the centenary edition of 1999[15] by Jane Starfield anticipated this, observing that 'historical change has enabled Plaatje's writing' – of which the *Diary* 'is now probably his best known text' – to 'migrate from quasi-pariah status on the periphery of South African literature and history into what may become a new mainstream South African reading culture'.[16] She comments on its 'inimitable style', arguing that it is 'one of the most literate texts written under wartime pressures', although the universe of comparison is not specified. Perhaps this has to do with the fact, as I suggested in the preface to the Centenary Edition, that the narrative moves between literary forms, playing not just with language but with a plurality of languages and cultural images, often to striking ironic, metaphorical and lyrical effect. It is a modernist work that exceeds received modernist aesthetics in favour of a wilfully creolised hybridity. The result is a personal literary experiment crafted in prose that is never prosaic. It is prose, Jane Taylor notes, that touches the uncanny. This is especially the case, she says, when Plaatje, 'a deft and wry story-teller', contemplates death from 'inside the event', revealing, as he does so, 'the structure of a haunting persistence', of a 'recurring trauma'.[17]

Consider, with this in mind, a reflection on the *Diary* by Kevin Davie. Writing in 2021, Davie evaluates Plaatje's account of the siege 'against the precepts of literary or narrative journalism', a mode of presenting 'factual stories using techniques more usually associated with fiction writing'.[18] Davie sets the bar exceptionally high – this in light of his view that 'Plaatje's writing casts a long shadow across the South African literary landscape' – by comparing the *Diary* with the work of George Warrington Steevens. Steevens, Cambridge-educated and academically pedigreed, was the 'pre-eminent British war correspondent of his era, ... [typifying] the highly commercial, personal and sensational British "new" journalism of the last quarter of the 19th century'. As it happens, Steevens also found himself under siege in the South African War, but in Ladysmith, where he was to die of typhoid. For Davie, well aware of Steevens's literary reputation, Plaatje's writing is 'every bit as good', despite being the work of a youth with no background in prose non-fiction and without much formal education: 'The difference ... is that over a century later Plaatje, who engaged and recorded the struggles of all who participated at Mafeking, stands the test of writing time. A blinkered Steevens, notwithstanding the poetic prose, appears as a propagandist for a dated imperial project.'

Like Colonel Robert Baden-Powell, so-called Hero of Mafeking, George Warrington Steevens, says Davie, erased black South Africans from his visually spellbinding accounts of the war – beyond passing racist, demeaning slights. By contrast – and here I add my own voice to Davie's – Plaatje's creolising, experimental, often edgy prose, like his multilingual allusions, gave voice to a critical imagination that saw the colonial theatre for what it was: a complex *mis en scène* of entangled predicaments, mutual dependencies, interwoven ironies and interlocking tragedies given shape by polite rules of brute violence.

Of all recent readings of the *Diary*, the most comprehensive, predictably, is owed to Brian Willan, whose grasp of the life, times and writings of Sol Plaatje remains unparalleled.[19] Willan begins by noting the 'inherently indeterminate genre of the diary ... being a private rather than a public document'. It was, as he reminds us, a narrative form favoured during the late-Victorian years; this precisely because of its ideological association with bourgeois selfhood, with the aspiration for self-improvement and with the modernist conception of life as an individual progress. Plaatje, endowed with the Protestant ethic, was deeply attached to this world view. Perhaps it explains his willingness to experiment: to play with metaphor and irony, alliteration and onomatopoeia, to give vent to his sense of humour and command of languages, to satirise and self-deprecate – all of which point to his turn to the diary form as both a means and a measure of his own self-making. But another wrinkle: the journal may well have been intended, also, as a memoir for his wife, who had taken refuge elsewhere in the Colony.[20] Several moments of poignant personal reflection, strikingly unselfconscious, suggest as much; and give insight into the sensibilities of a man coming to maturity in a colonial theatre of war. Willan adds, perspicaciously, that Plaatje's silences – especially on capital punishment and on British colonial interference in the political sovereignty of the local Barolong chief – are also telling.[21] They illuminate not just his own ethical principles and the moral economy in which he was situated astride two very different yet interlocked worlds, but also the limits beyond which he was not willing to go in serving his imperial masters.

As this implies, the *Diary* was, apart from all else, a self-exploration in the complex aggregation of elements that would come together, over time, in the construction of Sol Plaatje's identity and political subjectivity. Here Willan cites Karin Barber's landmark volume, *Africa's Hidden Histories: Everyday Literacy and Making the Self*, in which she makes the argument that established Euromodernist forms like the diary and the letter were readily adopted by African individuals and communities, but were 'refashioned ... to express new forms of being'.[22] Which returns us to the point that, while Plaatje-as-diarist documented the siege in a genre favoured by a number of Europeans in Mafeking and occupied a subaltern role in a colonial institution, he was, *pace* V.S. Naipaul, no mimic-man.[23]

I have already hinted at the complexities implicated in 'reading' Plaatje's identity-in-formation, circa 1899–1900, from the *Diary*.[24] I stress 'in formation'. According to Tswana vernacular notions of being-in-the-world, personhood is a lifelong process of becoming. It consists of partible elements that, together, compose the unfolding identity of a human subject over time, an identity built up through the work (*tiro*) of self-making in relation to significant others. *Motho ke motho ka batho*, goes the vernacular axiom, 'a person is a person by virtue of [other] people'.[25] Reading Plaatje, consequently, requires understanding that his maturing selfhood, played out in relation to many others of varying significance, involved multiple dimensions. His ethnicity expressed itself in his deep attachment to Setswana ('Tswana lifeways') and in his frequent observation of the differences between Barolong and other African populations in Mahikeng. Race, as invested in his blackness, his proud Africanity, manifested itself by contrast to whites and white lifeways (*Sekgoa*); also in the complicated, often breached yet archly maintained opposition between coloniser and colonised. Gender was given voice in his repeated concerns with his masculinity and his often demonstrably delicate references to the women in his life. Religiosity and class made themselves felt in his consistent efforts to essay, and behave according to, the norms of an emerging black Christian bourgeoisie and its sense of civility. And generation was interiorised in his marked respect for older people, itself taken for granted in a Barolong world that, in times past, emphasised the significance of age as a critical principle of social differentiation and authority.

The *Diary*, as a work of both self-construction and narrative rapportage, speaks to all of these elements. It does so in a profoundly kaleidoscopic manner, giving fluid shape and colour to an extraordinary chapter in the life of an extraordinary man, a self-making man early in the process of becoming a major historical personage. It does so also in a microscopic manner, offering the sort of grounded, experience-rich detail worthy of the finest of organic ethnographies. As an account of a late-imperial war, fought at the edge of a colonial theatre itself undergoing radical change, it is at once chilling, thrilling and unusually moving; besides being all the more informative for the standpoint from which it was written. Reading it as an exquisite exercise in the making of a 'new' African in a morphing world at the turn of the twentieth century – partly self-conscious, partly unconscious, much of it somewhere in the prose-poetics of the in-between – one gets the sense of reading backwards into the future. If we learn anything from it, it is – to rewrite one of Marx's most clichéd, most misquoted lines – *not* that all history is lived twice, first as tragedy then as farce. It is that much colonial history – the Siege of Mafeking being an epic instance – was at once tragic and farcical, deadly serious yet often absurd.

There is nothing more for me to say, 50 years on. Sol Plaatje has said it all for himself, at once volubly and eloquently, in his own inimitable voice. It is a voice that has spoken cogently across centuries and across worlds. And still does.

This chapter draws upon parts of the author's Preface to the 50th anniversary edition of Sol Plaatje's Mafeking Diary *(Xarra Books, 2023).*

Two

Sol Plaatje's Mafeking Pen and a New Imagining of the Anglo-Boer War

Bill Nasson

Once upon a time, I knew nothing of Mafeking except that it was an obscure place somewhere vaguely around Kimberley in the Northern Cape province. That ignorance included its 'historical associations', which, as the British journalist and writer Gary Mead advised some twenty-five years ago, is the only thing that saved Mafeking from being a complete 'waste of time'.[1] And as for that matter, since I had never been a member of the Boy Scouts, the grand imperial doings of Colonel Robert Baden-Powell in that northern patch of Britain's Cape Colony had flown over my head.

Equally, infected by an apartheid-era adolescent aversion to any South African history, I had absolutely no interest in the country's great war of 1899–1902, beyond feeling that a liberal and civilised British Empire ought not to have allowed the reprehensible Boers to grow too big for their boots despite having been defeated in that conflict. It was the reason I refused even to touch a thick book on the topic, despite its dashing cover, that my father had once been given as a present. The author's Afrikaner-sounding name, Rayne Kruger, was enough to damn it as suspect.[2]

England is where Mafeking and its encircling modern war first seeped into my mind. Finding oneself at a distance suddenly seemed to make South Africa's past more digestible. While I was an undergraduate student in English and History at the University of Hull in the early 1970s, the South African writings in a course on British Commonwealth literature included the short stories of Herman Charles Bosman. Seemingly out of the blue, up rose Bosman's *Mafeking Road*.[3] Hull city itself contained not only Pretoria Street and Kimberley Avenue, but also Mafeking Grove.

There was more. In History, an option on British imperialism 1850–1970 included 'The Second Boer War', which, although necessarily a skeletal outline, touched on the disappointment of those African and Coloured loyalists who had hoped for better results in 1902. Mafeking popped up in another course on English society 1870–1950, which paid some attention to the role played by empire in British national culture at the end of the nineteenth century.

One of the things we considered was the mass urban hysteria which greeted news of the British relief of the Boer siege of Mafeking in May 1900. Why all that fuss over some obscure, dog-eared little spot that I was then still unable even to visualise on a mind's-eye map of South Africa? Could it be explained entirely as a spontaneous explosion of proud, flag-waving, 'jingoistic' empire patriotism? Or could the Mafeking revelry also be seen more simply as crowds of ordinary people seizing an opportunity for an orgy of public high jinks and unrestrained drinking?[4] We also learned that Mafeking had spawned a collective verb – 'to maffick' or to indulge in 'mafficking', meaning to be embraced by a raucous, exuberant, crowd celebration. No longer inanimate, Mafeking now seemed to have acquired some kind of identifying significance in history – or, at any rate, at least that of imperial Britain.

On completion of my final year at Hull, to my great surprise I was awarded a departmental prize for joint honours in History. A book voucher, its value enabled me to acquire about half-a-dozen volumes. I opted for mostly British history, my sole South African concession being a copy of De Kiewiet's elegant and readable history of the country that had been recommended by a favourite lecturer.[5] That left the bookshop token equivalent of one pound unspent or, back then, roughly around five to six pints of Newcastle Brown Ale in a northern English pub. Eager to gain the full value of the prize, but at a loss over what affordable history book to choose, I turned to skimming through novels before by chance my eye was caught by a small corner display of titles.

A pyramid of covers announcing new paperbacks on 'War' that dealt with the world wars, the Spanish Civil War and the American Civil War included an oddity near the bottom. Pricking my curiosity, it was the solution to indecision not merely because of the promise of its title and the attractive sepia-tone montage on its front cover. At only 90 pence, it was also perfectly priced. A further clincher was the author of a glowing back-cover blurb which assured prospective readers of finding a 'diary of rare quality', kept by an 'outstanding character' who was 'gifted, energetic, full of humour and human sympathy', and whose 'shrewd' prose underlined 'the madness, as well as the vileness, of classifying men as superior and inferior according to the colour of their skins'. That endorsement came from the acerbic English journalist Bernard Levin, whose reviews and satirical writings I greatly admired. In the case of the slim book in question, it was also impossible to miss a little touch of irony. Levin was notorious for being picky about non-fiction works which lacked a proper index, singling those out for having been shoddily produced. The book for which he had supplied such a gushing personal puff lacked an index.

Thus it was that I acquired a 1976 Cardinal edition of *The Boer War Diary of Sol T. Plaatje*, a paperback version of the original 1973 hardback.[6] It was a book picked up entirely by chance, in a way almost as the original manuscript document had fallen into the hands of its editor over half a century ago. As John Comaroff reveals in his preface, it was 'discovered by accident rather than by design'.[7] While *The Boer War Diary* certainly made for marvellously brisk and intriguing reading during an unusually hot and dry British summer of 1976, it was also absolutely revelatory, a highly educative lesson which pricked unthinking assumptions about who the war affected, how it was fought, and what it encompassed.

In a way, *The Boer War Diary*'s impact is conveyed well by the notion embodied in an epigrammatic line from one of Rudyard Kipling's 1890s poems, 'and what should they know of England who only England know?'[8] In the revealing context of Plaatje's wartime record, it is tempting to adapt and rephrase it to pose a couple of other, similarly styled questions. Directed at anyone of my level of ignorance, these might have been, 'and what should they know of Mafeking who only Mafeking know?' and, by the same measure, if far more significantly, 'and what should they know of the Boer War who only the Boer War know?' On the striking personal evidence provided by Sol Plaatje, there was quite a bit more to Mafeking than had been imagined. And there was a great deal more to the Boer War than viewing it as just a conflict confined to white Boer republican and British Empire adversaries.

In a classic eye-opening manner, the 1970s publication of *The Boer War Diary* conveyed an essential historical truth by breathing a flesh-and-blood *individuality* – a voice expressing what conventional social history has termed 'real-life experience' – into early generalising reinterpretations of the 1899–1902 conflict. Plaatje first appeared in print only a year after the publication of Donald Denoon's pioneering and brilliantly suggestive essay on seeing the war as a total conflagration, grounded deeply within the fabric of black as well as white societies. As his chapter in the collected volume *War and Society in Africa* asserted, there was no simple, uncomplicated answer to the question of whose war the 'Boer War' actually became.[9]

The comparatively far broader impact of Sol Plaatje's *Boer War Diary* was undoubtedly its historical novelty as a document from the war – raw, original and immediate. A close and indissoluble link between the diarist and the war, it continues to retain the huge significance which it carried 50 years ago, remaining 'the only diary kept by an African during the war that has been discovered to date', and providing 'remarkable insight' into the writer's 'experiences and thoughts as an educated African of the time as well as those of the black people about whom he wrote'.[10]

It could perhaps even be suggested that Plaatje's Mafeking pen created a new angle of vision into, or a fresh understanding of, the breadth, depth and human cost of the warfare that was oozing across the South African interior. From an attritional corner of early action came an acutely observant African voice, providing a credible 'I am here' witness to day-to-day goings-on. In that sense, the *Diary* was almost as much the English-language literary-documentary creator of a fuller understanding of the war in our own time, as Major-General J.F.C. Fuller's mythologised 1930s version of the conflict as a colonial countryside clash between decent and chivalrous white warriors was the maker of a romanticised version of it in his.[11] Or, equally, for that matter, in throwing a corrective light on another partial – and ideologically partisan – image of the war projected by the heroic character of Boer diaries published during the 1930s–1940s blossoming of Afrikaner nationalism, like F.L. Rothmann's *Oorlogsdagboek*.[12]

While Plaatje's Mafeking entries had come as a surprise to my sense of what the Anglo-Boer War had amounted to, whatever interest it pricked at that point was really of a passing kind. By then, my mind had been captured by other sieges of empire, particularly those associated with British colonial India in the nineteenth century. Entranced by J.G. Farrell's masterly satirical historical novel about the 1857 Indian Rebellion (or 'Mutiny') against British rule, I had set my sights (depending on scholarship funding) on researching something or other about conflict in British India that would bring together literature and history, possibly the impact of the imperial shock of 1857 on Victorian fiction.[13]

But the complications of fate intervened and I ended up in the MA programme of the Centre for Southern African Studies at the

University of York. So it was that in 1977 my copy of *The Boer War Diary* accompanied me from East Yorkshire to North Yorkshire. There, my student time at York overlapped with that of Peter Warwick, then concluding his pioneering 1978 doctoral dissertation on 'African Societies and the South African War, 1899–1902'.

Naturally, Plaatje's *Diary* along with his *Native Life in South Africa* and *Mhudi* featured in Dr Warwick's subsequent pioneering book synthesis of the war's overall impact on the lives and livelihoods of the black population, most obviously in its chapters on the 'Myth of a White Man's War' and on 'Mafikeng and Beyond'.[14] The *Diary* was used sparingly but to telling effect in the author's *Black People and the South African War*, in revealing, for instance, the close eye that the nervous local Tshidi Barolong kept on 'the negotiations between the British and Transvaal governments during the middle months of 1899', and in showing Plaatje's acute distress at the wretched state of many of Mafeking's African refugees, 'hungry beings, agitating the engagement of your pity'.[15]

As a matter of course, the town's Colonel R.S.S. Baden-Powell's self-serving actions and attitudes were touched on fleetingly in my own mini-research dissertation on wartime British views on what they were experiencing in South Africa. Inevitably, where the calculating Robert Baden-Powell went, the astute and sharp-eyed Solomon Tshekisho Plaatje followed. The *Diary* was a handy source, and some of the wry observations which pepper it gently punctured Baden-Powell's public huffing and puffing over how his conduct of the siege defence was being viewed. As Plaatje noted at the end of March 1900, the 'Colonel Commanding has published a hot protest against alleged rumours by somebodies that he delays the troops and that he starves the inhabitants, etc. ... He threatens those fellows when their claims [prove false].'[16]

Sol Plaatje's *Diary* and Peter Warwick's research nudged me on towards the war of 1899–1902 and to a new way of exploring its impact and historical experience. That, inevitably, was bringing the history of the war's impact upon the black majority and the genesis and character of black involvement in hostilities. But as a broad field of doctoral dissertation research it had already been harvested by *Black People and the South African War*. Whatever the page Sol Plaatje had presented, overleaf it looked discouragingly full.

In due course, following an accidental encounter with J.P. Kenyon, professor of early modern English history at Hull, his kindly encouragement and influential patronage enabled me to land a PhD studentship at Gonville and Caius College, Cambridge, allowing for the resumption of postgraduate study. Initially, I grappled to define a viable South African War topic. But, as I was to discover, there were possibilities for a more regional, social history-focused approach to understanding the nature of black experience in wartime. That resulted in an early 1980s dissertation on 'Black Society in the Cape Colony and the South African War of 1899–1902: A Social History', which supplied chapter and verse for the present author's subsequent *Abraham Esau's War*.[17]

It has to be said that that study was not undertaken with either the Siege of Mafeking or *The Boer War Diary of Sol T. Plaatje* especially in mind. If anything, far from being woven in, they were intentionally dropped stitches. For, by the time of eventual publication in 1991, there seemed to be no point to fully integrating this already familiar dimension into the overall story. As *Abraham Esau's War* acknowledged, thanks to fresh research by and revisionist perspectives from more authoritative history scholars, there was little need to again dwell on 'the celebrated sieges of Kimberley and Mafeking; the latter engagement is probably one of the best-researched examples of how a community of African and Coloured civilians weathered the strains and bore a good deal of the destructive costs of conventional warfare'.[18]

Although mostly skipped over there, Sol Plaatje and the war could not but remain a twinkle in the eye of anyone with an interest in trying to understand black experience in the war, and through a remarkable set of worm's-eye siege observations. It was kept twinkling through the later 1970s and early 1980s over shared pints of bitter in North London pubs with Brian Willan, then also a research student and working on a University of London doctoral dissertation that would lay the foundation of his distinguished work as the definitive Plaatje biographer.

As the present volume's co-editor has emphasised in his recent magisterial new Sol Plaatje biography, what distinguishes the *Diary* is its 'sophistication and virtuosity', its general lack of 'distinction between black and white' in its recording of the writer's observations, its marked interest 'in individuals and their stories', and its even-handedness in depiction of 'acts of bravery, stupidity or cowardice'. Equally – indeed, if not more so – Plaatje's angle of vision was tilted towards the portrayal of 'a much fuller picture of the experiences of Mafeking's black residents' than that 'of any of the other siege diarists, all of whom were white'. Cumulatively, what his candid attention amounted to could not be expressed better than in the summary provided in his biography:

> We hear about the role of the Barolong contingents in defending their stadt; the 'Cape Boys' and their epic campaign in the trenches of the Brickfields; the situation of the black refugees and their desperate attempts to get out of Mafeking; the dispatch runners who risked their lives in keeping Mafeking in touch with the outside world; the exploits of Mathakgong and his band of cattle raiders; and, not least, his own role in liaising between the civil and military authorities and the African population, in supplying military intelligence, in interpreting at the Court of Summary Jurisdiction. It was emphatically not just a 'white man's war'.[19]

This, then, was the Plaatje whose siege diary was so seminal in stretching the historical universe of the Anglo-Boer conflict, in restoring to that world of war an assortment of lives and experiences which had been all but lost to posterity. More broadly, it is the pulse of his humane sensibility in wartime that gives his *Diary* its underlying value structure. At the same time, there was his self-conscious sense of identity as a loyal British subject, one 'of Her Majesty's loyal black subjects', anticipating that with the Empire's defeat of the Boer republics greater recognition and improved prospects for patriotic black subjects might come their way.[20]

In fact, the *Diary* has gone on to be assimilated by various modern histories of the war, even those not focused on the Cape Colony, let alone on Mafeking, as a slice of classic testimony to black British loyalism. Thus, in the course of his study of the Winburg district in the occupied Orange Free State, while noting the scale of black suffering in wartime and its crushing aftermath, John Boje turns to Plaatje on 29 October 1899 when his 'complete identification with the British cause is evident from a sentence on the first page of his *Boer War Diary*: "No music is as thrilling and immensely captivating as to listen to the firing of the guns on your own side."'[21] On the other hand, possibly by selective omission as being inconsequential, neither Mafeking nor Plaatje gets much of a look-in in the 2012 award-winning Dutch-language overview, *Den Boerenoorlog*.[22]

But this may also be to simplify or even to narrow the historical significance of *The Boer War Diary* as embodying only a valuable perspective on an early event of the war – coverage of a little over five months in the life of a Boer-besieged Mafeking – and reimagining its scope by bringing in the fortunes of black people to complicate the field of vision of the 'white man's war' in South Africa. In that sense, then, is the *Diary*'s imaginative place set to be fixed within a sort of sub-branch of South African War studies, perhaps best left to imperial siege-obsessives or to writers with a continuing interest in finding new ways to evoke, describe and explain black involvement in hostilities? Or can the life history of the *Diary* today be seen as taking on another dimension? After all, the historiography of the 1899–1902 conflict has undergone very substantial change over the past half-century. While the commonplace descriptive notions of the 'Boer War' or the 'Anglo-Boer War' still retain their figurative currency, they no longer express a literal sense of its multiple realities. Instead, the actuality of its *South Africanness* has become assimilated, nowadays almost a taken-for-granted ingredient of the mix of 'a wider war', to borrow the title of an early 2000s book that reassessed conventional understandings of the conflict.[23]

In that multi-layered sense, in which parts of the war are understood as parallel, coexistent and, at times, even complementary, Plaatje's Mafeking record may now be viewed as one of the defining emblems, even a distinguishing artefact, of the 1899–1902 hostilities. Thus, in an Afrikaans-language illustrated account of 'The Anglo-Boer War in 100 Objects', Sol Plaatje's *dagboek* (diary) joins General Christiaan de Wet's saddle and a cavalry sabre in conveying the history of the conflict.[24] In similar, or more obvious, vein, the Mafeking court interpreter and his 'famous diary of daily events' is a stirring sepia-toned insert in the massive wartime *Illustrated History of Black South Africans* historical album from the War Museum of the Boer Republics.[25]

More imaginatively ambitious is the wholesale absorption of Plaatje's account in a very recent semi-fictive evocation of life in an encircled and confined Mafeking, *Beleaguered and Besieged: A Year in a Place of Rocks*.[26] Here, the 'depressing and spirit-sapping' isolation inflicted by the experience of being under siege is compared allegorically to the 'lockdown' impact of the global coronavirus pandemic, 'the Covid-19 siege of 2020/21'.[27] A further inspiration for Mafeking as allegory through the mining of siege history as 'the starting point for fiction'[28] was – incidentally, for me a source of nostalgic delight – the empire historical fiction of J.G. Farrell.

Intermingling Mafeking fact and Mafeking fiction, the English biographical writer Hugh Gault has created a canny character, Sol Ventner, who relates a seven-month-long siege story in a loosely diarised manner. Appearing as a composite literary confection, Plaatje provides through his sensibility and eyes a key to understanding people and incidents as the eponymous Mafeking witness, 'Sol Ventner', who admits that his name 'does not sound very African. That's because it's not but I certainly am.'

Named after the Old Testament's King Solomon, he prefers 'Sol to Solomon', as among its 'advantages', leaving aside wisdom, was not having 'the tribulations of being a king'. The Ventner (a probable corruption of Venter) was a Dutch-language ancestral acquisition, 'passed down' and serving 'as an ideal name for an interpreter who must straddle as many cultures as possible if he is to remain employed in these volatile times'.[29] Located in a recognisable historical world, Gault's 'Sol Ventner' – reshaped and recombined to reflect the essential living properties of *The Boer War Diary* – peoples his Mafeking universe with a cast rooted in reality, from 'the showman Baden-Powell'[30] to the Boer general Jacobus Snyman, the fortunes of the Tshidi Barolong, and the fictive diarist himself, always self-aware, not least of his 'special and privileged position' as an employee of the administration, in effect 'an honorary white man, a feature that was most obvious in relation to food'.[31]

That sense of irony in wartime is perhaps as good a place as any in which to appreciate the life history of the original Sol Plaatje *Diary*. No longer needing to be read as an early illumination of black people's experience during 1899–1902, it can be placed – as a *civilian* record – among the classic personal testimonies to have emerged from the conflict. Candid, shrewdly observant, free of pretension and posturing, and marked by a humane outlook on the surrounding state of affairs, Plaatje's account can be joined by recently published Boer reminiscences which display a not dissimilar ironic sensibility. Margaretha Jooste describes a captured republican burgher in a concentration camp who was obliged to replace tattered trousers with skins. Washed and left out to dry overnight, they turned into 'blocks of ice'. With no alternative the following morning, he had to climb into the frozen legwear. 'It took the whole day for them to thaw. It is a wonder that he never became ill.'[32]

If the tone of that description of wartime life is distinctively modern or twentieth-century, so is that of *The Boer War Diary*. Thus, for a pair of British historians in their 2002 *The Boer War: A History*, Sol Plaatje features as an 'ironic and elegant' commentator on early Boer military shortcomings, whose diarist's smirk in November 1899 they quote: 'Goodness knows what these Boers are shooting: they kill on average only one goat, sheep or fowl after spending 1,000 rounds of Mauser ammunition – but very rarely a man.'[33]

In a small way, the style of *The Boer War Diary of Sol T. Plaatje* foreshadows eyewitness treatment of the cataclysm which lay just ahead in seminal First World accounts such as Edmund Blunden's *Undertones of War*.[34] Its dominant lens was that of quiet irony, for when in recording war's 'horror and violence, understatement delivers the point more effectively than either literalism or heavy emphasis'.[35] So when Plaatje records of weaponry that 'the big 94 pounder was on very splendid terms with me this morning',[36] this and other siege snapshots serve to confirm his spot as a diarist within the developing canon of a contemporary war imagination.

Three

Writing under Siege: Reading Sol Plaatje's Mafeking Diary 120 Years Later

Kevin Davie

How does one cope with incoming artillery shells sufficient to vaporise a horse or crush human skulls and mangle bodies into bits of flesh, all against the soundtrack of the incessant rattle of enemy rifle fire from not much more than a mile away? How do you deal with this, on a sustained 217-day basis, while managing to write – brilliantly – about this hell on earth?

So enraptured was I a few years back by Sol Plaatje's extraordinary record of the Mafeking siege, that I wanted to read it where he wrote it. I also wanted to evaluate his account against the precepts of literary or narrative journalism. This is a relatively recent area of scholarship: how well do Plaatje's words, written 120 years ago, stack up?

This is a high bar. Plaatje was just 23 when he authored his diary, had no tertiary education and was yet to begin his extraordinary writing career. He apparently did not even intend his siege diary for publication. He did not speak of it and its existence was not known even to close family and friends. It was discovered by the researcher John Comaroff who, in 1969, asked the family if there were any old letters or papers in their possession. This was 70 years after Plaatje wrote the diary and 37 years after his death.

Comaroff describes the find in the preface to *The Mafeking Diary of Sol T. Plaatje*,[1] an edition of the diary which he co-edited in 1999 with Brian Willan. Handed a tatty leather scrapbook by Victor Molema, a grandson of Plaatje's, Comaroff tapped its end against a table to remove the fine dust that permeated every surface. 'As I did so, probably more vigorously than I ought to, some sheets of foolscap slid from under the back cover … the paper was brittle and yellowed with age. But the script – including, astonishingly, long passages in pencil – was almost entirely legible.' The original, handwritten diary is now at the University of the Witwatersrand.

Plaatje's work and writing cast a long shadow across the South African literary landscape. Notable in this regard are his career as a newspaper editor; his authorship of the epochal *Native Life in South Africa* (1916) and the novel *Mhudi* (1930); his translations of Shakespeare into Setswana; and his compilation of a Setswana dictionary. This is not to mention his position in 1912 as the first general secretary of the South African Native National Congress, which later morphed into the ANC. Plaatje's story has been impressively told by Brian Willan in his 710-page monument, *Sol Plaatje: A Life of Solomon Tshekisho Plaatje, 1876–1932*.[2]

Educated at a mission school at Pniel near Kimberley, Plaatje began his first job, at 17, in Kimberley at the Post Office. But his linguistic skill – he could speak and write seven languages – and competence in shorthand and on the new-fangled typewriter, saw him subsequently secure a position as clerk and court interpreter 360 kilometres north at Mafeking.

He started the new job on 14 October 1898. War broke out a year later between the Boer republics and the British. In one of the first actions of the war, on 12 October 1899, the Boers ambushed the armoured train 'Mosquito' at Kraaipan 60 kilometres down the track.

Two black railway workers, their names not recorded, were killed. The mighty British Empire was at war with the two upstart Boer republics.

A 217-day siege began at Mafeking. The Boers pulled in their big artillery, including one of four Creusot 94-pound cannons, the most advanced piece of military hardware of the day, which they used to bombard the town relentlessly. Not that on the face of it there was much to fight about. Thomas Pakenham in *The Boer War* described Mafeking as on the 'borders of nowhere: a railway siding ... an oasis of tin roofs and mud walls in the sandy wastes where the Cape Colony, the Bechuanaland Protectorate and the Transvaal all touched fingers on the flank of the Kalahari Desert'.[3]

I was warned that the town was run-down. My expectations were not too high: the province had Supra Mahumapelo as premier between 2014 and 2018, when he stepped down following violent service delivery protests. But Mahikeng, as it is now named, largely conformed to my notion of a frontier town; busy, bustling, even though coronavirus restrictions had not been completely lifted.

'Mafeking' is a corruption of Mahikeng, a place of rocks, as the Setswana-speaking Barolong called it. This is the original settlement on the banks of the Molopo River. In Plaatje's time, as today, it was known as the *stadt*. Rocks of all sizes abound, many too large to be moved. Those of manageable size have been formed into walls, both straight and circular, to kraal animals and mark property boundaries.

One house was more prominent than the others. This, still in the Molema family, was home to Silas Molema, who took the young Plaatje under his wing and found him the job as clerk and interpreter. Plaatje lived in the house at times during the siege, and the diary was found here years later by John Comaroff.

Mafeking may be named after a place of rocks, but today it is a place of litter: plastic lies draped on its streets and public places. The residential areas, though, are neat, even the yards of modest homes being swept and tidy. Private cleanliness, public mess.

Plaatje lived in the *stadt* during the siege and worked at the civil commissioner's office in the town, over the railway line, about a kilometre away. The Barolong had opted to side with the British against the Boers and were to play a decisive role in the defence of Mafeking. A line of fortifications a couple of kilometres outside surrounded the town, the Boer positions being a few kilometres further out, the two within sniper range of each other.

My interest was in investigating how the siege diary measures up to the tenets of what some scholars call literary journalism, or narrative non-fiction, a style of storytelling which presents factual stories using techniques more usually associated with fiction writing. In it, writers draw on their imagination and writing technique to tell the story. Often associated with long-form work, such narrative writing requires that the writer be immersed in the story, soaking the text in details of place, scenes, characters and the spoken word. This approach, also termed the New Journalism, was defined by Tom Wolfe in the 1970s and is associated with American feature writers of the period.[4] But not all agree that the form emerged with Wolfe and his colleagues and that its practitioners are uniquely American. The telling of factual stories using the full suite of available writing techniques has a much longer history, and a far wider dispersion, than described by Wolfe.

Making this case, Andrew Griffiths has profiled George Warrington Steevens (1869–1900) in the journal *Literary Journalism Studies*,[5] arguing that Steevens, the pre-eminent British war correspondent of his era, wrote newspaper articles which read like short stories. Griffiths sees Steevens as typifying the highly commercial, personal and sensational British 'new' journalism of the last quarter of the nineteenth century. Like Plaatje, Steevens was under siege during the South African War, although not in Mafeking, but Ladysmith, where he died of dysentery. It would be instructive, I thought, even though Steevens was then on top of his game while Plaatje's published career was yet to begin, to compare the two.

I asked Sabata Mokae, who teaches creative writing at Sol Plaatje University in Kimberley and who has co-edited books with Brian Willan on Plaatje's novel *Mhudi* and his letters, whether he thought Plaatje's siege diary measured up to the prescripts of literary journalism. 'I'm sure Sol Plaatje will pass the test. But keep in mind that the diary was his first major work, which he didn't even intend to have published. It was also written at the time when he was only getting exposed to journalists and their work. So one could say Plaatje was quite courageous to undertake such a task as writing a war diary.'

Plaatje's first entry in his diary was on 29 October. His opening line sets up his relationship with the protagonist that was to define life under siege in Mafeking – the 94-pounder Creusot cannon, which he calls Au Sanna:

Haikonna [No] terror; and I have therefore got ample opportunity to sit down and think before I jot down anything about my experience of the past week. I have discovered nearly everything about war and find that artillery in war is of no use. I can say: no music is as thrilling and as immensely captivating as to listen to the firing of the guns on your own side. It is like enjoying supernatural melodies in a paradise to hear one or two shots fired off the armoured train; but no words can suitably depict the fascination of the music produced by the action of a Maxim, which to Boer ears, I am sure, is an exasperating grillery which not only disturbs the ear but also disorganises the free circulation of the listener's blood.

But while he mocks Au Sanna, there is also no denying the destruction it brought: 'Got up this morning and found very lovely weather. Sanna started at 7.00 and sent three shells into the town. I got there at 9.00 and met Sgt Stuart who told me that the second shell burst in the Civil Commissioner's stable and smashed the stable, Whiskey [Plaatje's pony] and all – poor fellow. When I got there I only saw his blood and nothing more of him, and a good thing too.'

Plaatje tells of a group of 22 Mfengu who had gone to an area known as the brickfields. Here they took shelter and killed several Boers, who responded with one of their seven-pounder guns: they 'cocked it right into the kilns'.

> Our men lay flat against the bricks, seven-pounder shells crashing among them with the liberty of the elements. They went for the bricks, knocked spots out of the ground they lay on, and shattered the woodworks of their rifles between and alongside them; in fact they wrecked everything except the flesh of human beings.
>
> It affused several of its mortal discharges over them and when convinced that everyone was dead, it cleared away leaving the 22 men quite sound, but so badly armed that if the Boers had the courage to come near they would have led them away by the hands.

Immersion and characterisation are often seen as two of the building blocks of good non-fiction storytelling. Plaatje was immersed in his story, if involuntarily. He tells us sufficient about himself and life under siege for us to engage with his fears and concerns, he being one of the two principal characters in the drama. Who is the other? You may now, over a century later, have expected that Colonel Robert Baden-Powell, the military boss of Mafeking, would be the other. But Baden-Powell hardly features.

Plaatje can't characterise the enemy, the Boers or their leaders – Piet Cronje and, later, J.P. Snyman – as they are invisible to him. So he makes Au Sanna the central character of the drama, putting the cannon front and centre, and imbuing it, as well as her progeny – shells and ordnance – with life and agency:

> Pleasant soft rains all day today ... I have never had a shell burst near me, but this afternoon while I was at the residency one of them exploded somewhere near to the east. A fragment came along, found its way through the roof, across the ceiling, hit the opposite wall and dropped onto the floor.
>
> This was in one of the rooms, but I thought that the whole

house was coming down on me and I could already picture to myself a number of volunteers picking up fragments of my body and piecing them together preparatory to them being laid out in the grave. This, however, did not come to pass, for then I would not have been able to write any notes on the occurrence.

How much of these siege times can still be seen today? There is a museum in the old town hall, built in 1903, which celebrates the siege. Adorning one of the outside walls is an outsized image of Plaatje. Memorials record the white lives that were lost during the siege. On the evidence of the inscriptions, it appears that you had a more or less equal chance of succumbing to disease as to a shot fired in anger.

Not all of the places where the siege played out are easy to find, an exception being Cannon Kopje, about two miles from the town centre. Plaatje calls the kopje Makane, telling how 800 Boers attacked this little fort from the east, south and west with the aim of provoking the townsfolk to rush across the plains to its defence, allowing them to be easily picked off. 'If this was their expectation they were sorely disappointed, for nobody cared ... nobody in the town troubled their soul about it. The volunteers round about the place, seeing that all the guns were trained on Makane, stood up and admired the operation as though it was a performance on a theatre stage.' Cannon Kopje, occupied by 70 officers and men, took about 20 tons of bombs on Plaatje's reckoning. 'Our losses were two officers and five men killed and six wounded ... This engagement was very unfortunate to me as it deprived me of one of my dearest friends in the place, in the person of the Hon Captain Marsham.'

Today Cannon Kopje, which is reached down a litter-strewn street, stands neat and tidy, a set of concentric rock walls under partial acacia shade. The site adjoins a psychiatric hospital. A replica cannon points (aimlessly) into the distance. There are a few dugout shelters; some rocks have soldiers' names engraved deeply into them.

Plaatje often makes light of the situation, combining weather reports ('Nice and pleasant rains') with daily counts of incoming shells from Au Sanna: 'We have this day received more shells than on any other occasion. But we are gradually getting used to them and it is getting more like a holiday than a siege.'

But Plaatje also captures the relentless bombardment and the horrifying deaths of some of the inhabitants too:

> Au Sanna seems to have been blessed now. The only shot she discharged yesterday did considerable damage. It came in at 1.25, just when I was returning from town. It cut across my track in a most sickening whizz and went for the BSAP [British South Africa Police] camp. It entered the stable and found several men of the Protectorate Regiment tending their horses, killed one and wounded two. The dead man was singing at the time it went for him.

The Boers, Plaatje tells us, are 'fond of shooting. They do not wait until they see anything but let off at a rate of 100 rounds per minute at the least provocation.' Not that he was impressed:

> While some prisoners were working in front of the gaol yesterday one of them was hit by a Mauser bullet (from the Boer lines) on the ribs. They expected the man to drop down dead, but the bullet dropped down (dead) instead.
>
> Immediately after, another hit a European's thigh. It penetrated the clothes but failed to pierce the skin; and just as if to verify his statement, another came round and struck the shoulder of a white man, who was shocked but stood still as though nothing had happened, when the bullet dropped down in front of him.

The constant bombardment meant everyone was on edge: 'Our ears cannot stand anything like the bang of a door: the rat-tat of some stones nearby shakes one inwardly. We often hear the alarm and run outside to find nothing wrong.'

A bullet flew close to Plaatje's cap with a *ping*, giving him 'such a fright as to cause me to sit down on the footpath. Someone behind me exclaimed that I was nearly killed and I looked around to see who my sympathiser was. When I did so another screeched through his legs with a "whiz-z-z-z" and dropped between the two of us.' Plaatje continued walking with the man, when he heard a screech and a tap behind his ear.

> It was a Mauser bullet and as there can be no question about a fellow's death when it enters his brain through the lobe, I knew at that moment that I had been transmitted from this temporary life on to eternity.
>
> I imagined that I had the nickel bullet in my hand. That was merely the faculty of the soul recognising (in an ordinary post-mortal dream) who occasioned its departure – for I was dead! Dead, to rise no more. A few seconds elapsed after which I found myself scanning the bullet between my finger and thumb, to realise it was but a horsefly.

He pokes more fun, amidst the mayhem and destruction, at the ineffectualness of the Boer weaponry: 'Mausers were also very brisk today. Goodness knows what these Boers are shooting: they kill on average only one goat, sheep or fowl after spending 5,000 rounds of Mauser ammunition – but very rarely a man.'

A siege map of Mafeking shows the Au Sanna site located about ten kilometres west of the town. We drove through a sprawling, rural township and saw an area which was slightly raised, about six or seven metres above the surrounding flatlands. This would be a good place to put a cannon, but driving around this raised area we could find no evidence that this ever was the spot.

I spoke to a resident, Galefele Molema, who had been recommended to me as someone who knew all things Plaatje. He said that the area had been taken over by a diamond mine and that there was no sign now of what had been the gun site. Sure enough, on a return visit the following day, this time to the other side of the naturally raised area, I came across the mine. It was clearly inactive, but a monstrous piece of mining equipment, presumably some kind of mechanical sorter, dominated everything, as alien and imposing today as Sanna, the Creusot killing machine, was back then.

George Steevens, the most famous British war correspondent of his day, regaled readers back home with his accounts of the British military expedition in Sudan, before arriving in Cape Town just ahead of the outbreak of the war. His reports, gathered in the posthumous volume entitled *From Capetown to Ladysmith*,[6] tell us of his travels through the Karoo to the front line at Stormberg: 'I wonder if it is all real. By the clock I had been travelling over forty hours but it might have been a minute or it might have been a lifetime. It is a minute of experience prolonged to a lifetime. South Africa is a dream – one of those dreams in which you live years within the instant of waking – a dream of distance.' The war was waiting to happen: 'The most conspicuous feature of the war on this frontier has hitherto been its absence.'

Steevens then reported first-hand from Natal where full-on hostilities broke out, for instance at Elandslaagte, and where the British raised the white flag:

> And then again that cursed white flag! ... The cursed white flag was up again over a British force in South Africa. The best part of a 1,000 British soldiers, with all their arms and equipment and four mountain guns, were captured by the enemy ... What bitter shame for all the camp! All ashamed for England! Not of her – never that! – but for her. Once more she was a laughter to her enemies.

Plaatje may have had only one big cannon to worry about: Steevens, under siege in Ladysmith, had four.

> November 10. Good morning, banged the four-point seven; have you used Long Tom?
>
> Crack-k—whiz, came the riving answer, we have.
>
> Whish-h—patter, chimed in a cloud-high shrapnel from Bulwan.
>
> It was half-past seven in the morning of November 7; the real bombardment, the terrific symphony, had begun.

He expresses a similar affection to that of Plaatje to his long-barrelled adversary, which 'conducted his enforced task with all possible humanity ... he is a friendly old gun, and for my part I have none but the kindest feelings towards him. It was his duty to shell us, and he did; but he did it in an open, manly way.'

As at Mafeking, there were no hostilities on Sundays:

> It must be said that the Boers made war like gentlemen of leisure; they restricted their hours of work with trade union-punctuality. Sunday was always a holiday; so was the day after any particularly busy shooting ...
>
> But the Boers had the defect of all amateur soldiers; they love their ease, and do not mean to be killed. Now, without toil and hazard they could not take Ladysmith.

For Steevens, life under bombardment meant

> if you have nothing else to do, and especially if you listen and calculate, you are done: you get shells on the brain, think and talk of nothing else, and finish by going into a hole before daylight ... If a hundredth part of the providential deliverances told in Ladysmith were true, it was a miracle that anybody in the place was alive after the first quarter of an hour. A day of this and you are a nerveless semi-corpse, twitching at a fly-buzz, a misery to yourself and a scorn to your neighbours.

But 'if on the other hand, you go about your ordinary business, confidence revives immediately. You see that a prodigious amount of metal can be thrown into a small place and yet have plenty of room for everybody else.'

After just a few days, Steevens was already growing weary:

> I was going to give you another dose of the dull diary. But I haven't the heart. It would weary you, and I cannot say how horribly it would weary me. I am sick of it. Everybody is sick of it.
>
> Weary, stale, unprofitable, the whole thing. At first, to be besieged and bombarded was a thrill; then it was a joke, now it is nothing but a weary, weary bore. We do nothing but eat and drink and sleep – just exist dismally. We have forgotten when the siege began; I know now how a monk without a vocation feels. I know how a fly in a bottle feels. I know how it tastes, too.

Steevens's last entry in *From Capetown to Ladysmith* was made on 6 December 1899. On 13 December he fell ill with enteric fever. He died on 15 January 1900, aged 30, six weeks before Ladysmith was relieved, after a 118-day siege.

Vernon Blackburn, who edited *From Capetown to Ladysmith* and authored the last chapter, said Steevens had a visual gift; out of sheer imaginativeness he could create for himself the style of a stately historian. Steevens, he said, had from earliest childhood a feeling for the prose of geography. His journalism contained much literature, Blackburn argued, quoting the magazine *Literature*, which noted: 'there never were newspaper articles that read more like short stories than his, and at the same time there never were newspaper articles that gave a more convincing impression that the whole thing happened as the writer described it'. Blackburn cites one admirer who speaks of Steevens's 'imperial pen' and another who wrote: 'What Mr Kipling has done for fiction Mr Steevens did for fact. He was a priest of the imperialist idea, and the glory of the Empire was uppermost in his writings.'

By some estimates over a hundred thousand black South Africans participated in this war, many of whom were armed, on both sides. This was true of Ladysmith, where both African and Coloured combatants participated in the fighting. You'd not know this from reading Steevens, as, with the exception of a few, mostly racist comments, black people are not present in the story. Griffiths, arguing that Steevens should be included in the canon of literary journalism, sees Steevens as having 'ventriloquised' black people out of his stories. They exist only for denigrating bit-references. Plaatje's diary, in contrast, is full of accounts of the critical, brave and decisive role played by Barolong combatants. Without them, Mafeking would surely have fallen to the Boers.

Just days into the conflict, General Piet Cronje sent a message to Colonel Baden-Powell, saying: 'It is understood that you have armed Bastards, Fingoes and Barolongs against us – in this you have committed an enormous act of wickedness ... reconsider the matter even if it cost you the loss of Mafeking ... disarm your blacks and thereby act the part of a white man in a white man's war.'

Baden-Powell too would have preferred to keep the Barolong out of the conflict, but there was no way to fortify the white town without including the adjacent Barolong *stadt*. While Baden-Powell may have had an ideological aversion to arming black combatants, as tensions rose and the outbreak of hostilities neared, the Barolong were armed, as were other black Mafeking residents.

Baden-Powell, Brian Willan tells us, did his best to maintain the fiction that Mafeking had been a white man's war 'and that the Barolong were not involved in offensive operations ... Baden-Powell had repeatedly prohibited the *Mafeking Mail* from giving a true account of the part they played in defeating the final Boer assault upon the town'. 'Black and white alike were critical of his heavy-handed misrepresentation, and Plaatje later went so far as to accuse Baden-Powell of "coolly and deliberately lying" in his evidence to the Royal Commission on the war, on the role of the Barolong during the siege.'

Some may think it unfair to compare a diary not written for

publication by the young Plaatje with that of Steevens, a Cambridge-educated and professional journalist pre-eminent among his peers, but for me Plaatje's writing is every bit as good as that of Steevens. The difference, though, is that over a century later, Plaatje, who engaged and recorded the struggles of all who participated at Mafeking, stands the test of writing time. A blinkered Steevens, notwithstanding his poetic prose, appears as a propagandist for a dated imperial project.

Four
The Missing Pages
Siphiwo Mahala

I am not a diarist. That is the forte of my brother, Tshekisho, or, as some call him, Sol Plaatje. In European terms you would call us cousins, but we regard ourselves as brothers. In fact, he is more than a brother to me. He is my teacher, my guide and my supervisor. He is a stickler for rules, this mentor of mine. I worked as a dispatch runner under his supervision. But before I became I runner, I was a rider, which is how I got the job in the first place.

It all started in August 1899 when I was sent to find brother David Phooko in Mafeking, to inform him about the demise of his grandmother. It took me four nights and five days to travel the distance from Maletswai to Mafeking on horseback. My majestic stallion, Motsamai, had carried me from Kimberley to Maletswai a month before. Our Maletswai is the place that Sir Harry Smith decided to rename Aliwal North, to honour the history of his people, as if our people who have occupied the area for years never existed. I digress.

When I got to Mafeking, abhuti David was sharing the compound with abhuti Tshekisho. I needed to rest Motsamai for at least another five nights, before heading back to Maletswai. The departure of David also meant that abhuti Tshekisho did not have enough support for interpreting and letter carrying. Whilst lodging with him, I assisted with carrying his letters to different people within the surroundings of Mafeking and Vryburg. It was due to my dedication that he recommended to the British to employ me as a dispatch runner. This is a task that I took with much enthusiasm, because Motsamai is a great travel companion.

However, on one occasion my enthusiasm to ride got abhuti Tshekisho infuriated to no end. He had this strange habit of recording everything that happened around him in his tattered scrapbook. He always carried his scrapbook wherever he went, and sat down to write his thoughts. When the siege started in October 1899, many of us could not anticipate that it would last for as long as it did, nor did we realise that it was a turning point in the history of the region. But abhuti Tshekisho had the foresight to jot down the daily happenings. In the midst of the sporadic attacks by the Boers, it so happened that he lost his scrapbook.

'Moses, my baby brother, will you please ride Motsamai to check if I didn't leave my diary near the Jackal Tree? In my quest for solitude I sat there to unwind and write,' he had asked me. Never reluctant to ride, and the ridden never reluctant to gallop, I readily agreed. 'Please be careful. The Boers can be very unpredictable. Although they claim that this is a principled white man's war, our safety as black people cannot be guaranteed,' he cautioned.

'There is nothing they can do to me, abhuti,' I said as I climbed on Motsamai's saddled back. My stallion galloped through the rocky gorges and slopes, all the way to the outskirts of Mafeking. It was a bushy area full of shrubs, save for the tracks that foretold the presence of the Boers in the vicinity. Indeed, there it was, my brother's scrapbook, abandoned under a tree where he seemingly sat and wrote. Its black cover stood out between the shrubs, glaring like the backside of a white goat going up a hill.

My journey back was equally swift, as my stallion had been feeling stifled after more than a week of virtually no activity. The Boers had just undertaken the siege of Mafeking, and a few incidents of sniper attacks and artillery bombardment at targeted sites had been reported. I could not wander much around Mafeking, as I would make a good sniper target for both the British and the Boers. But Motsamai did not know this. He was used to stretching his muscles every now and then, and his hoofs were yearning for the road now.

Motsamai was only a yearling when my father bought him from a white diamond trader in Kimberley. He had sacrificed two cows and a bull in exchange for the yearling. My father brought him all the way from Kimberley to Maletswai, hence we named him Motsamai – the traveller. Motsamai grew up to be a majestic and handsome stallion, outstanding for his well-built brown torso, a white blaze that began with a white spot on the forehead and extended down the bridge of the nose, a long shiny mane and white hoofs. I am yet to lay my eyes on a better-looking horse.

'Baby brother Moses, tell me that I was correct to think that I left the scrapbook there,' he said even before I could get off Motsamai's back.

'Yes, you were correct, abhuti Tshekisho. You left it between the shrubs next to the stone where you must have been sitting near the Jackal Tree,' I responded.

'That is wonderful news,' he said. 'You know, I have recorded the happenings of the first seven days of the siege in that scrapbook. It will serve as my war diary, told from a black man's perspective,' he added. 'Where is the scrapbook now?'

'Abhuti did not hear me well; the scrapbook is there by the Jackal Tree,' I responded.

'You mean you did not bring it?' His eyes were almost popping out of the sockets.

'Abhuti Tshekisho said I must go and check if he did not leave it there; I did just that.'

'Baby brother Moses, you were not supposed to just check. When you found it, you should've taken it and brought it back to me,' he said in exasperation.

'Abhuti Tshekisho always tells me to listen carefully to instructions. "Moses, my baby brother, will you please ride Motsamai to check if I didn't leave my diary near the Jackal Tree?" was abhuti Tshekisho's instruction.'

'Baby brother, it is a good thing that you listen to instructions, but next time you must also use common sense. I need the scrapbook here, because that is where I write my everyday observations.'

'I will go back to fetch it, abhuti Tshekisho.'

'No, it is too late now. The Boers might use you for target practice. Better go back tomorrow morning. I will use a different notebook in the meantime.'

'I will do so, abhuti Tshekisho,' I had said.

The following morning, I woke up early, harnessed Motsamai and led him out of the stable. After feeding on the lucerne and taking him to Molopo River to drink, I gave him some time to digest before we began the journey back to the Jackal Tree. We then left on our way.

When we got there, the scrapbook still cut a lonely figure among the shrubs. A few droplets of dew dotted its black cover like transparent beads. I tried to wipe the moisture off the cover, and put it in the pocket of the saddle. At that very moment a pair of soldiers emerged from behind a hill. Although I could not see properly because of the blinding rays of sun behind them, I knew their rifles were pointed at me. I heard the unmistakable sound of rifles being cocked behind me, and I realised that I was surrounded by a squad of Boer soldiers. Naturally, I raised my hands in surrender. The two soldiers that appeared first came closer.

'Name?' shouted one who was apparently the leader of the squad.

'Moses Moagi, sir!'

'Are you a spy?'

'No, sir. I'm a letter carrier, sir.'

'You want what here?'

'A scrapbook, sir.'

'What?'

'A scrapbook, sir. Here it is,' I said, trying to reach the saddle. There was a simultaneous cocking of rifles which stopped me in my tracks. I could feel the rifles pointed at me with bloodthirsty loathing, but I did not have the courage to lift my eyes and face them.

'Don't shoot!' said the leader of the squad, raising his right hand. I also kept my arms raised in the air, slightly higher this time. The soldier handed his rifle over to his companion to hold, and stepped forward. Only at that moment did I realise that the second soldier was a black man, probably one of the dissenting Barolong.

'Move away from the horse!' he commanded, and I obliged. He searched the saddle, and took out the scrapbook. 'What is this?'

'It's a scrapbook, sir!'

'Of course, I can see it's a scrapbook, but what is contained inside it?'

'I do not know what is inside, sir.'

The soldier looked at me irritably.

'He is playing with us, General,' said the black soldier standing behind me.

'I was sent to collect it, sir.'

'Who sent you?'

'My brother, sir.'

'Who is your brother? Doesn't he have a name?'

'Solomon Plaatje, sir. His name is Solomon Plaatje.'

'He's lying, General Cronje!' said the gruff voice of the Morolong soldier. I turned around to look as he stepped forward. He was wearing full military gear, along with rounds of ammunition draped across his shoulders. 'I know Plaatje very well; he has no brother like this one. This man does not even speak like a Morolong. He must be a spy!'

'Tell the truth, or we will have no option but kill you!' said the General.

'I am not a Morolong. I come from Maletswai, sir.'

'Maletswai! What then are you doing here?' asked the General.

'I came two months ago to report the death of a family member.'

'You report the death of a family member for a whole two months?' the General said mockingly. There was a chuckle from other soldiers.

'And what were you doing here yesterday?' asked the Morolong man. 'We have been keeping an eye on you, boy.'

'I was here to look for the scrapbook.'

'And then you decided to leave it here yesterday, only to come back to look for the same scrapbook today, hey?'

'Yes, no, sir, I—'

'Do you think we are fools?' the Morolong soldier said angrily. If he had not been carrying two rifles, he would have slapped me across the face. He turned to the General. 'This man is a spy. The horse that he is riding is a war horse. It's a get-away horse meant to travel long distances.'

'I have owned this stallion since it was a yearling six years ago. I was only 14 years old at the time. My father bartered it for two cows and a bull.'

'A two cocks and a bull story, maybe. What native would sacrifice a cow for a horse?' General Cronje said in a mocking voice. 'Check what this scrapbook entails.' He handed the scrapbook to his black companion, who took it and paged through.

'He has written stuff about the siege, sir,' he said. 'He is documenting the happenings from the first day of the siege. This man is dangerous. We must keep him until we have enough information about him.' There was excitement in the soldier's voice, almost as if he had made a major discovery.

'We have our first prisoner of war!' announced General Cronje. I felt like sinking into the ground at that very moment. I could not believe that retrieving a mere scrapbook might lead to my demise.

I was kept in a dungeon for what seemed like two years, but the Boer soldiers claimed it was just a little over six months. I could not tell the difference between day and night. Every day was the same. I was interrogated, tortured, deprived of food for long periods, and promised freedom in exchange for information that I did not even have. They gave me water when they saw that I showed signs of dehydration or near collapse. From time to time they took me to the open and presented me to some authorities who asked me the same questions about my spying activities. The final interrogation was with General Sarel Eloff, who ultimately released me after a very short interrogation. He said:

'I hear your stallion is as cheeky as you.'

'What do you mean, General?' I was happy to hear that they had spared Motsamai's life.

'It is refusing to be mounted. It injured one of my most experienced riders.'

'I'm sorry, General. Motsamai has never been mounted by anyone else before, including my own father who brought him from Kimberley.'

'Listen,' he said getting up, 'I believe that you are not a spy. You are an honourable native, unlike many of the Barolong here. You are very well mannered and articulate in different languages. You can read and write, something very useful in the current circumstances. We can work with a man of your calibre.'

'What do you mean, General?'

'We are going to release you, but that is not the end,' he said, offering me a cigarette. I declined. 'You will need to keep a diary. Write that we treated you very well when we held you captive as a prisoner of war. But I also need you to update us about the relief that the British are expecting. We have annihilated them and taken over most areas, but there will be a problem if they get reinforcements from Britain too soon.'

'I am not sure that I will have anything to report to you, sir. As it is, I doubt I am welcome in the community. Both the British and the Barolong will be suspicious of me, since I was relatively new and I disappeared for so long during the time of the siege.'

'You have a choice to be one of our native soldiers,' he said. 'But you are not the military type. You are a man of pen and paper,' he added with a chuckle.

'I would rather stick to pen and paper, sir, thank you,' I said with a suppressed smile. 'May I have the scrapbook back? I doubt you will have any use for it,' I added.

'A scrapbook? What are you talking about?' General Eloff seemed perplexed.

'The scrapbook that saw me spending six months in the dungeon. That's what I was arrested for, wasn't it?'

'Well, I wasn't there. But my advice to you is that you will have to choose: would you rather have the scrapbook and go back to the dungeon or opt for going home freely?'

'I'd rather go home. Thank you, General.'

'Get out of my sight!'

When I stepped outside the garrison, the rays of the sun shone brightly in my eyes. I heard Motsamai's distinct neigh. He was led by a Morolong soldier. He started trotting past the soldier, who then let go of the harness. I embraced his long face, and for the first time since I was taken captive in October the previous year, I found myself crying.

There was to be more crying when I arrived at the Molema homestead. I learned that since my disappearance, dispatches were sent to my parents to say that I had been captured and probably killed by the Boers. It was abhuti Tshekisho who never lost hope, saying there was no way that the Boers would waste their ammunition on me. His only disappointment was that I spent the whole six months looking for a scrapbook but still came back without it.

'We can go back and talk to General Eloff; he seemed like a nice guy,' I said.

'There is no need, brother Moses. I have recorded the largest part of the siege in my other scrapbook. But now it's getting too busy at work, I don't think I'll continue writing.'

'What about the missing pages; will you remember what happened in that first week?'

'The missing pages of a diary can be filled, but your life cannot be replaced. You have lived to tell the tale; that's all that matters right now.'

'I'm sorry that my six months' absence did not yield any results,' I said.

'Well, you can still redeem yourself. Now that the siege is almost over, the court cases are increasing. We are in desperate need of interpreters. Why don't you come and assist?'

'Most definitely. My Dutch has also been sharpened during my incarceration.'

The very next day, abhuti Tshekisho and I went to the court – he was riding his pony and I was riding on Motsamai. There was an air of sadness, as the world that I had returned to was quite different. It was a world where there was abject hunger among the Barolong. While I was in prison, I continued eating meat, and it later turned out that the Boers were stealing cattle from the Barolong. The natives were, in terms of the law of the British colonialists, restricted from arming themselves. It was inconceivable that natives should be allowed to shoot at Europeans of whatever origin. If they were allowed to shoot at the Boers, nothing would stop them from shooting at the British in the future.

Now the cattle of the Barolong were finished. There was hunger and starvation, and residents were dependent on rations. We passed men, women and children standing in long queues to receive their rations, which included dog flesh as one of the delicacies. Abhuti Tshekisho was lucky to receive the same food that was supplied to white people. I benefited from this, but the sight of helpless Barolong standing in queues waiting to be given rations, whereas only a few months previously they could produce their own food, was unbearable.

The first case in which I had to interpret was that of a Barolong man who refused to hand over his grain to the British authorities. He argued that, in the first place, the war that brought about hunger and starvation among the Barolong people was said to be a white man's war. The white man neither protected nor armed black men against the invading Boers. It did not make sense, therefore, that the British authorities demanded the grains that were the product of his own sweat and tears. I understood the man's argument, and I was sympathetic to his cause, but the court found against him. He had disobeyed the law.

It was at that point I realised that maybe interpreting was not for me. The court was adjourned for a lunch break and the officials seemed excited about the soup that was to be served. I took that opportunity to excuse myself from the court proceedings. My plan was to leave immediately, and to make my way back to Maletswai the following morning. I could not find Motsamai where I had left him. At the town hall next to the court, there was a long queue of Barolong people, waiting for their rations. There was much pushing and shoving, indicative of the eagerness among them to be served. This made me curious. 'What are they serving?' I asked no one in particular. 'Soup with horsemeat,' responded one man without even looking at me.

As I turned around the corner, a horse's head was placed next to the fire. The long face with a white blaze seemed very familiar. I looked at the long queue, and realised that before I started to cry over Motsamai, the story of how these people ended up feasting on horsemeat needed to be told. These are some of the missing pages in the history of the white man's war.

Five

The Music of 'Au Sanna'

Laurence Wright

This chapter sets out to explicate the extraordinary buoyancy and emotional lightness – the *jouissance* – we encounter in Plaatje's writing during the early stages of the siege. The matter is worth investigating because it distinguishes Plaatje's response from the work of other Mafeking and Boer War diarists and historians, offering a significant contrast.

Naturally, the Siege of Mafeking looks different depending on the historical perspective through which it is viewed. In contemporary parlance, the 'optics' change. This journalistic metaphor is intrinsically visual. Indeed, the word *perspectif* pops up in the late fourteenth century from the Old French *perspective* and directly from Medieval Latin *perspectiva ars* (the science of optics) and entails the notion of differing 'points of view'.[1] The numerous letters, diaries and histories that have come down to us from the Anglo-Boer War offer an array of contrasting perspectives, alternative points of view, reflecting the positioning of their authors. Concomitant with this spread of localised perspectives is the rich and varied range of prose styles in which they are expressed. By this means, the various Mafeking diaries and memoirs convey the discrete political outlooks, social status, educational attainments, and existential predicaments experienced by the different participants.

To give some examples, the brief, 2,000-word diary of Trooper William Robertson Fuller, aged 19, who served in the British Army's Protectorate Regiment, concludes with this heartfelt hope: 'Here endeth my diary and may I never be in a besieged town again' (n.p.). Fuller's laconic but precise perceptions constitute a personal record and are conveyed in succinct notes rather than fully developed prose:

> 14 April. An attempt was made to bring in 100 fat cattle last night. They were driven by 30 boys, but failed in the attempt. 23 Boys killed and all cattle captured by the Boers.
>
> Just as usual, Live and Learn.
>
> Troopers Maloy and Hassel were killed today by 12½ pound high velocity gun.[2]

The modest, laconic memories of Trooper Fuller contrast strikingly with the confident, almost bombastic pronouncements of Major F.D. Baillie, war correspondent for the *Morning Post*, who sets out an extended and technically informed military and political description of the siege for his readers, almost as if he were presiding over the conflict. His writing is clearly for publication:

> 28th, Sunday. A quiet day. I rode round the western outposts in the morning and found them considerably augmented in strength. They are now a series of bomb-proof block-houses, a zig-zag approach runs from the refugee laager up to Fort Ayr. So approach is possible without danger (which was not so before). A thousand yards to the front of Fort Ayr the new Boer fort is plainly visible, and flies a flag we have not seen before, blue, white, and orange, with a vertical green stripe. It is possible that there may be some political significance attached to this, possibly that our friends, the Transvaalers, by uniting the two Republics,

hope to get the Free State Boers to fight their battles further away from their own territory; but, after all, it is pure surmise, for we get but little news of any sort – and of political news none at all. Due south, and about eight hundred yards away from Fort Ayr, a new fort has been constructed, commanding the bed of the Molopo, and garrisoned by Cape Police. It is about on the position of the old look-out post. In the afternoon I rode round the eastern works. A trench now runs from Ellis's corner across the river, past the gun emplacement, past Webster's Kraal, up to and beyond the Nordenfelt position. It is hard to believe with the much stronger position we now have, and the reduced number of Boers, that they will attack again; but, on the other hand, it is harder to believe that they will leave Mafeking without a desperate effort to capture it.[3]

Compare Baillie's self-confident, matter-of-fact military analysis, sternly focused on strategy and tactics and airily unconcerned with the conflict's underlying rationale, with the desperate, passive suffering of Mrs Susarha Nel and her family, uprooted from their isolated farmstead by the British and transported to the Mafeking camp for women and children early in July 1901. This was the first camp Emily Hobhouse described in her report of the same year, alerting the world to what was being done to the families of Boer combatants. She wrote:

> Mafeking itself feels like the very end of the world, and the camp seems like driving six miles into space. There are 800 or 900 people, and is the oldest of all the camps I have visited. In fact, nearly a year old ... For miles around no habitation can be seen, and Mafeking folk are too bitter to do anything to help them.[4]

Susarha Nel's record of 'How I lived through 13 months in the Mafeking death camp', written sometime after the event in blunt vernacular Afrikaans, almost phonetic in its orthography, is harrowing in the extreme. The passage which follows, mild in comparison with many others, describes their traumatic arrival:

> hier lee en klompie en daar lee en klompie die kombeerse waf oor helle was die was hard van die rijp toe die zon op helle schijn toen tap die water ùit pertij se klere was zoo nat van die rijp maar helle moes maar zoo droog word ons het 8 dagen zoo op die kale vlakte geblij eer ons tente gekrij het toe word ons met trollies aan gerij elk een krij en ronde tent toe het ons bettere lijden begen van better geen hoùd om en vuurtie te maak o ik zal dit nooit vergeet hoe ik moes zùkkel om ver mij ziek kend en biekie kos gaan te maak graswortels en esel of mùil mes en moes ik bij mekaar maak om en vùùkie te maak o dan rook dit zoo ik moet blij blaas is die kosies wat van biekie meel en water gemaak is o dan is ik dek gehùil en die aù ziek kendkie aan die slap met die où hanger magie ja die better kelk zal ik nooit vergeet

> [Here and there lay clusters of people. The blankets covering them were stiff with frost. When the sun started shining, water dripped from them. Some people's clothes were wet from the frost, but they just had to dry out [in the sun]. We lived for 8 days out in the open on the bare ground with no shelter, before we were given tents. We were taken [to the camp] on trolleys. Each was given a round tent after which conditions improved a little but there was still no wood to make a fire. I will never forget how I had to struggle to make a little food for my ill child. I had to gather grass roots and donkey or mule dung to make a small fire. The fire was so smoky I had to keep blowing [to keep it alight]. The food was made from a bit of meal and water. O, and then I cried until my eyes were swollen at the sick little one asleep on an empty little stomach. Yes, that bitter cup I shall never forget.][5]

Different perspectives, different kinds of writing. The Anglo-Boer War has generated a cacophony of disparate voices of which these three examples are perhaps representative instances. However, most of them share a roughly congruent, commonsense world view in which, whatever the author's particular bias in the conflict, the commonalities of wartime hardship, suffering, deprivation and disruption are accepted as deplorable contingencies. The authors are mainly outsiders, trapped in a town with which they have no intrinsic connection, simply because a deep-seated international political contention is playing itself out there, as it is across the country as a whole, and perforce in their own lives. They are caught in a tense military predicament from which they hope to be extracted as soon as reasonably possible. Sol Plaatje shares this baldly factual outlook, but there is in his writing a further, richly rewarding dimension which is missing or less emphatic in other records. This dimension has two aspects. The first is that by birth Plaatje *belongs* to this place in a way other writers do not. He is rooted, not just in the besieged town, where he had lived for little more than a year, but in the area as a whole, its history and the history of the surrounding areas. The second is that there is an exhilaration to his writing about the siege, a unique spiritual afflatus, which other writers don't have. That at least is what I want to argue.

Before I illustrate the contention, an obvious objection must be put to rest. It could be argued that Plaatje's freshness of style and approach is simply the natural concomitant of his youth, his immediately satisfying career prospects, and generally congenial personal circumstances. There is much to be said for this.

Here is a young man, only 23, freshly entered into the business and legal world of Kimberley and Mafeking, becoming newly conscious of his extraordinary linguistic and literary talents. He is caught in an extraordinary situation which typifies *the* international conflict of the times, the Anglo-Boer War. The young man has behind him not only the rich cultural legacy of a traditional rural upbringing in the Orange Free State – he was of Christian Barolong parentage, born on a farm in the region – but also some formal learning, including formal grounding in the Christian faith and some slight exposure to the international nineteenth-century culture of books and letters, thanks to his time at the Pniel mission, north-east of Kimberley, under the tutelage of the Rev. Ernst Westphal and his wife Marie. After school (mission education took him nominally only to the end of Standard 3), his subsequent experience in the rumbustious environment of Kimberley, the diamond-mining vortex, where he worked as a messenger for the Post Office, introduced him to stimulating civic excitements such as the South Africans Improvement Society (founded in 1895), a club run and patronised largely by urbanised mission-educated Africans (Xhosa and Mfengu) from the eastern Cape. The club's activities reflected the ubiquitous Victorian passion for intellectual self-cultivation, evidenced in a devotion to the English language and an unchallenged faith in the British Empire. The non-racial franchise of the Cape Colony, with its cherished principle of equality before the law regardless of race, gave this privileged coterie in Kimberley large hopes for the future, a real confidence that history would be on their side, thanks to the beneficence of the British Empire. Young Plaatje flourishes in this environment, participating in political and social debate, attending musical concerts, and relishing his exposure to exotic events such as live Shakespeare performed at the Kimberley Theatre. He learns languages – Dutch, German, isiXhosa and Sesotho – in hopes of scoring a position as a legal interpreter. Then he marries Elizabeth M'belle, younger sister of his friend Isaiah Bud-M'belle, a cross-tribal union which initially scandalises both families (he being Barolong, she Mfengu) but which proves to be a thoroughly happy one. Such unorthodox marriages were de rigueur in sophisticated Kimberley circles, even if extended families struggled to adjust to the idea. Everything is going well for him. Eventually a suitable post as clerk and court interpreter opens up north of Kimberley in the small town of Mafeking, a place Plaatje knows well, and he begins work there in 1898, just a year before the start of the siege.

Surely this general background is sufficient to account for the exuberance of Plaatje's prose and the spirit of inner happiness which so patently pervades these pages? Is there need for further explanation?

Two of the most impoverishing approaches to the diary, valid in their own terms but devastating to an appreciation of the special 'lift' that gives Plaatje's diary its charm – and charm is by no means a negligible artistic achievement – are, firstly, the tendency to read the work simply as factual historical corroboration for what other siege diarists or historians affirm; and, secondly, to read it merely as a foretaste of the sterling literary and socio-political achievements to come later in Plaatje's career. The first response is that of the 'dry-as-dust' historian (to quote the nineteenth-century trope), the second that of the rear-view-mirror biographer. To rest in such perspectives, however adequate their baked-in teleological intent may seem, is to miss the quiddity of the Plaatje diary – the feature which makes the book such an exhilarating read.

Consider the diary's extraordinary opening statement, its fourth sentence: 'I have discovered nearly everything about war and find that artillery in war is of no use' (27). Written just two weeks into the war, on Sunday, 27 October 1899, the remark is a show-stopper. What on earth could it mean? True, the day is peaceful – there is no bombardment: 'Divine Services. No thunder. Haikonna terror' (27). But the siege has barely begun. On what basis could this young man claim to have discovered 'nearly everything about war', let alone assert that 'artillery in war is of no use'? Something here needs to be understood, and not merely passed over.

Plaatje does his best to explain:

> To give a short account of what I found war to be, I can say: no music is as thrilling and as immensely captivating as to listen to the firing of the guns on your side. It is like enjoying supernatural melodies in a paradise to hear one or two shots fired off the armoured train; but no words can suitably depict the fascination of the music produced by the action of a Maxim, which to Boer ears, I am sure, is an exasperating grillery which not only disturbs the ear but also disorganizes the free circulation of the

listener's blood. At the city of Kanya they have been entertained ... with the melodious tones of big guns, sounding the 'Grand Jeu' of war, like a gentle subterranean instrument, some thirty fathoms beneath their feet and not as remote as Mafeking; they have listened to it, I am told, with cheerful hearts, for they just mistook it for what it is not.[6]

The bombardment to which the inhabitants of Kanya (today Kanye) had supposedly listened with such equanimity was in fact the first major assault launched by General Piet Cronje, commander of the Boer forces, hurling an estimated 300 shells in the direction of Mafeking.[7] The attack featured for the first time the 94-pound Creusot siege gun Plaatje was to call 'Au Sanna' (or Big Ben or Creechy), which was destined to punctuate audibly and indelibly lives (and deaths) among the inhabitants of Mafeking for months to come. Naturally enough, several of the Mafeking diaries use enemy artillery fire, especially the resonant reports and changing positions of Au Sanna, to mark the passage of time and the 'progress' of the siege, almost as if the scope of the bombardment established a military-style *temenos* beneath which the drama of the siege was playing out. Plaatje's treatment of 'Au Sanna' is often jokey – humans regularly try to domesticate or tame palpable threats by means of familiar naming – and his running quip about the big gun's 'bad-night', a shot fired usually at about nine o'clock of an evening, becomes a refrain through the diary. The dismissive familiarity of the female name perhaps also hints at Plaatje's underlying attitude to his Boer assailants. If the British and their empire represented thrusting modernity, as Plaatje implicitly assumed, perhaps 'Au Sanna' (Old Susanna) signalled retrograde rusticity – 'sanna' can also indicate *voorlaaier* or muzzle-loader, a relic from the Great Trek – even though at the time, and internationally, this formidable weapon was 'state-of-the-art' ordnance. Plaatje details the munitions employed by the two sides as fully as possible, as do many of the Mafeking diarists. But none recounts the prolonged artillery assault as having the characteristics of musical performance.

His musical fantasia continues on the same page, this time invoking particular musical ensembles and mentioning specific musical forms, references based presumably on performances he has heard:

> I was roaming along the river at 12 o'clock with David [Phooko][8] yesterday when we were disgusted by the incessant sounds and clappering of Mausers to the north of the town: and all of a sudden four or five 'booms' from the armoured train quenched their mettle. It was like a member of the Payne family silencing a boisterous crowd with the prelude of a selection she is going to give on the violin. When their beastly fire 'shut up' the Maxim began to play: it was like listening to the Kimberley R.C. [Roman Catholic] choir with their organ, rendering one of their mellifluous carols on Christmas Eve; its charm could justly be compared with that of the Jubilee Singers performing one of their many quaint and classical oratorios. But as in everything desirable it ceased almost immediately.[9]

This is an unusual reaction to the experience of artillery bombardment, even if the predominating assault is from your own side. Fleeting reference to artillery fire as a kind of 'music' could be passed over as a simple emotive analogy: a noisy percussive discharge signals to hearers that systematic defensive action is being undertaken on their behalf, and the toneless cacophony may engender a corresponding emotional impact, 'rejoicing the heart', as music so often does. But Plaatje's extended musical encomium is light years from such an ordinary response to artillery fire, especially when the assault is possibly set to last for weeks and months. Far more usual would be the description offered by Mafeking's resident auctioneer, Edward Ross, who asks the readers of his diary to 'conceive if possible the smashing, crashing, bashing sound that was going on all round us, from 6.15 in the morning until 6 in the evening and then don't be surprised if we tell you that we shall not go looking for any more besieged towns, if we once get out of this'.[10] Smashing, crashing and bashing: this is the unconscionable din everyone in Mafeking has to put up with, at least sporadically, during the siege. This was the racket Plaatje actually heard, the empirical basis of his musical encomium. How and why does he manage to transform this tuneless cacophony into the well-mannered musical evocations which grace the opening pages of his diary? It is hardly conceivable that his mellifluous language lauds some primitive anticipation of *musique concrète*, transposing the empirical sounds of war into a strange conceptual music.

Some of Plaatje's linguistic exuberance can be accounted for by his sheer joy in 'languaging'. One can feel the zest in the young man's coinages – 'grillery', 'clappering' – the fun of being able to capture 'the world', or your immediate slice of it, in words. He is learning to make articulate what is really an inner feeling, to write back from sense impressions so that the intersection of interior response and external impression becomes intersubjectively available. So much is clear. But how can 'one or two shots fired off the armoured train' be like 'enjoying supernatural melodies in a paradise'? How can the enemy's discharge of 'Au Sanna' and her collaborators register as 'the melodious tones of big guns, sounding the "Grand Jeu" of war, like a gentle subterranean instrument'? Deeper investigation is required.

The Jubilee Singers were a black American ('Negro') choir, popular with both black and white audiences, which had sung in Kimberley on several occasions in the 1890s to great acclaim. The Payne family, from Australia, comprised vocalists, violinists, pianists, flautists and bellringers, in an equally popular musical ensemble which played for Kimberley audiences in March 1895 and January 1897. Clearly Plaatje retained fond memories of such concerts. The editors of the Centenary Edition of the diary note soberly that 'Plaatje was a keen music-lover and musician. In the diary this is reflected in his predilection for musical metaphor.'[11] Musical metaphor indeed, but in this extended form, and pinned to identifiable musical examples, how does Plaatje's predilection work? The empirical vehicle seems so stridently at odds with the elevated tenor.

Of course, the likening of coordinated gunfire in a general way to 'music' is not wholly unusual. Writing from the Siege of Ladysmith, one of the three prolonged sieges which dominated public response to the war, namely the assaults on the railway centres of Mafeking, Kimberley and Ladysmith, the dashing war correspondent for the *Daily Mail*, G.W. Steevens (he was to die of typhoid before the siege's end), wrote jokingly of the intervention of one of Au Sanna's siblings, another Creusot given the nickname 'Long Tom', as the Boers' bombardment of Ladysmith begins:

Ladysmith, November 10th
    'Good morning,' banged four-point-seven; 'have you used Long Tom?'
    'Crack-k—whiz-z-z,' came the riving answer, 'we have.'
    'Whish-h—patter, patter,' chimed in a cloud-high shrapnel from Bulwan. It was half-past seven in the morning of November 7; the real bombardment, the terrific symphony, had begun.[12]

There it is, the musical analogy, 'the terrific symphony', this time music writ large to evoke the emotional impact of the impending bombardment which was to be directed at the writer and his compatriots in the coming weeks. But musical analogy exhausts itself here with little need for comment.

    To regard Plaatje's musical predilection as merely another instance of the same thing, a routine figure evoking the emotional impact of bombardment, perhaps pressed beyond usual limits, or even viewed as a stylistic excrescence, might be a legitimate reading, unexceptionable, but it would nevertheless miss an important key to understanding the exuberant joy of Plaatje's diary. From a mundane empirical perspective (that word again), it becomes difficult to relate the specific musical performances, artists and genres Plaatje cites, which have their own character and historical positioning, to the rhetorical purpose for which they are invoked in the diary. How could cherished performances by an American choral group, a Roman Catholic church choir, and a consort of Australian musicians – these actual performances, not music in general

– be accounted apposite in Plaatje's figurative response to the artillery defence of Mafeking? A catalogue of past musical pleasures retrieved from memory is referenced to characterise the present experience of remote artillery fire. From the empirical perspective we are for the moment adopting, something seems missing. A Western musicological approach regards a concert or performance as a defined, bounded event, often text-based. Memories may linger and be described, but they belong to a time and a place. Music in general may function as a loose metaphor for artillery action, but hardly specific memories of specific performances by specific musical ensembles. Or can they?

What if we were to shift our sense of the diectic impact of Plaatje's utterances? In other words, let us explore the possibility that while their semantic meaning remains fixed, the denotational reference of these utterances may be other than is normally assumed by typical speakers of English. We need perhaps to get closer to Plaatje's main theme, the topic sentence of his linguistic structure: 'no music is as thrilling and as immensely captivating as to listen to the firing of the guns on your side. *It is like enjoying supernatural melodies in a paradise* to hear one or two shots fired off the armoured train' (emphasis added). This is much more than hyperbole.

Across the continent, African musical sensibility is attuned, not to localised empirical contexts of historical genre and performance, where printed score or repetitive and practised performance fixes the artwork in time and place – the typical Western aesthetic – but to music as mediating for the community a holistic cosmic response in an instant of spiritual meaning, inculcating immediate physical attunement and social responsiveness in participants or hearers. This statement is a whopping generalisation, egregious in its vagueness, but it nevertheless captures something of the linkage between musical performance and the open, unbounded cosmos within which African music operates to humanise participant 'audiences' and communities. I am not here talking about the variety of musical traditions in Africa, or the often stultifying debates about how to write intellectually about African music without muddying the waters with exogenous

Western perspectives. There is nonetheless an overarching unity in the metaphysical assumptions and procedures of African musicality which render it an intrinsic part of African sensibility.

Most academic articulations of the place of music in African cosmology emphasise music as integral to human life: 'Music accompanies and celebrates every rite of passage, birth, and christening, initiation into adulthood, and finally death and mourning' (Onwuekwe); 'In African tradition, music is an integral part of life linked with the worldview of the society in which it is produced. It has social, ritual, and ceremonial functions as well as some purely recreational purposes. Furthermore, quite a few African musical activities are ritualized and intended to link the visible world with the invisible' (Odunuga and Ogunrinade); 'The logic of indigenous African musical arts is the systematic management of natural resources and metaphysical imagination to encode society, and transact relationships, health, mores and an ordered polity' (Nzewi).[13]

Moreover, although they may express the issue in different ways, ethnomusicologists are unanimous that the experience of African music is immediate (literally 'unmediated') and invokes ontological connectedness in a manner which is inexpressible in any other way. Meki Nzewi makes the point as follows: 'The issues and perceptions of life in the tangible world have equivalence or complementation in the spirit or supernatural realm – "the ethereal world". Humans live in the physical earth plane, and manipulate the energies of the cosmos while they perceive the essence of the immaterial spirit immanence of the non-physical world in the material earth plane.'[14]

From this dualistic ontological embeddedness of musical response follows the widespread discontent with Western-influenced academic approaches that seek to articulate the significance of African music in abstract meta-language. This irreducible immanence is often asserted as a unique identifying feature of African music (though it is probably shared to some degree by musical inventories in traditional societies the world over), but it is less widely recognised that the issue is bound up with the disturbing emergence of symbolic forms expressing reflexive 'consciousness' of the innate musical experience. These forms are traceable diachronically or historically (as text) but are also experienced immanently wherever musical performance unites intuition and form without supervening intellectual analysis or interpretation. Philosophers like to develop such issues beyond specific anthropological or ethnographical instances. For instance, in his magnum opus, *The Philosophy of Symbolic Forms* (originally published in 1923), the Marburg neo-Kantian Ernst Cassirer (who was, incidentally, uncle to Nadine Gordimer's husband Reinhold Cassirer) observes that 'The mythical world is concrete not because it has to do with sensuous, objective contents, not because it excludes and repels all merely abstract factors – all that is merely signification and sign: it is concrete because in it the two factors, thing and signification, are undifferentiated, because they merge, grow together, concresce in an immediate unity.'[15] In other words, immanence eschews diectic gesture, that empirical pointing which is so much a part of language as 'sign', in favour of the holistic resonance and response which prefigure it. Describing and understanding the *form* of music is never the experience of music.

Philosophically speaking, Cassirer is rehearsing and recalibrating Kant's baseline distinction between 'phenomena' – things as they appear to the subject – and the 'thing in itself' (*ding an sich*) – things as they actually are, immediately, uncontaminated by thought.[16] Kant's direct philosophical descendant, Arthur Schopenhauer, developed this position, arguing that phenomenal experience gives rise to intellectual activity, thus establishing the a priori, the tendency of human intelligence to direct itself towards an object.[17] Cassirer retraces the intellectual forms which result, 'symbols' he calls them, back to their originating noumenal impulse, which is not only implied by them but actually present.

Cassirer's philosophy sets out in detail the emergence of conceptual thought in Western intellection. He is insistent that the development of language and, much later, of Western scientific thought does not (or need not) leave behind the immanent 'mythic' awareness in which it is grounded. The gradual disjunction between sheer experience (feeling, emotion, intuition) and a growing capacity for analytical awareness of that experience may indeed mask an underlying unity of intuition, but at some deeper level this unity remains ever available. An important implication of the potted philosophical excursus we have been following is that 'African' and 'European' epistemologies, however much they differ in surface manifestation and polemic, remain at fundamental levels in profound conversation with each other, even if this congruence is seldom heralded. The synergy remains as cogent for African performance in dance and praise poetry as it is for music. Any rift between African and Western musical thought-ways at their most fundamental is more apparent than real.[18]

The issue is important, because what I am arguing is that the 'music' Plaatje hears or finds in the sounds of artillery fire is not an empirical echo of past concerts seen as replicating or even representing the sounds of the siege. That is mere linguistic analogy, an empirical 'signing' or 'pointing' to satisfy the imagined (Western?) audience for whom he is writing. The diectic reference is entirely different. Plaatje's musical efflorescence presents a transcendent apprehension of this particular moment, the start of his diary, an apprehension which is outside mere history and which resonates with an inner awareness of who he is, where he comes from, his spiritual *habitus*. This is the moment, the process, whereby transcendental *being* slides into contingent *becoming* at the instance of the written word.

The music of Plaatje's diary is poetry, not mundane prose. It is significant that the diary's opening musical fantasy is encoded neither as memory nor as avid imaginative anticipation. This is definitely not Wordsworth's 'emotion recollected in tranquillity'; indeed the episode is much closer to the creative invocation of a Wordsworthian (and South African) 'spot of time'.[19] We need to adjust our mode of reading, from a diectic, empirical *perspective* towards our own noumenal or poetic appreciation, in order to savour the manner in which the diary opens. This is what makes Plaatje's so different from other records of the siege.

Plaatje writes his opening diary entry on Sunday, 29 October 1899. Having mocked the Boers' profligate habit of randomly deploying their Maxim in response to fire from the British Mausers, with no observable target in sight, he recounts two incidents where enemy bullets prove surprisingly ineffectual. A prisoner is hit in the ribs by fire from the Boer lines, but the bullet drops off harmlessly; another strikes a 'European' in the thigh, penetrating his clothing but not his skin. Then Plaatje notes that during the previous Wednesday's general assault on Mafeking (the one mistaken by the inhabitants of Kanya as friendly defence of the town) it happened that 'not one person was killed – while the Dutch ambulances were busy all afternoon'.[20] On the following Friday a raid led by Barnabas Samson, a well-regarded teacher in Mafeking, resulted in the death of eight Boers, with Samson receiving only a slight shoulder wound. On the Saturday, a foray by 22 Mfengu to the brickfields, about a mile outside the town but within the military investment, attracts the attention of the Boers, who deploy rifle-fire and their seven-pounder to good effect. The Mfengu take shelter among the piles of bricks to keep themselves safe, suffering damage only to their weapons.

The impact of these four days of intermittent combat, from Wednesday, 25 October, to Saturday, 28 October, creates for Plaatje a picture of limp military ineffectuality. Weapons *work* but seem not to have the impact they are supposed to. The impression he conveys is even-handed, impartial, although his own side, the British, comes off marginally better. Earlier, Plaatje has pondered whether the weapons of the Republican forces 'were imprecated by some empyrean authority', or their 'ammunition has been cursed'.[21] The besieged town seems possessed of a charmed immunity. The cumulative significance of these various 'hair-breadth scapes i' th' imminent deadly breach',[22] to misuse Othello's phrasing, goes a long way to substantiating Plaatje's opening clarion call, his flamboyant finding that 'artillery in war is of no use'.[23]

To this point in the diary, one might assume that Plaatje is utterly impervious to the human impact of the military siege. This is far from the case. Things had changed radically for Plaatje just the previous day. Having recounted the fortunate adventure of the 22 Mfengu in the brickfields, he follows this immediately with a passage in which the psychic trauma of war is all too apparent, though the precipitating cause seems at first unclear. Plaatje appears to be speaking for himself, or for the occupants of the house in which he is living (and where in 1969 the diary was found), or perhaps for the inhabitants of Mafeking as a whole: 'Our ears cannot stand anything like the bang of a door: the rat-tat of some stones nearby shakes one inwardly. All these things have assumed the attitude of death-dealing instruments and they almost invariably resemble Mausers or Dutch cannon; and such alarm was often the motion of the pillow if one was lying down.'[24] Quite what that last phrase means is unclear. Either the pillow's motion registers a blast (unlikely, it would have to be very close) or the pillow moves because Plaatje convulses while clutching it (more likely). Either way, writing on the very day that produced his opening musical encomium to artillery fire, perhaps in the same writing session, Plaatje tells of abject terror. His rapturous account of artillery assault as a kind of heavenly music flips to one of palpitating fear. The reason is not hard to find. The previous day, Saturday, the same day as the Mfengu escape in the brickfields, Plaatje has been through a very scary experience:

> yesterday I came through the gaol yard onto the Railway Reserve's fence as Mauser bullets were just like hail on the main road to our village. I had just left the fence when one flew close to my cap with a 'ping' – giving me such a fright as caused me to sit down on the footpath. Someone behind me exclaimed that I was nearly killed and I looked round to see who my sympathizer was. When I did so another screeched through his legs with a 'whiz-z-z-z' and dropped between the two of us. I continued my journey in company with this man, during which I heard a screech and a tap behind my ear: it was a Mauser bullet and as there can be no question about a fellow's death when it enters the brain through the lobe, I knew at the moment that I had been

transmitted from this temporary life on to eternity. I imagined
I held the nickel bullet in my hand. That was merely the faculty
of the soul recognizing (in an ordinary post-mortal dream) who
occasioned its departure – for I was dead! Dead, to rise no more.
A few seconds elapsed after which I found myself scanning the
bullet between my finger and thumb, to realise that it was but a
horsefly.[25]

From terror to bathos in a sentence. Plaatje's poised rhetorical smile triumphs ineffably over potential tragedy, his own and others'. The passage exudes personal fright. He knows full well what might have happened. Yet this is the same young writer who a page earlier – having just the day before been through this terrifying experience – starts his diary by writing so exhilaratingly of military bombardment as a kind of heavenly music.

The episode underlines just how special and untoward Plaatje's opening invocation of the music of war really is. Whether or not he wrote Sunday's diary entry at one sitting, it is absolutely certain that the young man who indicted his thrilling eulogy to 'musical' artillery fire has himself just experienced the narrowest of personal escapes. He knows, first-hand, what the grim meaning and outcome of the sounds he is lauding might well be. The musical encomium does not, cannot, spring from naive unawareness of the implications of war.

Nor can it be simply a hyperbolic encomium drawing on his musical experiences in Kimberley. Those empirical gestures are mere diectic 'signage', a 'perspective': trite musical exempla drawn on to sketch a slightly awkward factual vehicle validating his inner experience, which is inward and ineffable; a *mentalité* which infuses the opening of his diary with a metaphysical uplift that resists all attempts to reduce it to empirical quanta. He politely asks his readers to extrapolate from their own experience of Western music to enable them to imagine, or commune with, his inner state of being.

Consider again the diary's opening words: 'Divine Services. No thunder. Haikonna terror'.[26] (Both sides at this stage of the siege respected Sunday observance.) Having read some way into the diary, and harking back, the reader knows exactly what Plaatje has just been through; that the respite from terror to which he refers is not just the general community's, but his own. It is from this standpoint that he launches into his 'short account of what I found war to be': 'no music is as thrilling and as immensely captivating as to listen to the firing of the guns on your own side'.[27]

The intervention of the big gun on the town's armoured train, those four or five 'booms' which silence the 'clappering' Mauser fire from the enemy, remind him somewhat capriciously of a violinist from the Payne family ensemble stepping forward to silence a rowdy Kimberley audience, prior to embarking on a musical prelude. This would, one imagines, be a courteous intervention in a concert hall. A stilling of impolite noise, scarcely a violent rebuff. Immediate silence. Then musical harmony displaces discord and transmutes the space. It is as if the whole psychic energy of Plaatje's life is caught up in this moment, and the visionary forward momentum it captures is not the impulse of the war in which he finds himself trapped, but the stuff of life itself. He is confident in his capacities and in the future possibilities that seem to lie ahead.

The music Plaatje celebrates in his diary's opening passages is not really analogy at all. It has no obvious diectic reference. Certainly there is no bellicose animosity directed to an enemy. What is expressed is his inner life at this moment. What the reader responds to is Plaatje's joy in being who he is and where he is. Existential confidence in his own history, the history of his people, the bright future prospects beckoning for both and, beyond this, a happy openness to the cosmos, his inherited world view melding with the religious teachings to which he has been introduced; all this is latent – if unspecified – in this opening riff. We respond to noumenal resonance rather than empirical sign, lifting us above and beyond mundane perspectives to the inner life the opening passage expresses.

It seems important to recognise this young man's immanent vitality, because here is the first literary expression of that inner sprightliness, the cultural and spiritual self-confidence, which is to be the hallmark of Plaatje's future writing, and which will carry him through years of difficult political campaigning. This is the same charming courage and tenacity we are to meet in the character Mhudi, heroine of Plaatje's famous novel; the same cultural self-belief which inspires Plaatje's efforts to transmute Shakespeare into the Barolong universe. Perhaps, too, here is the energy of the cultural enterprise which would drive his recuperation of Setswana proverbs and sayings, as well as his work with Daniel Jones in devising phonetic orthography for Setswana. Above all, here is the brimming inner conviction with which Plaatje tackled the issue of land expropriation in *Native Life in South Africa*, confronting head-on the legislative chicanery (the Natives Land Act of 1913) which denied South Africa the future which Mhudi and Ra-Thaga hoped for.[28]

For whom was he writing? Plaatje evidently cared very little whether his diary was published or not. Probably he forgot all about it. There is no evidence that he pondered its fate. Was he writing for his family and friends? For posterity, should he not survive? On the evidence, it seems safest to assume that he wrote the work primarily for his own pleasure and satisfaction. In addition to the diary's obvious documentary value, it remains extraordinary that, all these years later, readers are privileged to overhear this remarkable young man's communion with himself, his inner being, at this unique historical juncture.

Six

The Personal Thoughts of Two Black Britons? Comparing Sol Plaatje's Diary and Tiyo Soga's Journal

Vivian Bickford-Smith

Sol Plaatje's *Mafeking Diary* stands as a sharp corrective to any thought that the siege was simply part of a 'white man's war'. Recently, though, Brian Willan has rightly lamented that Plaatje's diary has received little attention as a 'literary artefact' or 'text in its own right' – despite its rarity for the colonial period in having a black South African author.[1]

In his assessment of Plaatje's literary approach, Willan notes Sol's delight in playing with the English language and improving his use of it.[2] Facility in reading, writing and speaking in English – the language of commerce and governance in the Cape – was central to his sense of self-improvement, as it also was with the Rev. Tiyo Soga. It was an essential skill for upward social mobility, in pursuing career opportunities not (yet) barred to their ilk by white racism, and one that underlay shared elements of their complex self-identities as black Britons.[3] Such an identity was never seen by either Plaatje or Soga as incompatible with also being African, or Barolong or Xhosa.

Part of playing with English was Plaatje's experimentation with unusual words, or similes that could compare gunfire with musical recitals (a 'respectable' bourgeois recreation, like debating societies and reading), or metaphors that drew from the Bible or English literature.[4] Hence an entry that compared a black dispatch rider's ability to conceal letters when intercepted by the Boers in November 1899 to the acumen of Sherlock Holmes, Conan Doyle's fictional detective. Runners conveying messages from the besieged were described in similar fashion in March 1900.[5]

Willan has also wondered about Plaatje's authorial intent. Many diarists probably have some sense that they might be read by others even if they do not have plans to publish. Willan believes Plaatje had no such plans, but that his putative audience was his wife Elizabeth, parted from him by the siege. Yet while one reads the diary's vivid descriptions, linguistic experiments and character sketches, it is difficult to believe that Plaatje did not consider the possibility of drawing on some of this material in a more public outlet one day.

Be that as it may, Willan suggests that the *Mafeking Diary*'s neglect by non-military historians might be the result of its immersion in the drama of the siege. Such immersion is readily apparent to the reader: in the enumeration of the number of shells fired daily by 'Au Sanna', and with what (injurious or otherwise) results; or detailed accounts of local military actions; or rumours about the war beyond Mafeking; or the dreadful hunger and rationing inflicted disproportionately on the besieged. All this may have diverted attention from other less spectacular or remarkable elements the diary revealed, or indeed concealed, about the South Africa of its period.[6] These included Plaatje's arresting observations as translator at the Court of Summary Jurisdiction, or as a census compiler counting how many mouths there were to feed. There is also the question of Plaatje's broader (cultural, aesthetic) sensibilities, or racial, ethnic or gendered self-identities, or descriptions – their significance in this respect – of others in Mafeking.

The diary may also have been neglected as a result of its not fitting neatly into the 'grand narrative' of African nationalism. This, Willan argues, has largely been a political or historical chronicle uninterested in individuals – or elements of individual lives – that do not easily fit this narrative, not least when they demonstrated attraction to elements of British loyalism, identity or culture, and the tangled web of cultural hybridity that accompanied this.[7]

A diary that has probably been neglected for similar reasons was Presbyterian minister Tiyo Soga's 'journal'.[8] This was perhaps the only other diary, and the earliest, written by a black South African in the colonial era. Soga kept his intermittently between 1857 and 1870, while pursuing missionary work in the eastern Cape. Consequently, it might appear to be only of interest to historians of missionary work, and might also not fit well with an African nationalist grand narrative. Like the *Mafeking Diary*'s detailed account of the siege, Soga's focus on indigene conversion – 'enquirers' about Christianity; numbers of converts; levels of attendance at services or Bible readings given; or where Soga travelled on evangelical expeditions – may have distracted from its other components. These include Soga's views on 'traditional' culture perhaps, including burial practices, or his discussion of internal Xhosa politics, the character of particular chiefs and their attitudes towards missionaries.

Soga's record of evangelical activity provides a corrective to any lingering notion that missionary activity was exclusively a white activity. Instead, 'native agency' lay at the heart of its effectiveness. Soga's journal explains how and why. Yet beyond this, it is as equally worthy of analysis as Plaatje's as a literary artefact in its own right.

As it is, beyond Willan's cited reflections, there seems to be little else by way of analysis of the South African diary as a genre, despite the presence of diary keepers throughout the colonial period, from Jan van Riebeeck onwards. Many have been published by Historical Publications Southern Africa.[9] Indeed there is little analytical work on diaries in general, whether overview histories of their origins, evolution and changing preoccupations and styles, or their varied possibilities as historical sources.[10]

Hopefully, this comparative chapter as well as the book as a whole might prompt further discussion and academic exploration of the South African diary as a genre and source. Looking at Plaatje's and Soga's diaries in comparative perspective is an initial attempt to suggest ways this might be approached and perhaps to suggest a few new insights into each.

Understanding and comparing diaries requires knowing something of the lives of the diarists. Plaatje needs no further introduction here. Yet his equally extraordinary diary-keeping precursor may do so. Tiyo was born in 1829, the son of Jotello and Nosuthu Soga, in the eastern Cape. Jotello retained Xhosa religious beliefs, served as chief adviser to the Ngqika chief Sandile during several wars against the British, and was a pioneer of commercial farming in the region. Nosuthu converted to Christianity, was allowed to separate from Jotello, and saw to it that their son received a missionary education, initially at a school in Chumie (later Tyhume), later at the historically famous Lovedale College.[11]

Soga's education was interrupted by the War of the Axe (1846–7), which saw Lovedale damaged by Xhosa forces. He was then taken to Britain by a Presbyterian missionary to attend the Normal School in Glasgow, and was baptised there in 1848. Returning to the Cape the following year, Soga worked as an interpreter, evangelist, catechist and writer of hymns in isiXhosa alongside a white missionary. Yet their evangelical efforts, already insubstantial, fell into almost complete disarray following the War of Mlanjeni (1850–3).

Soga was taken to Scotland again and enrolled as a theology student at Glasgow University. He was ordained as a Presbyterian minister in 1856 and married the Glaswegian Janet Burnside in 1857. Unfortunately, we know little of Janet's background except that she came from a weaving family in Saltmarket, one of the worst slums in the city. An 'interracial' marriage of this kind was predictably rare in the Victorian British imperial world. When Tiyo and Janet arrived in Port Elizabeth, they encountered 'wonder and amazement' from all who saw them. 'In walking through the streets, black and white turned to stare at us, and this was the case as often as we went out.'[12] Once they were greeted by cries of 'Shame on Scotland', aimed at Janet for having married Tiyo, revealing the considerable settler racism in the region.[13]

The Sogas travelled to an area inland newly devastated by the Xhosa Cattle-Killing. It was in this context that Sandile allowed Soga to establish a mission in the region at Mgwali.[14] Janet worked alongside Tiyo in his missionary endeavours, chiefly as a schoolteacher, while also giving birth to seven children. Soga raised funds for buildings on the mission station, preached to the small but growing number of converts, and went on evangelical missions to Xhosa chiefs and their followers. Apart from his diary, Soga's literary endeavours included corresponding in English with fellow Presbyterians in South Africa and Scotland, writing articles in isiXhosa for the Lovedale journal *Indaba*, and translating John Bunyan's *Pilgrim's Progress* and the Gospels into isiXhosa. He met Queen Victoria's son Prince Alfred, who came to Mgwali in 1860, and travelled with both Alfred and Sandile to Cape Town on a British warship. In 1868 Soga opened a mission at Tutuka in the territory of Chief Kreli of the Gcalekas, who had supported the Cattle-Killing. Soga died in 1871 of TB at the age of 42. The earlier onset of the disease helps to explain why his entries become progressively intermittent, with large gaps between entries from the mid-1860s onwards.[15] He bequeathed revealing advice to his sons, who had been sent to Scotland to be educated.

Soga and Plaatje recorded their thoughts in and about different places, people and events in South African history. Their jobs and ethnic origins were dissimilar, as was the fact that Soga had travelled to Britain and Plaatje had not. Yet commonalities between the two men are readily apparent as well, be this their initial missionary schooling which had given them their literacy and facility with English, or their gradual immersion in British culture more broadly.

An element of this culture was diary-keeping. It had expanded greatly across north-western Europe and beyond from the late sixteenth century onwards, accelerating with globalisation and the rise of literacy, itself facilitated by and further fuelling the accessibility of writing materials and instruction. The emergence of Protestantism, emphasising the desirability of individual relationships with God and thus the ability to read the Bible, acted as an additional catalyst. Diary-keeping was seen as central to spiritual 'self-examination' and the monitoring of self-improvement. Over time, it became a less strictly spiritual exercise for many.[16] Both the rise of Protestantism and the growth of capitalism, seen by Max Weber as symbiotic, encouraged self-conscious individualism, the sense of 'interiority' and self-reflection, which diary-keeping further promoted.[17]

Diary-keeping in the anglophone world probably peaked in the late nineteenth century. This partly explains Soga's and Plaatje's involvement in the activity, readily observed as practised by others they knew well from their work.[18] An authority on British diaries of the period, Rebecca Steinitz, argues that diary-keeping's popularity stemmed from its effectiveness as a means of conveying the 'dominant discourses of the century': 'the enactment of Enlightenment observation and organization, Romantic interiority, Evangelical and secular self-improvement, Victorian domesticity, and imperial geographies and ethnographies'.[19]

Willan sees all these elements present in Plaatje's *Mafeking Diary*. The same could be said, though to varying degrees, of Soga's journal.[20] So, displaying Romantic interiority and Victorian domesticity, Plaatje lamented that he had spent 'the second Christmas of my wedded life ... so very, very far away from the one I love above all [his wife Elizabeth] ... I wish I could drive the thought from my mind.'[21] Soga's entry for 9 September 1863 demonstrated similar sensibilities:

> I cannot forget this day – I parted in Kingwilliam's Town, with

my dear wife and child – the boy Johnny – on their way to Scotland on acct of his deformed leg ... I never believed that I should have felt so much ... In this house everything proclaims my wife, & I sometimes am ready to sink down with sadness – Oh God preserve those dear – dear ones!'[22]

Both diaries convey details of imperial geographies, including climate and topography, and ethnographies in describing local cultures. Soga's does so for the eastern Cape, and the journey there. Plaatje's is full of thick descriptions of the built environment and varied inhabitants of Mafeking. The town's name became imperially iconic, an empire-wide synonym for public celebrations after the siege was lifted.

Soga's journal began with daily entries, but their regularity tapered off, particularly from the mid-1860s, owing to a combination of escalating missionary work and declining health. Throughout, Soga used word shortening and dashes by way of punctuation. Initial entries were usually brief observations of places passed, weather encountered, sights seen and services conducted. The first entry was on 20 April 1857, as Tiyo left London by ship down the Thames, a geographical beginning for many imperial ventures and one that famously appears in fictional form in Joseph Conrad's *Heart of Darkness*. Tiyo wrote: 'Left London this day for Gravesend where we rejoined "the Lady of the Lake" bound for Algoa Bay [i.e. Port Elizabeth] – All well – but in anticipation of the horrors of seas-sickness, from which none expect to be free – Mr J. and I went on shore at Gravesend to make a few necessary purchases.'[23]

The next few entries trace the slow journey toward the Channel, through 'still waters', 'squals' – 'All our company are sick – I alone am left comparatively well' – past the Isle of Wight into open sea and 'the roughest day we have yet had' on the first Sabbath: 'In the Evening I conducted worship in the mess room of the Second Cabin Passengers – Probably 20 persons joined in our exercises – ... a number of individuals on board, who delight in holding communion, privately as well as publicly with God, & with the people of God.'[24] The captain had 'very cordially agreed to assist us' in the conducting of 'worship' every Sabbath. A few days later, he asked Soga to read the burial service for the death by disease of an infant: 'aged fourteen months – Coffin – two holes – to let in the water – Revulsion of feeling.'[25]

If less often than Plaatje, Soga allowed his diary to be a place where he could express, perhaps release, inner emotions discreetly in this way. Could his journal be what Rebecca Steinitz dubs a 'book of the self', of 'interiority'?[26] Yet far more so than Plaatje, Soga used diary-keeping as an exercise in the observation of spiritual affairs, his own or those of others, within that long Protestant tradition. Plaatje, while not ignoring religious matters, dwelt on secular ones, including his work attire: 'in knickerbockers and without a jacket ... more like a member of a football team or a village cyclist than a court interpreter'.[27]

Soga also used his entries, in nineteenth-century missionary style, to record – often in detailed numerical form – the ups and downs of his evangelical efforts. On 2 March 1860, Soga noted the opening of an evening school at the mission that had attracted 'an astonishing number of 44 adults – young men & women ... I hope & trust that through God's blessing good will come out of it.'[28]

Engagingly, he recounted lengthy debates with Xhosa groups or individuals – including Chief Sandile himself – over Christian beliefs.[29] Some of this recording, surely revealing part of its purpose, subsequently found its way into correspondence with Glasgow Missionary Society members or other missionary colleagues.[30] Equally, thoughts noted on other matters such as the cultural traditions and future of the Xhosa, resurfaced later in articles or letters that appeared in *Indaba* or a regional newspaper, the *King William's Town Gazette and Kaffrarian Banner*.

This combination of Soga's diary-keeping intentions becomes more obvious in his entries once he is settled at Mgwali. A violent hailstorm in 1859 prompted an entry where he threw himself on God's mercy:

Ndsikelele Bawo, Umsubenzi wako namhla – wusikelele kodwa umpefumlo -Mabati abo bazilelayo ngezono zabo bandisulele ndililele ezam iizono – Undincede ndikolwe koko ndikushumayela kwabanye – Bawo ndifuna? Ukuzilahlela kuwe ngemilo yam. [You bless me, Lord, your work today overwhelms me, but the spirit – Let those who are crying over their sins move me to cry over my own, and help me to believe in what I am preaching to the others. Father, I throw myself at you as I am.][31]

Soga may have used the vernacular, isiXhosa, because he felt it conveyed his emotional thoughts in a way English could not. This is also a reason Plaatje may have done likewise in Mafeking.[32] Perhaps Soga was also subconsciously demonstrating solidarity with local inhabitants. A month later, Soga slipped from English to isiXhosa within a sentence, berating himself for letting his congregation down by insufficiently preparing his sermon: 'Never preached more wretchedly – indeed Andize nkikoliswe kushumayela kwam [I am never pleased with preaching] unless I have fully and carefully prepared my forenoon Kaffir discourse.'[33] If Plaatje used his diary to practise his English, Soga – educated so extensively in Britain – may have done so to refresh his isiXhosa.

Further self-reflection by Soga was frequent. On 17 December 1859: 'Much gratified by the admission of two young women into my Enquirer's class ... These enquiring souls should awake me to greater concern of my own state before God.'[34]

Steinitz has argued, though, that a nineteenth-century diary was not just a 'book of the self' but reflected 'dominant ideologies of the time' potentially 'complicit' in 'hegemonic social structures'.[35] Adoption or adaptation, to use more neutral terms, of such ideology is omnipresent in both Plaatje's and Soga's diaries. This can be demonstrated through their Christianity – in Soga's case, central to his sense of self – their belief in auto-didacticism and the merits of European education, their aspiration to Victorian respectability, and their thoughts on gendered domestic arrangements.[36]

Such beliefs accompanied and underpinned their waxing and

waning (depending on circumstances) enthusiasm for British identity and empire loyalism. This is made abundantly clear in Plaatje's diary, more indirectly so in Soga's. Plaatje's enthusiasm for the British cause was expressed in jingoistic fashion in plenty of entries, understandably perhaps given that the besieging Boers posed a realistic threat to his life, liberties and career as a black Briton.

One entry recalls the scoreboard deployed to reflect casualties in the First World War in *Oh! What a Lovely War*, that satire on imperial folly:

> The following is the result of the season's fixtures between Baden-Powell's 400 and Cronje's 10 times that number:
> Baden Powell 287 ⎫
> Cronje 19   ⎬ What a licking!
>   ⎭
> Mind you, this does not include the fight on October 14th and the bayonetting on October 21st. These games were against the Snyman and Botha teams called the Marico commando.[37]

Such a *Boy's Own* equation between war and sporting contests diminished in Plaatje's entries as the siege lengthened and conditions deteriorated, but returned towards its end.[38] By January 1900, Plaatje had begun to question his earlier unwavering faith in British martial prowess: 'I am inclined to believe that the Boers have fully justified their bragging, for we are citizens of a town of subjects of the richest and the strongest empire on earth and the burghers of a small state have successfully besieged us for three months – and we are not even able to tell how far off our relief is.'[39] Yet this faith never disappeared entirely, and towards the end of February it was revived by news of the relief of Kimberley 'and the [railway] line … being constructed north'.[40] By early March, after the surrender of Cronje and his army to the British, Plaatje noted: 'Boers bolted before Buller', 'Glorious slaughter of women slayers'.[41]

Direct declarations of Britishness or empire loyalism were absent from Soga's diary, being reserved for sermons and correspondence:

'I am the loyal subject of the best Government for the aborigines that ever existed under heaven. What would I not do, to have all the natives brought, in God's providence, under the influence of the English government.'[42] Such declarations have been deemed – by some post-colonial academics – to be but strategic public avowals of loyalty, perhaps for career purposes (whether as missionary or court interpreter). This despite the fact that Plaatje's loyalism was strongly reflected in his private diary. In this vein, some have argued that at heart Soga was a proto-African nationalist or pan-Africanist or Black Consciousness advocate. Soga could certainly be critical of specific imperial policies or of the immorality of many white settlers, and he was certainly committed to the spiritual and material upliftment of the Xhosa. Yet his support for the British presence in Africa seems sincerely based on his belief that this had allowed and protected evangelism. He could be a British loyalist in this respect, while still seeing himself – like some of his Scottish Presbyterian mentors – as belonging to a different 'race' from other Britons, such as the English.[43]

Soga's diary entry of 25 April 1865, headed 'The Kaffir Race', is significant here. It consisted of notes towards a letter he subsequently wrote responding to an article by a (white) missionary in the *King William's Town Gazette* predicting 'Kaffir doom'. Soga's counter-argument was that 'my Race' was not doomed, partly because 'Africa God has given to Ham – & all his descendants ... and nothing shall ever dispossess them of this inheritance', but also because Africa would ascend from the 'Barbarism & heathenism' in which it was currently sunk through the introduction of 'Xty & civilization'. As with Europe, this might take several generations. Yet missionaries were 'good men, [and] they would have done vastly more – had the silver and the gold of this world been theirs'.

If Soga explained the slow process of Christian upliftment as in part due to a shortage of missionary funding, he saw the coming of European settlers to the region as a further hindrance. Some brought with them vices such as promiscuity, alcoholism and exploitation of local 'ignorance' that corrupted black inhabitants. The British imperial government should not have allowed this, and should instead have fulfilled its valued – hence the loyalist exhortation cited above – duty to protect missionary efforts to introduce the gospel and essential 'social well being'. Soga contended that missionary work had been most successful in remote places like 'South Sea' islands where 'fatal vices' had (supposedly) been excluded. By implication, this model could serve the eastern Cape and its people well.

This implied protection of Xhosa landholding and, it would seem, traditional chiefly rule under the British. Soga drew parallels between the Xhosas' and the Scottish Highlanders' supposed 'love and attachment to their hereditary native chiefs', hoping this would continue under 'one benign [i.e. British] rule with the English people', believing the Xhosa were 'bound to their chiefs by the same devoted attachment'.[44] In apparently similar fashion, Plaatje also seemed to believe that different 'races' (a nineteenth-century synonym for 'nations') could retain separate identities under overall British sovereignty, like 'that gallant Britisher – the Barolong herdboy'.[45]

Unlike Plaatje's, Soga's diary overtly reveals his hopes and fears in this respect. Yet Plaatje's expectations for Africans like him who had acquired British cultural attributes are implicitly conveyed: that of being accepted as equal citizens, with no racialised limit on personal aspirations. These are expectations that Soga believed he'd achieved. The advice he gave to his sons suggests as much: 'I have got to a point of respectability in society, to which many considered impossible for a black man, yet it *never* was impossible ... God has made ... no race of men mentally or morally superior to other races ... but education, civilization, and the blessings of Christianity have made the differences among men.'[46]

There are moments when both diarists implicitly perceive difference between themselves and others of their 'race' along these lines. For instance, Soga deemed the majority of the Xhosa to be in a state of 'barbarism', while Plaatje noted that '*we* have very great difficulty in feeding the Natives ... about 7,000 of *them* in the stadt' (my emphases).[47] Both diarists also make occasional patronising statements in similar vein. Soga referred to people near the Bolo River as 'willing and docile', while Plaatje wrote about herders as 'piccaninnies', or the 'contented little black faces' of children receiving Christmas gifts from a white benefactor.[48]

Yet Soga and Plaatje decisively parted company with dominant 'settler' ideology in their refusal to accept that there were inherent barriers to the potential of members of different 'races', or that one 'race' was superior to another. They were perfectly aware of extensive white racism. Hence Soga's rebuttal of the notion that the Xhosa might be inherently incapable of ascending from 'barbarism' to 'civilization'. Equally, there is Plaatje's observation of 'very great difference [discrimination] between white and black even in a besieged town' in the allocation of rations. By March 1900, as food shortage intensified, he noted that some black refugees supplemented a diet of horsemeat soup by digging up the corpses of dead dogs.[49] Four months before, he criticised the *Mafeking Mail* for regarding 'the Native as a mere creature' while reporting that it had finally given credit to information that 'Kaffirs' supplied.[50] Plaatje's diary was a prolonged testimony to the loyalty, martial prowess and bravery of black defenders, including their cattle raiding which damaged the enemy. Yet it also recorded white bravery. Indeed, Plaatje often stressed interchangeable human characteristics: for instance, that 'white ladies' celebrating the relief of Kimberley could scream 'just as loud as Native women'.[51]

Part of refuting notions of inherent racial difference lay in the way that both diarists depicted those around them as individuals, not merely anonymous members of social groups, whose character traits, like those of the diarists themselves, owed more to this individuality than to particular 'racial' or other group membership. The possible exception was the wartime enemy Boers. Both diarists introduce us to a plethora of individuals. Soga refers to chiefs like Mhlana of 'fine – benevolent – and gentlemanly – amiable disposition'; congregants like Notasi of 'unwavering faith – of patient, uncomplaining suffering'; Mr Ross from Lovedale with his 'practical wisdom'; or Sandile, who challenges Soga to explain why the gospel was 'not sent to our

Forefathers' rather than being 'withheld' by God if 'considered so good'.⁵² In Plaatje's diary, we meet his close friend David Phooko: wondering why he had ever left Aliwal North, unexpectedly turning up with two chickens for Christmas, or weak and emaciated but back at work. There is also his employer, the 'patient' magistrate Charles Bell, with an 'acumen in fixing sarcastic phrases and aptitude in putting comical jokes', who speaks fondly of Sol's father and gives the diarist some of his best grapes, yet failed to deliver a Christmas dinner promised to his servants.⁵³

Writers of books 'of the self' might be expected to see others as relatively rounded individuals. But not all do. Perhaps it was Plaatje's and Soga's cultural hybridity and interracial or ethnic friendships (in Soga's case, marriage) that freed them from what Kwame Appiah dubs the 'lies that bind' – racial or ethnic senses of belonging, often accompanied by ideologies of inherent difference, that blind adherents to commonalities with people of other groups.⁵⁴

Plaatje could write that the death of the British soldier Captain Marsham 'deprived me of one of my dearest friends' and could sympathise with a white soldier convicted of illegally selling government supplies, 'such a pretty young fellow … he has a wife and child'.⁵⁵ If Plaatje's diary has been neglected in part, as Willan suggests, because it defied what became the grand narrative of African nationalism, it also – like Soga's – defied apartheid's grand narrative of the desirability of racial and cultural purity under the auspices of white supremacy. Such disruption is greatly to Plaatje's credit, a reason why his diary reads so freshly and refreshingly today.

Seven

'Part of a Longer Story': The Sieges of Mafeking 1882 and 1899–1900 Compared

Andrew Manson

'To the English-speaking Victorian public, and in the chronicle of imperial facts of arms, there was only one siege of Mafeking: in the long history of conflict between the Tshidi and Rapulana it counted [in Plaatje's view] as the sixth ... From such a perspective the events of 1899–1900 were just part of a longer story.'[1] Brian Willan's observation about Plaatje's understanding of the Siege of Mafeking from October 1899 to March 1900 as being part of a continuum of conflicts (or part of a longer story) is taken from an editorial in *Koranta ea Becoana*, dated 20 December 1902. Plaatje does not elaborate further, but clearly his comment should be seen in the context of a long-standing enmity between the Rapulana and Ratlou factions of the Barolong on one hand and the Ratshidi on the other; an enmity that found expression in both events.

The intention of this chapter is to provide some background to this state of affairs and to compare and contrast what is very evidently a

First Siege of Mafeking from January to October 1882 with its more acclaimed counterpart 17 years later. This helps us to understand Plaatje's references in his diary to the earlier siege, and to shed some light on the historical memories upon which it relies. I have drawn directly on material from Plaatje's diary or accounts of Plaatje's view of the siege written by other writers, especially the biography by Brian Willan.

INTRA-BAROLONG RIVALRIES

To trace the origins of the 'longer story' of conflict, one needs to follow the division of the Barolong from the 1780s. Rolong traditions record that there was a major schism in the chiefdom after the death of their famous warrior chief, Tau, in about 1760. This occurred in the context of protracted contests for dominance triggered by economic upheavals in the western Highveld from the middle of the eighteenth century. This period of crisis was the product of a variety of factors, including drought which led to food shortages and cattle raiding, and to competition over trade.[2] This caused the chiefdom to split into factions bearing the name of the sons of Tau: Ratlou, Tshidi, Makgetla, Seleka and Rapulana. Ratlou, as the first-born, was the senior. There is no evidence of any bad blood between the Barolong factions in the remaining decades of this century, however.

A chronicle of Barolong events and histories from approximately 1820 to their resettlement in the Cis-Molopo (the territory south of the Molopo River) in 1858 is contained in Dr Silas Molema's excellent biography of their eminent *kgosi* (chief) Montshiwa Tawana. However, Molema is not alone in recording this dramatic period in the Tswana past. Plaatje himself dramatised these events in his novel, *Mhudi: An Epic of South African Native Life a Hundred Years Ago.*[3] In brief, the majority of the Barolong were driven from the Cis-Molopo in 1833 following a devastating attack by Mzilikazi's Ndebele in 1833, who themselves had fled from south-east Africa following a sustained period of conflict there in the 1820s–1830s. This was the final straw for the Barolong, who had earlier been attacked by raiders bursting onto the Highveld from south-east Africa from 1823. Historians call this phenomenon the Difaqane, a period of intense conflict and dislocation that swept across the interior of South Africa. These initial attacks had forced them out of the Cis-Molopo to seek sanctuary as far south as the confluence of the Harts and Vaal rivers.[4]

As most readers familiar with these events on the western Highveld will recall, the Barolong, one of the first African societies to convert to Christianity, and consequently familiar with the ways of European missionaries, took shelter with the Wesleyan Methodist missionaries on the Platberg mountain along the Vaal River. Subsequently, they moved to a defensible mountain top, Thaba Nchu (in the later Orange Free State), paying tribute to the rising Sotho kingdom. Having rebuilt their cattle herds, the Barolong in 1841 decided to embark on what was an epic trek (one of many that occurred during these middle decades of the century) back to their homeland. The Rapulana, Ratshidi and Ratlou lineages moved in a northerly direction, which brought them into the orbit of Boer control. Hendrik Potgieter's trek party had established itself at Potchefstroom in 1836 and claimed suzerainty over the territory seized by Mzilikazi on the grounds that his trekker party had driven the Ndebele out of the western Highveld. It was at this point that disagreements and possible former enmities between the Ratshidi and their Barolong relations resurfaced and intensified. It would seem that the common threat posed by sets of interlopers on the western Highveld and a shared attachment to the Wesleyan doctrine provided some form of adhesive unity up to the middle decades of the nineteenth century. This was undone by the complexities and opportunities caused by the establishment of new and more militaristic and extractive Boer states on the Highveld.

It was the differing tactics and policies pursued by the Ratshidi in the face of the complex circumstances presented by Boer mastery of the region that drove a deep wedge of division between them and the Ratlou and Rapulana. Put as simply as possible and to reduce a fairly complicated situation to its barest elements, though all Barolong chafed under the restrictions imposed on them by the newly formed

South African Republic (SAR), it was the Ratshidi who took the initiative by trekking away from the heartland of the white state to its western margins, where they thought they would be safer from Boer depredations. Thus they moved to Lotlhakane (the source of a number of considerable springs) in 1849 just before their *kgosi* Tawana died and Montshiwa took over. At this stage the SAR basically considered its western border indeterminate and the Ratshidi were still their vassals. The Ratshidi had a different view on matters, believing that the British would act to prevent any aggression mounted by the Boers, Britain's former colonial subjects, against Africans in the interior of the country. Unfortunately the signing of the Sand River Convention in 1852 between Britain and the SAR put an end to any such niceties and allowed the citizens of the SAR free rein to expand their western border.

Refusal to obey Boer demands for labour and tribute led to open conflict in 1851, when a commando was sent to punish Montshiwa for his disobedience. From Montshiwa's point of view, the Ratshidi had broken free from the shackles of Boer domination by moving further westward. Eventually, realising his followers had little option if they wanted to avoid repeated attacks, Montshiwa responded by establishing settlements even further west in the Cis-Molopo, and then opted to negotiate a deal with his northern neighbour, *Kgosi* Gaseitsiwe of the Bangwaketse in modern Botswana, by which he was granted residence at Moshaneng. However, in no way did he abandon his right to possession and control over lands in the Cis-Molopo, signalling this by posting his younger brother, the Christian convert Molema, to occupy the upper Molopo River at the site called Mahikeng. Clearly, the Ratshidi had made their choices and were from henceforth avowed enemies of the SAR. They had also stolen a march on the Ratlou and Rapulana by being the first to move and establish possessions in the Cis-Molopo, to which the latter two chiefdoms felt they had a historical claim.

The Rapulana and Ratlou allowed themselves to be drawn into a contrasting position to that of their kinsmen. In order to avoid the restrictions imposed by the Keate Award of 1871, which was intended, among other objectives, to demarcate a western border for the Transvaal, President Thomas Burgers concluded a treaty with the Ratlou *kgosi* Moshete, acknowledging his paramountcy and agreeing to advance his ambitions in the Cis-Molopo. The Ratlou thus became surrogates of the Transvaal, and Moshete (perhaps unknowingly) ceded his territorial rights to the SAR. Emboldened by this support, Moshete in 1875 moved a section of his supporters to Lotlhakane. President Burgers similarly championed the ambitions of the Rapulana under *Kgosi* Matlaba and gave practical expression to this by displacing some of Montshiwa's followers from the all-important headwaters of the Molopo River at Polfontein and allowing Matlaba's people to settle there. Worse was to follow; in 1875 Matlaba ordered a section of the Rapulana to move from Lotlhakane 'probably without ever consulting Molema or Montshiwa'.[5] 'All the Tshidi clan', Molema writes, 'now clamoured for the blood of the Rapulana "dogs"'[6] and a party of Ratshidi warriors counter-attacked, seized a number of Rapulana captives (including Matlaba's son) and took home cattle, sheep and horses as booty. Sensing the seriousness of the attack and its likely repercussion, Montshiwa left Moshaneng in December 1876 with approximately ten thousand followers and trekked initially to Sehuba (Rooigrond) 15 kilometres east of Mahikeng before settling with his brother in the 'Place of Stones' itself. Here he found himself at the centre of the evolving crisis. He 'was now in a position to exercise his authority at close range upon his recalcitrant subjects – the Rapulana'.[7] His confidence in achieving this control was no doubt bolstered by the British annexation of the Transvaal in 1877. However, the divisions between the Ratshidi on one hand and the Ratlou and Rapulana on the other were further deepened when the Boers in the Transvaal rebelled against British control in November 1880. In this short-lived war, the first Anglo-Boer War, Montshiwa declared himself an ally of the British while Moshete and Matlaba sided with the Boers.

MAHIKENG BESIEGED, JANUARY–OCTOBER 1882

This conflict provides a background to the siege of 1882. Montshiwa acted upon his support for the British cause in a number of ways, for example, by sheltering those 'loyalists' resident in the Transvaal. On the one hand this invited reprisals from the Boers, while on the other it provided him with a cover for the Ratshidi to 'attempt to control the whole of the Molopo'[8] and reverse the losses experienced in 1875–6, thereby concurrently intensifying competition with the other Rolong factions. In February 1881, he 'ordered all the Rapulana living in Lotlhakane, on the wagon road south of Sehuba', to vacate the village.[9] He also accused the Rapulana of shooting at some of his followers returning from work at the diamond fields in Kimberley. Such interventions of course 'provided the opportunity for the South African Republic to offer support to the Rapulana and Ratlou'.[10] A force under Commandant Carl Hendrick Webers, one of the more determined leaders of the freebooters, encamped at Polfontein for three weeks. Allegedly, it was Webers who instigated the launch by Moshete's Ratlou of a full-scale attack on Mahikeng. (Webers later lost his life in the battle.) Matlaba's Rapulana also threw themselves wholeheartedly behind Moshete's efforts. When Captain H. Nourse, an official under the authority of the British Resident at Pretoria, George Hudson, visited Matlaba's town at Polfontein on 27 January, he found only a handful of men there, the remainder being at the front assisting Moshete.[11] Nourse further informed Hudson that Moshete was being supplied with arms both by individual burgers and by the landdrosts of the border towns.[12]

Montshiwa wrote to the British military authorities in the Transvaal informing them that the 'Boers are very bitter with me and are inciting Matlaba and Moshete to attack me'.[13] On 2 May he decided to take the initiative and attacked Lotlhakane, routing the Rapulana and a Ratlou regiment sent to assist Matlaba's men, killing 73 of his opponents and finally setting fire to the settlement. The action simultaneously enabled the Ratshidi to extend their control over the irrigable land at Lotlhakane. Commandant-General Piet Joubert reacted swiftly to protect his African allies, even sending a commando of 300 men to assist Matlaba in regaining Lotlhakane, but the cessation of hostilities saved Montshiwa from an inevitable and possibly devastating counter-attack. The fault lines were clearly drawn, and in the ensuing Siege of Mahikeng from January to October 1882 the Ratlou in particular further cemented their friendship with the Transvaal burgers and their government.

As is well known, the British lost the war, and the concluding peace treaty of 1881, the Pretoria Convention, showed scant regard for Africans living in the Transvaal or its neighbouring territories. The Ratshidi were effectively thrown to the wolves. Even worse, they were now exposed not only to the full wrath of their Rolong adversaries but to the depredations of white filibusters – more commonly known in South Africa as freebooters. These were men who were mostly (but certainly not all) impoverished individuals who became mercenaries in the hope of quick booty in cattle or grants of land, a phenomenon, one historian has asserted, that was 'rooted in piracy'.[14] They were a motley bunch. Some were deserters from military duty in the Transvaal, others 'Englishmen, who appeared to be chiefly deserters from the Imperial Army and English sailors both from the navy and mercantile service'.[15] The majority, however, were drawn from the ranks of Boers resident in the western Transvaal districts of the Marico, Lichtenburg and Potchefstroom. Thus, when Matlaba's Rapulana, five months after the signing of the truce, 'declared war' on Montshiwa's followers, he was enthusiastically joined by rapacious bands of freebooters. On 22 October, Moshete and Matlaba led their followers in a combined attack with the freebooters on Sehuba, driving looted cattle back to the safety of the Transvaal.[16] Another raid followed on 12 November when Matlaba's and Moshete's forces carried away more cattle and set fire to Sehuba. Under the direction mainly of Christopher Bethell, an Englishman who had befriended the Ratshidi and taken a Tshidi wife, Montshiwa attempted to raise his own mercenaries.[17]

The siege of 1882

Mahikeng was eventually besieged on 21 January 1882. On that day Moshete's Ratlou attacked Mahikeng alongside about eighty freebooters carrying three 'ship's guns'. They constructed a redoubt about three kilometres outside the town and conducted nightly raids for the next three weeks. It later emerged that the attack was not confined to Mahikeng itself but included its local environs. The village of Disaneng 50 kilometres west of Montshiwa's capital, occupied by subjects of the Ratshidi, was destroyed and at least fifteen men were murdered (it was later ascertained) after surrendering to the attackers. While the motives of the freebooters were predominantly focused on profiteering, the officials of the Transvaal were happy to allow 'volunteers', raised from within the borders of their state, to exact punishment on Montshiwa for having thrown his political hat into the British ring. The freebooters were their proxies as much as the Ratlou were those of the motley crew of white volunteers who invoked Moshete's name to justify their atrocities. Meanwhile, the Earl of Kimberley, Britain's colonial secretary, could do no more than remind the Transvaal government about the proclamation of neutrality it had signed under the Pretoria Convention and sent officials employed at the Resident's Office in Pretoria to monitor the course of the conflict.

By October Montshiwa was forced to fly the flag of truce, so devastating was the conflict's overall impact. The Ratshidi were unable to plough and, with no harvest in sight, in Molema's memorable phrase, 'the gaunt spectre of famine stalked through the land'.[18] This perilous state of affairs was 'exacerbated by the arrival of hundreds of people who had evacuated Sehuba … [causing] the rapid spread of diseases'[19] – two of Montshiwa's councillors died of dysentery.

Consequences

Montshiwa was forced to accept humiliating 'peace terms' after he surrendered. However, many of these conditions he simply ignored; in effect, once the freebooters had claimed their booty they had little interest or capacity to enforce the terms of the treaty. Significantly, as many readers will recall, the treaty led to the establishment of the

Boer republics of Goshen in Montshiwa's territory and Stellaland further south in Mankurwane's land. Both were essentially feeble states, but from the perspective of the Imperial power they posed a threat to stability in the Bechuanaland region and to control of the 'Road to the North' and the economic opportunities it presented. The death knell of the republics was sounded by the possibility of German imperial advance into the region from present-day Namibia and the news of the gruesome murder of Christopher Bethell, whose politically well-connected family demanded justice for this atrocity. The result, though it never played out with such symmetrical neatness as its architects might have envisaged, was of course Charles Warren's military expedition to dismantle the Boer republics, the extension of colonial control over the southern Tswana, and the declaration of a protectorate over those people living in modern-day Botswana.[20] Thus the siege of 1882 was to provide the motive for Britain's clear intervention in Bechuanaland and the blueprint for future intervention in Kruger's Republic, which was given impetus by the discovery of gold in the mid-1880s. This finally came about with the Jameson Raid, a botched attempt to overthrow a legitimately constituted state and the ensuing South African War, which, again, held dire consequences for Montshiwa's Rolong, though the wise old *kgosi* was personally spared its shocking consequences, as he died in 1896.

To reiterate the point, at the risk of possibly being overly deterministic, there was a linear political connectedness between the two events, both of which were located in the same geographical theatre. In similar vein, John Comaroff observes that Mafeking 'represented the confluence of competing interests in South Africa at the time; its significance was more than merely logistic'.[21] In another important development spawned by the Bechuanaland wars, the Ratlou, far from extending their lands, found large swathes of their territory had been ceded to the freebooter states. Moshete and his followers realised they had been duped; in the words of the Rev. John Mackenzie, 'living in a veritable fools' paradise apparently ignorant of what had been said and done in their name'.[22] (The freebooters referred to themselves as

'Moshete's volunteers'.) In 1885 Moshete asked to be placed under British protection. He died four years later.

COMPARISONS

There is a distinct dissimilarity between the two events, in that in 1882 the freebooters (though aided by the Transvaal state) were the aggressors and the Ratshidi the direct object of their belligerence. In 1898–1900 the Ratshidi under their *kgosi* Wessels Montshiwa were ostensibly bystanders in what was meant to be a 'white man's war' between the Imperial power and the Boers. In other respects, however, there are several striking likenesses and continuities in the conduct of the respective sieges.

Intra–Barolong schisms and antagonisms

As we have mentioned, in July 1885 Moshete, realising he had gained nothing from supporting the efforts of the Transvaal authorities and the freebooters, and that he was but a pawn in their hands all along, asked to be taken under British protection. Simultaneously the Ratlou and Ratshidi put aside their long-standing enmity. However, the same did not hold true for the Rapulana, who saw the 1899 siege as an opportunity to continue their long-standing feud with the Ratshidi. The Boers under General J.P. Snyman engaged the services of African allies and armed them, a precedent he had personally established in 1882. These individuals included, but were not limited to, the Rapulana. *Kgosi* Saane, a nephew of Wessels Montshiwa, was arrested by the Boers in early January 1900 'after they rightly suspected him of supplying the garrison with information'[23] about their tactics and movements. The Rapulana were entrusted with the task of keeping him captive at their capital town, Rietfontein, but nevertheless he managed to impart information to the garrison during his incarceration. Later Saane reported his captivity 'at the hands of [*Kgosi* Abraham] Matuba and his headmen' to the British authorities, 'providing details of how his captors had been issued with arms by General Snyman in January 1900'.[24] The Ratshidi sought revenge for this act and simultaneously took advantage of the conflict to 'settle their own score' with the Rapulana. Brian Willan records that Silas Molema led an expedition to Lotlhakane (Rietfontein) to capture Chief Abraham Matuba and his headmen, returning in triumph not only with the chief as their prisoner but with 'large quantities of livestock and loot',[25] amounting to 200 head of cattle, 500 sheep and goats, and a few horses. A number of Rapulana men were later imprisoned in Mafeking for taking up arms against the Ratshidi. Plaatje regarded these incidents as stemming from a 'long-standing quarrel between them [the Rapulana] and ourselves which made up a case of treason'. However, in his biography Willan casts doubt on whether the charge of treason was an 'appropriate' assessment of the situation.

The Ratshidi conversely hoped their loyalty to the British and the assistance they rendered would result in the restoration of land at Polfontein (Bodipe) occupied by Matlaba's people. In this presumption they were proved correct. After the Bechuanaland proclamation of 1885, the then magistrate of Mafeking, Charles Bell, had ratified the appointment of Ratshidi headmen at Lotlhakane. Further evidence of Rapulana aggression against the Ratshidi only confirmed and strengthened the conviction that this was a correct and appropriate measure. Thus, the dispute over the area 'dragged on until well into the third decade of the next century, when, after investigations lasting "thirty-three years by successive officials and representatives in the Bechuanaland region" the Supreme Court ruled that the Rapulana were the rightful claimants to Lotlhakane'.[26]

The same cast of characters
From the Boer perspective the siege of 1899–1900 was indeed part of a longer story. It can be assumed that several of them, frustrated by the relative scarcity of booty accruing from the first war with the Ratshidi and the failure to gain a long-term foothold in the irrigable farms at Sehuba, saw another opportunity to plunder Barolong cattle and the other profits of war. It is also likely that some members of the Boer forces had been participants in the earlier attacks on Mahikeng.

Their spirits would have been lifted by the appointment of General Piet Cronje of Potchefstroom in charge of the western theatre of war.

A veteran of the first Anglo-Boer War, Cronje was among those officials of the Transvaal who 'conducted a long and at times acrimonious correspondence about conflicting territorial claims, spoliations and reprisals' between Montshiwa and the Transvaal and its African allies after the Ratshidi attack on Matlaba's followers at Polfontein in 1874.[27] This sense of confidence would most likely have been reinforced by the appointment of none other than J.P. Snyman as his successor. Snyman was a long-term resident of the Marico, who in 1882 had 'crossed the [Transvaal] boundary in charge of Transvaal border guards [and] attacked the Ratshidi'.[28] It was this definitive assault that forced Montshiwa to accept the duplicitous Snyman Treaty of 24 October 1882, negotiated, as the secretary to the British resident in Pretoria, R. Rutherfoord, informed the British high commissioner, 'at Cannon's mouth by the Boers'.[29] Undoubtedly the older men and residents of the Mahikeng *stadt* remembered the devastating consequences of this 'treaty', which forced the Ratshidi to assign most of their country south of the Molopo River to the freebooters, thus depriving them of almost all their fields for cultivation and about 70 per cent of their grazing land.[30] Snyman, it seems, adopted a similar tactic to that which he employed in 1882: one of long-term attrition. 'Starvation', Plaatje notes, 'appears to be the fate for which Snyman planned for his enemy.' By January 1900 Plaatje records that sickness, 'which has not formerly troubled us very much during the siege', was now badly affecting the Barolong, with the result that Silas Molema's sister had 'setlhabi [a severe chest pain] – she can hardly breathe'.[31] This starvation was to lead to the repatriation of many Barolong from the town. The crisis was worsened by the continuing disease of rinderpest, which decimated the Rolong herds.

Plaatje was certainly aware of the persistence of memories held by both the Boers and the Ratshidi regarding the 1882 siege. Indeed, many of the older Rolong residents of Mafeking must have experienced a sense of déjà vu during the 217 days of the siege. (Both events incidentally were of almost identical duration, the 1882 siege lasting 229 days.) Plaatje records that 'these west Transvaalers ought to remember that Mafeking has always held her own against becoming Dutch and the only Boer who owned Mafeking was the one who swore by the honour of the King'.[32] Comparing the effects of the artillery bombardment of Mafeking, Plaatje asserted that 'the Barolongs who fought Snyman and Cronje, many years ago, freely admit that if, at the time, the Boers brought something half the size of "Sanna" [a highly effective siege gun] to bear on them, they would have started a mutiny if Montshioa [Montshiwa] had refused to hoist the white flag'.[33] We can presume that among the Boer forces was a sprinkling of former freebooters.

In addition, a few of the individuals caught up in the crisis of 1882 were participants, though in different ways, in 1899–1900. One of these was James Honey, a colourful character based in Taung, a settlement which it would appear was a centre of organised brigandage in the early 1880s. One of the leading criminal instigators was Scotty Smith, the alias of George Lennox, a Scotsman popularly remembered as South Africa's Robin Hood, and his gang of both 'Europeans and Natives'. Honey initially was arrested by the Stellaland authorities in 1881 on a charge of theft and conspiracy to incite an insurrection against their puny state. Honey escaped and, ever the opportunist, enlisted as a volunteer with Mankurwane's Batlhaping in 1883, thus confirming the suspicions of the Stellaland authorities. Declared an outlaw, he was thought to have been murdered by the Stellalanders; this at the time caught the attention of the British press. However, it proved to be untrue.[34] Interestingly, it is very likely that he was the same 'Mr Honey' who in March 1900 assisted 'two Rolong despatch runners ... to reach Kimberley'. One of the runners had encountered Honey at the Vaal River and the other, Plaatje's own brother Gabriel, who lived near Taung, was a personal friend of Honey's. Honey, Plaatje informs readers, was 'on excellent terms with the Boers, and they allow him to move about freely' and was therefore a useful contact to have.[35]

Enduring tactics

It would be safe to suggest that a number of tactics learned during the 1882 encirclement were re-employed during the later conflict. This applies mainly to the capturing and smuggling of livestock into the town from the surrounding countryside. This intensified as starvation set in during both sieges. While in the various accounts of the 1882 siege there is no direct evidence of the Ratshidi purloining or by other means securing livestock from the invading force or from Batswana allies (such as the Hurutshe in the Transvaal, who were severely punished for this loyalty), it would undoubtedly have formed part of their response to the crisis. It is worthy of mention that the attack on Disaneng was partly a punishment for the local chief Jan Masibi's having supplied Montshiwa with cattle.

Furthermore, in 1882 the dire need to secure arms and ammunition led to parties of men breaching the surrounding redoubts during the night to try to obtain these supplies wherever they could – Kimberley, Kanye and elsewhere. It was in these operations that Christopher Bethell displayed his initiative and almost reckless daring.[36] In 1900 it was the exploits of the cattle raiders such as Mathakgong (and others) who attacked Boer farmsteads and ran cattle back to Mafeking, that 'boosted the morale of blacks and whites alike' in the town when food stocks were low.[37] There is another similarity in the way the Barolong deployed spies to observe and gather information on enemy activities during both incidents. The besiegers were alert to this and intercepted any movement by the Ratshidi (or their Tswana allies) suspected of spying or carrying messages, such as 'Freddy', who expertly avoided detection by the prying eyes of a party of Boers in 1900.[38] It was surely due to their knowledge about 'escape routes' out of Mafeking that enabled a large number of Barolong to abscond from the town when conditions became unbearable.[39] To reiterate, it seems plausible to suggest that the means and ways of clandestinely exiting and re-entering the town for whatever of these reasons mentioned above were those learned and employed during the earlier encirclement of the Tshidi capital.

In conclusion, then, Sol Plaatje was correct in his observation about the connectedness of certain elements of the Siege of Mafeking in the South African War to past events and in his recognition that they were part of a longer trajectory of conflict in Bechuanaland that had engulfed both the Barolong and white societies in the region. In significant ways, the experiences of the Barolong in 1899–1900 were a refraction of previous episodes that arguably formed part of an ongoing historical consciousness.

Portrait of Sol Plaatje, taken around the turn of the century

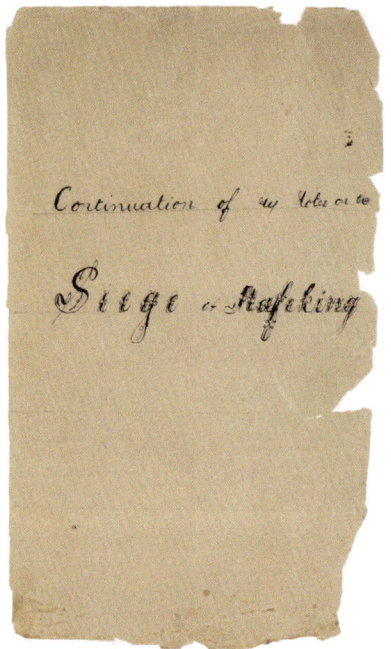

Title page and first page of the manuscript of Plaatje's diary, 29 October 1899

Church and school buildings at the Pniel mission near Barkly West, early 1890s, where Plaatje lived until 1894

Photographs taken by the journalist Angus Hamilton of the stadt, *Mahikeng. 'I went to town early this morning to fetch Mr Hamilton to take pictures in our village for* Black and White, *which paper he represents besides the* London Times,' *Plaatje wrote on 11 December 1899.*

Plaatje's wife Elizabeth (left), often mentioned in his diary, and Charles Bell (right), Mafeking magistrate and civil commissioner, for whom Plaatje worked

Barolong chiefs and headmen during the siege
Sitting, left to right: Silas Molema, Wessels Montshiwa, Lekoko Montshiwa

Boer artillerymen preparing to fire their 94-pound Creusot siege gun ('Big Ben' or 'Au Sanna' as Plaatje called it)

War correspondents in front of their dugout during the siege
*Left to right: J.E. Neilly (*Pall Mall Gazette*), Vere Stent (Reuters), Major F.D. Baillie (*Morning Post*) and J. Angus Hamilton (*The Times *and* Black and White*).*

Plaatje and other members of his family, c. 1900, including his nephew Ebie Schiemann (front left), who is mentioned several times in his diary

The Court of Summary Jurisdiction in session, meeting outside the courthouse. Plaatje is standing next to the table. 'Myself in knickerbockers and without a jacket looked more like a member of the football team or a village cyclist than a court interpreter.'

A 94-pound shell explodes in the Market Square, Mafeking, February 1900.

Interpreting for Charles Bell and Major Hamilton Goold-Adams. Two unidentified African 'runners' (sitting, front) convey news of the relief of Kimberley, 15 February 1900.

An unidentified armed guard, one of many Africans who took up arms during the siege

An armed African raiding party about to leave Mahikeng, March 1900

Issuing rations in the stadt, *Mahikeng.*

Page from manuscript of Plaatje's diary, 1 January 1900. The first paragraph (in pencil) is in Plaatje's hand, while the other two paragraphs were written by David Phooko, dictated to him by Plaatje.

Horses and rifles captured from the Boers by an African raiding party, after what Plaatje described in his diary as 'a brief but very hot battle'

Shell damage to the offices of the Mafeking Mail, *inflicted by the Boers' Creusot siege gun*

Top left: Ernst and Marie Westphal, Plaatje's two missionary mentors. Plaatje recalled in his diary his differences with Westphal over whom to vote for in the 1898 Barkly West election (above).
Top right: Silas Molema (1852–1927), inspiration and financial backer for Plaatje's career as newspaper editor

Boer 'rebels' captured after the siege, lining up outside the Mafeking gaol. Plaatje would later interpret at their preliminary examinations on charges of treason.

Crowds gather in the stadt *to witness Colonel Vyvyan present a letter from Lord Roberts, commander-in-chief of British forces in South Africa, commending the Barolong for their part in the siege. Plaatje interpreted at the speech-making.*

Tiyo Soga (1829–1871), missionary, writer and diarist, and John Tengo Jabavu (1859–1921), editor of the English-isiXhosa newspaper Imvo Zabantsundu

Plaatje, Molema and the staff of Koranta ea Becoana, *1903*

One of the early issues of **Koranta ea Becoana** *(Newspaper of the Batswana), started in April 1901. A new enlarged version, in English as well as Setswana, was launched in August 1902.*

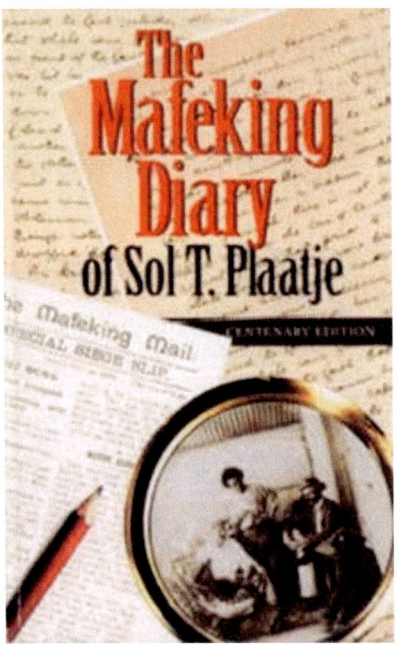

Four editions of Sol Plaatje's diary: Macmillan (1973); Cardinal (1976); Meridor (1989); David Philip (1999)

Eight

The Interpreter

Andries Walter Oliphant

1

The entries in my diary, anyone familiar with my record of the siege knows, break off on the penultimate day of the third month of the new century. This was just a day before the end of the first quarter of the new age. This time had no special meaning except that the sun, scorching the sand and stones all summer, suddenly fell further west and away from us. Autumn set in. The earth cooled but I lost none of my desire to write.

At the end of March, I wrote: 'The Colonel Commanding has published a hot protest against alleged rumours by somebodies, to the effect that he delays the troops and that he starves the inhabitants, etc., in the *Mafeking Mail*. He threatens to catch those fellows when their claims …'

There is nothing after this. Not a word. Yet the empty pages in my diary, 20 sheets to be exact, continue to produce a great deal of conjecture. I have heard many speculations. One of the wildest has it that the rest of my diary is written in invisible ink.

To confess, I have toyed with the idea of calling this story

'Invisible Ink'. But since there is nothing to decipher, I decided against it. Also, I do not want to fuel further conjecture.

This then is the story. It is not written from the shadows or the margins of time but dredged from what has been expunged from memory. It is the story I did not tell.

2

Back home after a day in the Summary Court, I sit down to record some events. Hearing what could only be the sound of feet falling on the steps leading up to the threshold, I stop writing in mid-sentence. I wait for the knock. There it is: a tentative percussion of knuckles on wood. Placing the pen next to my open diary, I rise and go to the door.

It is the boy Tshepo who works as court messenger, with a note from Morena. Before he leaves, I read the note in case I have to send a reply. It is written in code. As it turns out, I have to respond.

On a sheet of paper, I write in code that I understand the message and will do as instructed. I place the paper in an envelope. After sealing it, I scribble Morena's name on the front of it and hand it to the messenger. As he turns to go, I call him back and give him a lump of jelly sweets. He runs off into the growing darkness of the evening. Somehow he reminds me of my own son, down south with his mother in the city of diamonds. I smile and turn, not back to what I was busy with before the interruption, but to the urgent business of packing a few things.

3

So, on the second last night of that month, I move from my book-crammed house adjacent to the Chief's Residence. With everything I need in a knapsack, I lock the house and hide the key. Under the cover of darkness, I walk towards the railway lines. Once I have crossed the lines, I will leave the *stadt* and enter the white town.

A light, unseasonable downpour patters on the roofs of the houses. The water glistens on the grey boulders. The sandy ground is damp and soft and pleasant to tread on. The air is nippy.

I make a wide berth around the Chief's Residence before cutting across the veldt, passing the fort and barracks between the *stadt* and the settlement. My stocky body moves with the stealth of a *phokojwe*.

I reach the Railway Reserve. There I cut across the road leading north. Once in the area of the siding, I hop over the lines, avoiding the Prison and the Shell Factory. I wait in the shadows for the sentry guarding the Commissariat Store to pass. When darkness swallows him, I enter the town at its northern limit where the grid of the settlement gives way to the sandy recreation fields.

From there, I walk across Government Square and slip into the yard behind the Court House. Skirting the main inner defence emplacements, leaping over dugouts and trenches, I reach my new quarters undetected: a disused cell behind the Court House. This is my new home.

4

On my second foray out in the field we capture Mafura Motswalle. He is one of the two men from the *stadt* who recently lured 25 cattle raiders, sent by the Colonel Commanding to replenish the beef stocks of the town, into a trap. They were decimated by Maxims hidden among the reeds of the Molopo River. We catch him as he crosses the river on his way to the encampments of the enemy. I have to restrain Mgugu from killing him.

'Kill the dog!'

'No! Not me,' Mafura slobbers as the tip of the rifle grazes his head.

'Yes, you. *Ntswa!*' Mgugu swears, thrusting the barrel of his gun into the chest of the captured man.

'We were fishing. Only fishing. They were hiding in the reeds. Someone shouted … there were shots … I can't remember,' Mafura pleads as he is kicked.

'Traitor!' Mgugu sneers.

'Shoot him and get done with it,' Mara, the woman in our unit, eggs him on.

'Killing is not justice,' I say in a ridiculous court-like tone to distract them.

'Justice? My arse,' Mara laughs.

'Yes, the law.'

'*Masepa!* This is war,' Rajane sniggers.

'He's our prisoner,' I say feebly.

'Shoot the shit!' they shout in turns.

Mgugu leans forward. He presses the nozzle of his rifle hard into the captive's chest. He pulls the trigger. The gun barks. As he lunges to one side to evade the shot, the bullet rips into Mafura's left shoulder, hurling him to the ground.

'Are you mad?' I shout, pushing Mgugu aside.

They back off. I raise the wounded man onto my horse. I ride into town after dark, the others straggling behind in silent disapproval, reach the Prison and ask the guard to call the captain.

'What is this?' the captain points at the bleeding man.

'A traitor, one of those who lured the raiders to their deaths,' Mgugu explains.

'Aha, I see. But why bring him here? What must I do with a wounded man?'

'Ask him,' Mgugu says, pointing at me.

'He can only die here,' the captain says but nevertheless calls for assistance.

'Get someone to look at his wound. When he is fit, he will go on trial,' I say as if I have the authority to instruct the prison captain in such matters.

'Only to face the firing squad,' he laughs as the wounded man is carried off.

I greet the other men. We go our separate ways. I know where to find them. Where I live is a secret.

Mounting my horse, I head in the direction of my house in the *stadt*. There I leave the horse in the stable and walk back to the town.

5

I stop at Morena's house and deliver my intelligence reports. We greet each other without shaking hands, then I hand him some sheets of paper. He will read them and in turn pass them on to the Colonel Commanding.

'You look the worse for wear,' he remarks drily.

'I need a rest,' I mutter and shrug my shoulders.

'What are you waiting for?' he grins.

I leave with a feeling that things are starting to get at me. After a quiet beginning to the month, matters have taken a turn for the worse. The siege, no doubt, is coming to a head.

6

I am on horseback all day long, gathering surplus people: refugees and other foreigners. The Colonel Commanding wants them out of here. They are parasites, he writes. They feed on the precious food stores of the siege like locusts. They must leave or starve to death.

Ferrying them through the lines while armed detachments from the Black Watch open gaps in the circle of guns thrown around the town, we manage to get more than a thousand out in a matter of a few days. How many reach safety? No one knows.

This is what the Colonel Commanding wants. It is the only way to save the townspeople and those who rightfully belong in the *stadt* from starving, he announces. He brooks no dissent and in earnest we obey. Not to do so would be a crime.

On the last census I conducted for Morena with Philemon and Gates, about a month ago, there were just over five and a half thousand people in the *stadt*. That was four months into the siege when almost half the population had left. Now, early April, I estimate that two-thirds of the population have gone.

The siege drags on. The tension, like the death tolls, mounts. The *stadt* is a cemetery.

7

We expected it to be over before the end of summer, that the Imperial troops would arrive from the south at the beginning of January. The only relief that came was the summer rains. The showers now are only a memory. The dry season is here. We are still waiting.

The casualties grow. The toll is heaviest among the people in the *stadt*. Nobody but I bothers to keep count. Sketchy as they are, my own figures suggest that, between the victims of war and starvation, many more have died to keep the townspeople fat than the official figures show.

We are fast running out of supplies. The sorghum, barley and oats are low. We are supplementing whatever meat we have with the flesh of horses. In the *stadt* dog meat sustains many. Those who will not eat dog or horse flesh live off the bark of fern trees. Wherever one turns a starveling totters. One dreads to look for fear of seeing another 'fall over backwards with a dead thud', as I write in my diary on March the 21st.

We whisper in the *stadt* that the settlers and the merchants are hoarding grain and other food. The merchants and the inhabitants of the settlement go about openly accusing the people of the *stadt* of concealing their harvests. Such are the recriminations of people facing starvation. It poisons the air with suspicion. I, who live on the rations allotted to the town, am in the middle of all this. Many envy me. Others resent my privileges. Some insinuate I have forgotten my own people.

In this matter no one mentions the name of the Colonel Commanding nor that of Morena. He, Morena, issues Sowen Passes – a ration of oat porridge – to the most destitute. We report to him, he reports to the Colonel. The Colonel Commanding knows everything. Why doesn't he instruct Morena to put out these smouldering fires?

The Colonel Commanding, instead, issues eloquent but sinister proclamations. He demands Obedience, Unity of Purpose, and Harmony. Anyone who Shames the Fame of the Heroic Defence of the Siege, he threatens with Stringent Measures.

To me, an interpreter, this is a strange form of speech. The words, drained of meaning, are recharged with the emphatic tones of power. This is enough to silence even the most outspoken among us.

8

I escape from the choking atmosphere in the besieged town and from the walking skeletons of the *stadt* when I am on spying expeditions. The veldt between the investments of the enemy and the plains behind their lines is, at times, so tranquil, it is difficult to believe that the country is at war.

I sleep under the stars of the autumn sky. Lying on my back in a hollow between the rocks, I gaze up into the heavens where the galaxies wheel above me. The earth rolls through the sparkling skies.

During the day, I gaze with the eyes of a raptor out over the veldt. At every opportunity I peer into the laager of the enemy. Pale, stout and bearded, they are a rough, uncivilized people. They are stuffed with meat, their encampments dens of smoke. If they overrun the town, we will, if not taken into slavery, become pariahs in our own land. Their greed for land and servants knows no limit.

My main task is to compile intelligence reports on their activities. I watch where they position their artillery. I assess the strength of the commandos. From Morena's comments and the favours bestowed on me, I deduce that these have served the defence of this outpost of the Empire well. The Colonel Commanding bases a great deal of his strategy on my reports. How he does this is not entirely clear to me, but this does not matter, I do my work.

Sharp as my eyes are, how I miss my field-glasses. If I was caught with them by the enemy, they would be the end of me, so, reluctantly, I leave them in my quarters.

I live on the small things I can catch. Creatures within the grasp of a spy who must go about his work with stealth: *mmutla wa sekgoa*, francolin, sparrows, and whatever I can trap or shoot during the exchanges of fire between the warring forces. Most days the fare is locusts, *mokgatitswane*, worms, wild spinach, berries or *noga*.

It is a furtive life. But subterfuge has its own exhilaration and rewards. The money I complained about in my letters to Morena and others a few months ago seems so trivial now. The pressing demands of action outweigh the calculations of career and cash. How anyone can become rich from war escapes me.

9

I am part of a unit, the Jackal Scouts. No one but Morena and the Colonel Commanding knows of our existence. He, the Colonel Commanding, conceived us.

Only the most able and trusted are part of it. Counting not more than the fingers of one hand, each one of us has a purpose. We are no motley band of raiders but part of the new science of war.

On missions I operate independently. I make sure the most vital information reaches them. I keep abreast of the enemy's movements and try to divine their plans. I sleep away from the rest; in case the unit is surprised at night. This is the art of reconnaissance. I am the eyes and ears of the unit.

If you look at it dispassionately, it is no different from my job as interpreter. I read the signs of war and write reports for those entrusted with the destiny of the Empire. I do my bit for freedom and progress.

He, the Colonel Commanding, never leaves his Headquarters. He is stationed in a storeyed building adjacent to the market square. From his observation post he has a view of the entire settlement and well beyond it. This includes the *stadt*. His view takes in the veldt, the *rantjies* and the river. His eyes, day and night, sweep over the world in all the directions of the compass.

Linked to telephones, mirrors, field radios, dispatches, runners, flags, forts and trenches – his eyes and his words, his decisions and his very wishes, reach into places no mortal confined to one space ever can. It is a marvel. No one, not even Morena, can divine his thoughts.

Information and cunning, not bravery, are the keys to success in war. His axioms are knowledge and calculation. This is what the few who have contact with him say counts in his estimation. His estimation, everyone in the settlement and the *stadt* knows, counts for everything.

His desires are passed on to us in whispers. The defence of the town, and how we will be relieved, is his precious knowledge. I am a small but vital part of it. What else but brutality is there beyond this?

10

It is night. The boulders are dark ruminating elephants. I meet with my unit in the blue darkness below a rock. I brief them on the movements of the enemy. Dealing in truth, I underplay the risks I take. I amplify what is in their safety. They listen, their eyes shining like planets in the dark.

When it is their turn to brief me on their activities, there is silence.

Someone coughs.

'It is not the brave who succumb in war but the foolish,' Surrbuss Setehabi, speaking through a tight throat, remarks like a ventriloquist.

We laugh. His utterance has a ring of truth to it, though it is difficult to see what he means. It is a relief to hear it from him and not from some slouch-capped loafer in the garrison. This, I suppose, is what makes it so funny.

'You look strange,' Mathakgong, staring at me, says.

What? I want to ask but the others laugh and I choke on the question.

'That's right,' Mara, dressed in the clothes of a man, responds to my puzzlement.

'You have two faces,' Rajane adds.

'What?' I exclaim, finally getting the word out.

They laugh, falling about in the dark. I wait for them to answer but they lose interest.

'I am hungry and tired,' Rajane yawns.

For days I ponder the meaning of their remarks. How should I interpret them? I forget them for a while only to return as to one's shadow at sunrise.

I look at myself in my field mirror. I can see no change in my face. It is a shade darker from the sun. The pools of my eyes are not as untroubled as they were before the war. There is nothing strange about this.

Two faces? What was he hinting at? Is it some kind of joke? I resolve to banish it from my mind.

11

I quench my thirst from a hidden loop of the Molopo. At midday, I scoop the blue sky from the stream running over the smooth stones below the canopy of reeds.

At night, I drink the stars sparkling in the water cupped in my hands. The smoky taste of water drunk in the dark lingers in my mouth. I sleep with one eye shut and both ears open.

With the passing days I drink deep from the waters of this new time. I have never felt better in my life. This war, to be sure, will change our fortunes, and not only mine and those of us engaged in it. It will touch all our people. It will change things forever.

More than most, I greeted the outbreak of hostilities with a sense of expectation that somehow our freedom was at hand. The first skirmishes with the enemy held the promise that when the last shot was fired, we who have fought on the side of the righteous, will take our place among the civilized and the just.

Now, several months into the siege, I am beginning to have doubts. I thought the war would pass but it hasn't. I must nevertheless see this through to the end.

12

Back in my quarters behind the Court House I feel I need a bath. My body reeks of smoke, grass, sweat, and death. I scoop water from the barrel in the corner of the room and pour it into the kettle.

There is much to do before I turn in. I must fix something to eat. I must write down what is not in the reports I handed over to Morena. I must do some reading. There is a passage in Shakespeare about spying which I must look up. I must prepare myself for the trial of Mafura. They will patch him up and haul him into court tomorrow. My testimony will be needed.

How I long to hear some music. A time will come when the

human voice will be recorded, and I will sing our Anthem of Freedom to the world.

I sit by the fire slicing a pumpkin. When done, I clean the chaff from a small heap of sorghum. I place it in a saucepan and add a few grains of coarse salt. I take what is left of the rabbit I shot a day or so ago from my knapsack and season it.

A sliced onion braises in some lard in a pan on the fire. I place the pieces of rabbit, ribs, and half a rump into it. My mouth waters.

When the water boils, I pour some onto the grain. A bit more goes into another saucepan with the pumpkin. The rest goes into the tub on the floor half filled with icy water. In 20 minutes supper will be ready, I think, reminding myself of my good fortune in these hard times. With the low supplies and the high prices of food, I have done better than most.

13

Now I strip and get into the warm water for a scrub. I work up a lather from a chip of blue soap and rub the soapy water into my skin. I am rinsing the suds from my body when suddenly there is a violent knock at the door.

'Coming,' I shout, taking my gown from the hook behind the door. When I turn, barefoot on the stone floor, the door opens. Who but Morena walks into my abode? He has never done this before.

'You must keep your door locked, you …' he says without completing his sentence.

'I have no enemies. Not here in town nor in the *stadt*,' I say, unable to make sense of the incredulous expression on his face.

'What on earth is the matter with you?' he snarls.

'Back from another excursion,' I explain.

'I know. I saw you earlier this evening when you delivered your reports,' he says tonelessly and pulls in his angular chin.

'Good,' I say, and add to flatter, 'You've already read them?'

'That's what I came to see you about.' He is unable to mask the irritation in his voice.

'Oh …?'

'Come down to the Prison. Right away,' he turns to leave.

'Yes sir,' I say, watching him go to the door.

'And for God's sake lock your doors,' he bellows before the night closes round him.

I rinse my face and leave. I turn the key and place it in my pocket.

14

Leaving the shadows of the backyard, I walk around the Court House on to Market Square from where I have a view of the Colonel Commanding's Headquarters. The double-storeyed building is in darkness. This makes me wonder whether there is any truth to the legend that he never sleeps.

It is said that after midnight his favourite Imperial officers from the Protectorate Regiment have lunch with him until daybreak. He does everything in reverse. He has breakfast at sunset; lunch at midnight; dinner before sunrise. These are the habits of a hyena.

Looking at the dark quarters, I cannot help but wonder why, if the Colonel Commanding is omniscient, he values my reports as much as I am led to believe. Is it a case of the hyena guided to carrion by vultures? If so, who guides the hyena at night? A shot rings out and disturbs my train of thought.

Crossing the railway lines, I reach the entrance of the Prison. I identify myself. The sentries, one on each side of the gate, are nonchalant. I hand over my rifle. One frisks me. He finds the key to a prison door in my pocket and holds it up in the dark, shaking his head before returning it. The other one watches but without following this silent exchange in the dark. They let me in.

There are two more sentries on the inside. I am asked to wait. One tugs at a rope dangling from the wall: once, twice, pauses, and tugs again. A bell chimes within the Prison building.

Two soldiers stride across the grass towards us. Without a word they turn, waiting for me to step into the space between them. In silence we walk across the sandy inner court to a large wooden door leading to the cells. The grass I saw a moment ago, except for a few dried and stubby clumps, is gone. Sand crunches under our feet.

Someone opens the door from the inside and lets us in. We walk along a dark passage, one soldier ahead of me, one behind me. I am out of step with their measured footfalls.

At the end of the passage, I am shown into a large bare room. The soldiers turn and leave.

15

I am alone in a space where the glow of the night-sky falls through a high barred window. It casts a strange grey light over the floor and against the opposite wall.

When my eyes eventually adjust to the dimness, I see that there is no place to sit. Standing in the middle of the bare space, it strikes me how different the place feels compared with the holding cell behind the Court House in which I now stay. The single cell in the Court House is comfortable if somewhat crammed. This large empty space, a group cell no doubt, holds a strange feeling of extreme constriction.

Stories told to me about the Prison have it that the place is overcrowded. It should be. Every day in the Summary Courts, not counting those fined, in one session after another, legions are sent here and only a few to execution by firing squad.

All this is done with the utmost civility. Not a trace of savagery is to be found even in the executions. It is not a flawless procedure but its objectives are, as far as I can see, governed by justice and above reproach.

16

About prison I know nothing, really. It is, after all, a place behind walls. I have listened ruefully to the stories told me. A grunt of pity, a grimace of dismay at the vision of broken bodies piled upon each other, what more can I offer?

How then is this place empty? The muted moans rising from

somewhere within the thick-walled body of the building are so faint, they seem no more than sounds issuing from my imagination.

A door opens. No one calls me, no gesture beckons. Still I walk towards the open door. I hesitate for a moment, then enter.

'Why have you taken so long to get here?' a voice I have never heard before but with the same measured intonation of Morena's asks tersely.

I see four figures. The hands of one concealed behind his back, two standing erect, a fourth prostrate on the floor. In the dark space of the cell their bodies are blurred like charcoal sketches.

'Black bastard, take off your bloody hat. Who the hell do you think you are?' Another, even stranger voice spits out the words I have heard so often all over the colony and in the republics.

'I don't have a hat on,' I reply and turn to see if there isn't another person behind me.

Looking over my shoulder, I see the door swing on its hinges. It shuts without making a sound.

17

After what seems a lifetime, I emerge from the Prison like from a lair into the dead of the night. The guns are silent, yet it feels as if some vast yet obscure activity is going on everywhere in the opaque night.

I walk in the direction of my residence in the *stadt*. Moving along the track, I realise that I am right below the Headquarters of the Colonel Commanding. I look up on to the roof from which I and so many have diverted our gazes, observing the saying: he who even once looks into the eye of the sun shall have no eyes to look again.

In the starry darkness a shape looms above the gables. I peer up into the dark but can't fix a clear image to it. Where I thought the head was, I see eyes, large and round, glowing like polished glass.

Then suddenly, from the south-east where the enemy have constructed a fort, the 94 pounder flashes, lighting up the sky. In the second between the illumination and the boom that follows it, I see into the night.

I see the figure of a person, its head small and shaped like that of a hyena, its face cadaverous as if powdered with ash. A fabric coloured dull-yellow and smudged dark-brown flutters like a flag draped over the erect figure. It is like a cloak worn in the manner of warriors draping themselves in the skins of leopards.

As the shell whooshes harmlessly overhead, I retreat. I fall into a trench behind me. Dazed and witless, I crawl out of the hole and stagger home.

18

I reach the house, feel for the key hidden in the doorpost groove and stumble in. I sink into the couch in the living room. Slowly I regain my senses. I light a lamp. It burns for a while, flickers and dies.

While it burnt, I saw that the house was covered in the fine red dust of the desert. Whatever I touched, my hands were printed in the dust.

I find a candle and I light it. I rummage in the drawers looking for my diary. It is gone. The drawers are filled with sand. Surely I did not take it with me to my new quarters? Or did I? Definitely not.

I find some paper. Clean folio sheets: Irish feint without margins. The dry fragrance of paper is like the scent of some desert flower. The thick dark blood of the ink appals me.

Sitting down, I dip my pen into the inkpot. Turning the shaft as I lift it, I take care to drain the nib and so avoid blotting the page. I raise my pen over the paper and begin to write. My hand moves over the sheet, swift and deliberate. The subtle captivating screech of inked steel pressing gently against the delicate fabric of paper is a cry which does not carry further than my ears as I stoop close to the page in the dim light.

19

I pause to look at what I have written. Where there should be words, the image of the town with its roads and the inner circle of trenches and defence positions is spread across the page. The fort and garrison of the Protectorate Regiment, situated between the town and the *stadt*, all are in place.

On the edge of the desert, the besieged city is an image of enclosure. Buttressed by the Black Watch in trenches dug by the dead, by the Cape Corps in the Brick Fields, spattered in blood, by the Mfengu Raiders crawling along the greasy banks of the Molopo disguised in the feathers of ostriches, the starved stagger across the veldt armed with nothing but their own bones.

The outer defence positions around the divided settlements are tracings of fire in the landscape. The air here is a sulphurous glue of boiling horsemeat. The earth stinks.

Further afield, in a laager drawn like a diamond around the two settlements, the *stadt* and the white town, is the investment of the enemy: forts, blockhouses, encampments, roaring guns. Behind it, in every direction, a myth burns.

20

The sun rolls like a burning stone in the autumn sky. The Colonel Commanding stands smiling beside a ruminating ox. It is a gift from the Royal Family. His eyes glow with the sky's fire. With his officer's staff he lightly taps the uppers of his shining black boots.

Listening, I try to interpret his message without thinking of a hyena snapping its jaws. Involuntarily I remember my first day in the Magistrate's Court. I had just done my first clerical task. It was a summons to the father of the traitor we took as a prisoner on my second expedition.

The ink was hardly dry when a hand silently returned the page to me. I looked up. It was a messenger. His expression, in which I saw another face, left no doubt that whoever had read it wanted me to redo it. I could not see what was amiss but tore the paper up and rewrote the summons, changing every single word. Then I signed my name, Sol T. Plaatje, in the summons logbook and turned to attend to some other work.

This story was first published in Kunapipi: Journal of Postcolonial Writing and Culture, *21 (3), 1999.*

Nine

Sol Plaatje's Diary and African Views of the Pax Britannica

Stephen Volz

'The Imperial Government may be as good as we are told it is, but one thing certain is that it does not care a hang over the lives of its distant subjects.'[1] Thus wrote Sol Plaatje in February 1900, expressing frustration at the apparent inability or even unwillingness of the British to lift the siege of Mafeking four months after it had begun. At the beginning of the South African War, he was optimistic that British forces would quickly defeat the 'Boer rebels' and expand their rule over all of South Africa. But as rumours of their impending arrival repeatedly proved to be untrue and the hardships of life under siege became increasingly severe, Plaatje lost faith in both the vaunted military supremacy and the professed benevolence of the British Empire.

Similar doubts about British capabilities and intentions also arose among Africans elsewhere on the continent during that time. Plaatje was one of many mission-educated Africans who had adopted some elements of British culture and who hoped British imperialism would benefit Africans through an expansion of humanitarianism, commerce, the rule of law and other liberal goals. That optimism, however, was soon challenged by experiences of discriminatory and exploitative British rule, and African educated elites struggled to reconcile their idealism with the reality of becoming colonial subjects.[2] Like the Pax Romana (Roman peace) of the Roman Empire, ostensibly providing security and civilisation for all within its borders, the Pax Britannica proved to be more beneficial for those closer to the imperial capital of London.

The idea of a Pax Britannica has long been treated with scepticism by scholars, from the time of anti-imperial critics in the early twentieth century, through the era of African independence movements, and up to the present day.[3] Many of those studies have also tended to portray imperialism primarily as a binary opposition between coloniser and colonised, minimising various local and personal concerns that often only partially aligned with one presumed side or the other.[4] As described in the writings of Sol Plaatje and other literate Africans at the turn of the century, however, the expansion of British rule provoked conflicting feelings, promising a more enlightened and prosperous order while at the same time threatening to denigrate and disempower Africans.

African-edited newspapers in British West Africa and their coverage of the South African War, in conjunction with Plaatje's diary, provide a valuable glimpse of the complex ways that anglophone Africans viewed Britain's participation in the violent 'scramble for Africa'. Most studies of the war have tended to focus on its importance within the history of South Africa, but it was part of a broader wave of conflicts throughout the continent that raised intense concern among literate Africans. While hope in the promises of British liberalism proved to be quite durable in both southern and West Africa, with instances of oppression being blamed on the failure of particular officials or policies rather than on imperialism in general, West Africa's lack of European settlers and the concentration of anglophone elites in coastal towns gave rise to different views of colonialism and how it should operate. In both regions there also emerged a defensive pride in African cultures and an insistence on the ability of Africans to play leading roles in their own economic and social development. However, at that time they did not see those ideas as intellectual foundations for later African nationalism but rather as ways to maximise the potential benefits of the Pax Britannica.

African intellectual responses to British colonisation

In both southern and West Africa during the early and mid-nineteenth century, a booming trade in commodities and relatively benign missionary activity indicated the potential advantages of cooperation between Africans and Europeans. But by the end of the century, the rapid growth of European industrial, economic and military might instead precipitated the conquest and colonisation of most African states. Using skills and ideas acquired in European-built schools and towns, Sol Plaatje and other similarly equipped African individuals adapted well to those changes, as they found employment in colonial society and presented themselves as models of sophistication and progress for fellow Africans. At the same time, however, many of them also maintained connections with African-led communities and, to varying degrees, joined with them in seeking to harness elements of European power for their own purposes. The 1890s was therefore a time of great upheaval and uncertainty, accompanied by contradictory and fluctuating strategies among Africans on how best to respond to European rule.

In southern Africa, Africans' receptiveness to British imperialism varied depending on their proximity to areas of European settlement and their level of assimilation to colonial society, yet they generally all insisted on the innate equality of African and European people even if perhaps not their cultures. The history of African responses in the eastern Cape has been particularly well studied, as isiXhosa-speaking graduates of mission schools in that area wrote extensively about British colonialism, which arrived there earlier than elsewhere.[5] Their writings reveal recurring disagreement about whether Africans were subjects of the British Empire primarily as individuals or instead as groups with shared interests. Those intellectual tensions during the 1890s were most apparent in response to John Tengo Jabavu's newspaper *Imvo Zabantsundu*, which, while promoting Xhosa language and culture, generally accepted segregation between white and black and emphasised the responsibility of Africans to adapt to European rule.[6]

Among Tswana-speaking people further north, whose chiefdoms confronted British expansion several decades later than those of the Xhosa, there was a stronger expectation that their communities might retain much of their cultural, economic and political integrity, side by side with European farms and towns. Those hopes were severely undermined by a series of conflicts and treaties after 1870 that gave Europeans increasing control over Tswana land and labour, but Tswana rulers and their followers continued to demand some level of independence, as exemplified by the visit of three rulers from the Bechuanaland Protectorate to Britain in 1895, seeking to avoid being taken over by white settler forces.[7] Evidence of Tswana efforts to adopt some elements of European culture while rejecting European domination can be found in letters that they wrote to the missionary-edited newspaper *Mahoko a Becwana*, which Plaatje also read as a teenage boy.[8] Plaatje and other literate Tswana of his generation grew to be impressed by and dependent on the British Empire, but that cooperation was tempered by an expectation that Tswana rulers and culture would continue to be respected.[9]

In areas of West Africa that were colonised by the British, there was a more pronounced separation between mission-educated Africans who resided mostly in coastal towns and Africans in the interior who remained under the control of African rulers. With the support of British abolitionists and missionaries, Sierra Leone's coastal settlements had been founded by diasporic Africans relocated from the Americas, and their primary cultural and economic orientation was toward the Atlantic and its distant shores. As they and their descendants were joined by re-captives from intercepted slave ships and gradually became more rooted in Africa, self-described 'educated

Africans' were drawn toward an idealised 'African' identity, but they continued to regard 'tribal Africans' who resisted colonisation as inferior and uncivilised.[10] Yoruba-speaking Sierra Leoneans who moved to southern Nigeria were generally more sympathetic to Yoruba communities threatened by British expansion, but most nevertheless preferred to live in Lagos and sought to mediate, rather than resist, British imperialism.[11] Educated Africans in the Gold Coast during the late nineteenth century held similarly complex views, embracing the cosmopolitanism offered by a Pax Britannica while insisting on the equal humanity of Africans.[12]

Such views were expressed in a variety of written formats. Although detailed eyewitness accounts of colonial conquest in West Africa, comparable to that of Plaatje, have apparently not survived, the journals of Yoruba evangelists during the nineteenth century and later diaries by other Africans provide valuable glimpses of the quotidian cultural and personal changes that accompanied colonisation.[13] More prominent writers such as Edward W. Blyden in Sierra Leone and J.E. Casely Hayford in the Gold Coast published several books and pamphlets on African responses to colonialism, but their time and attention were frequently occupied by their work as newspaper editors. Like Jabavu's *Imvo Zabantsundu*, the newspapers of British West Africa were the leading means by which literate Africans publicly shared reports and opinions about events in their own region and elsewhere in the empire, exhibiting an eclectic variety of perspectives.[14] Much of each issue consisted of material copied from newspapers elsewhere in Africa or the metropole, as well as several pages of advertisements for consumer goods, with only occasional commentary by the editor. The resulting news and analysis was frequently contradictory, leaving it up to readers to draw their own conclusions.

In the *Sierra Leone Weekly News*, descriptions of imperialism during the 1890s tended to welcome greater British control. In commenting on an article from the London-based weekly *The Spectator*, the editor agreed with the liberal view that military campaigns were needed to impose a 'Pax Britannica' over the 'childish caprices and puerile ambitions' of troublesome chiefs in the interior, but peace could only be maintained 'by something more deep-seated than mere physical force. It reposes on a wise, just and generous Civil administration, the aim of which is the welfare and content of the people.' The editor expected Britain to 'conquer by her language, her commerce and her laws numerous tribes, who will be glad to take refuge under the flag of the Empire from their own blindness and stupidity – and feel that such refuge is necessary for their public and domestic peace. *Confugiendum est ad Imperium.*'[15] At the same time, however, the editor was thankful that West Africa's tropical climate deterred European settlement, and an editorial in the *Lagos Weekly Record* warned its readers of 'the disastrous results attending the adoption by the African of European forms of civilization without any modification'.[16] As in southern Africa, support for British imperialism in West Africa was contingent on its delivery of benefits, and there was some concern about the potential costs to Africans.

PAX BRITANNICA AND THE SIEGE OF MAFEKING

During his youth, Sol Plaatje had grown to admire the British and their achievements, and his employment as a clerk and interpreter at the magistrate's court in Mafeking instilled in him a respect for British government and a conviction that British rule was preferable to that of the Boers. He and other African residents of Mafeking took 'refuge under the flag of the Empire' during the seven-month Boer siege not from 'blindness and stupidity' but from the threat of violent Boer seizure of their land, cattle and labour. Plaatje felt, reasonably enough, that his safety and that of fellow Africans depended on the strength and skill of British troops, and he was encouraged by any sign of their success. Shortly after the siege started, Plaatje declared, 'no music is as thrilling and captivating as to listen to the firing of guns on your own side', and two months later he asserted, 'The English are among the foremost warriors of their day', praising their 'wisdom' and inventiveness.[17] In reflecting on a Sunday sermon by the Methodist preacher Stephen Lefenya, 'who warned his hearers to be very careful in their prayers, and remember that their God was the enemy's God', Plaatje objected that the Boers were the aggressors, not the inhabitants of Mafeking.[18]

As the siege dragged on for several months, however, Plaatje became increasingly disappointed by the failure of the British to liberate Mafeking. In late December, he acknowledged the different view that Boers had of the war, and a few days later he lamented:

> Instead of getting brighter, the prospect in front of us is darkening itself. I am inclined to believe that the Boers have fully justified their bragging, for we are citizens of a town of subjects of the richest and the strongest empire on earth and the burghers of a small state have successfully besieged us for three months – and we are not even able to tell how far off our relief is.[19]

He further criticised 'the Imperial Government' for provoking the war: 'Now they let us square the account while they lounge on couches in London City, reading their newspapers and smoking their half-crown (2/6) cigars.' Plaatje was also dismayed to observe that Africans' food rations were inferior to those given to European residents of Mafeking, concluding, 'there is a very great difference between white and black even in a besieged town'.[20]

As the siege continued, Plaatje looked less to the British for securing peace and prosperity and more to Africans themselves. Both the British and Boers officially refrained from recruiting African soldiers out of fear that well-armed Africans would pose a threat to all Europeans, but they nevertheless provided guns for some African allies and they could not prevent African militia groups from occasionally mounting their own raids.[21] During the Siege of Mafeking, some of its Rolong inhabitants daringly crossed through Boer lines at night to gather provisions and information about Boer troop placements, leading Plaatje to declare, 'Too little, if anything, has been said in praise of the part played by that gallant Britisher – the Barolong herdboy.'[22] Although Plaatje himself did not engage in the fighting, recognising that his education made him better suited to contributing in other ways, he praised a group of Rolong raiders led by Mathakgong, who exclaimed during a battle at a Boer fort that the Boers were mistaken in their disregard of the raiders as merely 'basimane ba likoalo' (schoolboys) who were unable to defend themselves.[23] Plaatje saw Africans not simply as colonial subjects who depended on the British for protection but as important allies in a war against the 'abominable' Boers.[24]

That opinion came to be shared by most other educated black South Africans, with the prominent exception of John Tengo Jabavu. Viewing the war from the relative safety of the eastern Cape, Jabavu felt that the British were too quick to abandon negotiations and to take up arms, recklessly ignoring overtures from more moderate Boers.[25] Jabavu denied accusations that he was being disloyal, arguing that he was simply calling on the British to pursue more diligently their professed preference for peace, but military authorities nevertheless ordered *Imvo Zabantsundu* to suspend publication in August 1901. Based on his own experiences in Mafeking, Plaatje disagreed with Jabavu's analysis of the war, but he defended Jabavu's right to voice a contrary opinion.[26] Meanwhile, the majority view was to hope for the triumph of British liberalism over settler policies that would disenfranchise Africans, thereby making 'African pro-imperialism' also 'a kind of anti-colonialism'.[27]

WEST AFRICAN DEPICTIONS OF THE SOUTH AFRICAN WAR

Because the newspapers of British West Africa did not have their own correspondents wiring reports from South Africa, they relied on Reuters for regular updates and on other newspapers for analysis of events, but the articles that they chose to reproduce and their own editorial comments revealed a range of perspectives on the South African War. In general, they supported the British effort and hoped for a British victory, but, like Plaatje, they were also concerned about British motives and methods, questioning whether the British really had the best interests of Africans at heart. In reflecting on the war and other events elsewhere in the British Empire, that scepticism grew steadily, and West African educated elites became increasingly doubtful that their own situations would benefit from British imperialism.

Although some readers were unclear about the identity of the Boers at the beginning of the war, wondering if they should be regarded as fellow Africans, most of the West African newspapers soon put forward reasons to support the British.[28] In a letter to the editor of *Gold Coast Aborigines* from 'One of the Aborigines', the author explains that the Boers are not black Africans but rather they 'despise and hate the black races', and people of the Gold Coast therefore should pray 'that this war may soon end in success to the British arms; and bring quietness and peace, freedom, humanity and justice to the men of South Africa'.[29] In a detailed article on the outbreak of the war that cited evidence from multiple sources, the *Sierra Leone Weekly News* similarly concluded that 'the natives have infinitely more to hope from British rule than from the other foreign occupants of their country', and 'British rule, in spite of all drawbacks incident to human limitation and frailty, is necessary for the peace and progress of Africa'.[30] Nevertheless, the Siege of Mafeking was later compared to the Asante siege of British residents at Kumasi, and another article, while praising the idealism expressed in Rudyard Kipling's 1899 poem 'The White Man's Burden', averred that in carrying his burden, the white man 'may be assisted by the intelligent sympathy and judicious co-operation of the non-Imperial races, whom, not understanding them, he is disposed in moments of poetic fervour to describe as "half devil and half child"'.[31]

Anglophone Africans in Lagos were more sceptical of British motives at the beginning of the war, reproducing anti-imperialist articles from *The Spectator* and comparing South Africa to other colonies. An 1896 article in the *Lagos Weekly Standard* argued in favour of autonomy for the Boer states, and when hostilities appeared imminent in 1899, the newspaper questioned British justifications for war and their claims to be the guardians of liberty, citing the experiences of British Indian subjects in Natal and blacks in Jamaica.[32]

Quoting from the *Jamaica Standard*, the Lagos newspaper declared, if 'the Christian government of Great Britain ... aims at Empire in Africa, she can secure it by convincing the native race that the Empire of the Englishman is *one* with the Empire of the African'.[33] In its own editorial a week later, the Lagos newspaper argued that the British would not need to wage expensive wars 'if the colonies had been governed upon sound equitable principles and with due regard for the interests of the people governed'.[34]

Gold Coast Aborigines was even more provocative in its use of anti-imperialist articles from British publications. An editorial from the *Manchester Weekly News* objected to 'barbaric' British eagerness to wage war against the Boers rather than seek a peaceful solution, and an anti-capitalist editorial from the *Morning Leader* suggested, 'We might do something worse than "abandon" the Natives "to the tender mercies of the Boers". They at least protect them from the financiers who have openly made this war that they may establish some form of slavery on the Rand.'[35] In a report on the Pan-African Conference of 1900 in London, *Reynolds's Newspaper* sympathised with the plight of black people around the world and boldly predicted, 'We talk of Boer and Briton in South Africa, as if that were a statement of the whole matter. What if, at some distant date in the future, South Africa should belong neither to Boer nor Briton, but to the negro – his by right, by superior numbers, and superior power? We may smile at the idea, but it may easily become a tremendous reality.'[36]

When the Siege of Mafeking ended in May 1900, most of the West African newspapers published brief reports of the event and of the subsequent celebrations in their towns. Ships in Lagos harbour were 'decked with flags' to commemorate the 'indomitable courage' of Mafeking's 'plucky garrison', and in a public demonstration 'the loyal citizens of Freetown participated in the Mother country's joy' over the success of 'the gallant B.P. [Baden-Powell] and his band of heroes'.[37] As the war thereafter devolved into a relatively static stalemate, news from South Africa appeared much less frequently, and the *Sierra Leone Weekly News* instead called on British authorities to pay more attention to the needs of their colony.[38] When the war finally ended in 1902, that newspaper's editor congratulated Joseph Chamberlain, the British colonial secretary, on his victory but then sardonically commented, 'It is hoped that the energies of Downing Street will now be somewhat disengaged so as to enable the brilliant statesman at the head of the Colonial Office to devote a little more of his great abilities to the consideration of West African Affairs.'[39]

As the Boer republics and other states in Africa fell under British rule, educated elites shifted the focus of their attention from the spread of 'civilisation' to the perspectives and agency of Africans within the 'Pax Britannica'. As Philip Zachernuk explains, 'it was no longer a matter of retaining what was acceptable to the West within Africa but of discovering what was acceptable to Africa within the West'.[40] With the completion of British colonisation, anglophone Africans closely watched the new rulers to see if they practised what they preached, and they increasingly embraced collective ethnic and other identities that might strengthen their position as colonial subjects.[41] That effort was reinforced by news from other colonies and expanded by the experiences of Africans who spent time abroad, producing the new identities of 'Black' and 'African' in response to the racism and oppression of European imperialism.[42]

CONCLUSION

Three years after the end of the South African War, the *Lagos Weekly Record* published a report from the *Rhodesia Herald* expressing concern about a newspaper in Mafeking 'financed by a native chief, which has for its aims the inflammation of hate against the white man on the part of the black, and the fostering of the contention that he is an invader of the land properly owned by the native'.[43] In 1901, Sol Plaatje built on the skills he had practised in writing a diary to become a journalist, and with support from Silas Molema, a member of the Rolong royal family, he began producing the newspaper *Koranta ea Becoana*. In the first issue, Plaatje commented on tentative peace talks between the British and Boers and hoped that the interests of 'Bancho' (Blacks) would be taken into consideration.[44] Published mostly in Setswana with occasional English articles, *Koranta* proudly defended the value of African cultures, but, contrary to Rhodesian claims, Plaatje also promoted cooperation between the races and insisted that European fears of a 'black peril' were baseless.[45] He instead repeatedly called on British authorities to grant Africans the rights they had earned as loyal subjects of the Empire. Demonstrating the growing solidarity of Africans against unjust rule, he also on one occasion cited an article from the *Sierra Leone Weekly News* that criticised discriminatory land-ownership laws in South Africa.[46]

The Siege of Mafeking was only one episode in a wave of destruction that accompanied European 'pacification' of Africans who resisted colonisation. In almost every part of the continent, efforts by African rulers to retain control over their realms were brutally crushed, compelling them to submit to Europeans. The Tshidi Rolong chiefdom in Mafeking gained a temporary reprieve from Boer expansion, but British victory did not result in the restoration of their former territory and independence. Like anglophone elites in coastal areas of West Africa, Plaatje initially expected to benefit from British rule, but it soon became apparent that he and other Africans would all simply be grouped together as 'natives', thereby revealing a contradiction between 'the logic of the Empire, which told them that they were British, and the logic of the metropole, which persistently and often violently told them they were not'.[47] Although Sol Plaatje stubbornly continued to hope that a Pax Britannica might someday bear fruit for Africans, his experiences as a young man during the Siege of Mafeking taught him that Africans could not depend solely on the British and would have to take matters into their own hands.

Ten

Past and Present in Sol Plaatje's Mafeking Diary: The Making of a Diarist

Brian Willan

Sol Plaatje's *Mafeking Diary* is a remarkable testament to what he saw going on around him during five months of siege and to the thoughts and memories that his observations inspired. As an eyewitness account of the siege by a black writer, it has no parallels and is one of the best of the many first-hand accounts of the South African War. Yet Plaatje's diary has sometimes puzzled its readers. On the one hand its very uniqueness and extraordinary qualities have sometimes made Plaatje seem like a lonely genius, unrepresentative of anybody but himself and free from either social or literary context. For how else could such a document be explained given the widespread ignorance of the level of sophistication of black South African social and intellectual life in the late nineteenth-century Cape Colony?

On the other hand, Plaatje and his diary have been expected to take on too much of a burden of representation, and have had to stand in for countless others who experienced the war but whose voices have not been heard. Plaatje has thus become, almost by default, the black voice of the war, frequently quoted, with scant appreciation of the issues raised by such a broad-brush characterisation.

Such contradictory responses are rooted not only in a failure to understand the circumstances in which the diary was written but also the ideas and qualities that its author brought to it, and how and where these originated. To understand these things requires an exploration of Plaatje's experiences in the years leading up to the war, and the siege, in 1899. This provides the context for making sense of the many specific references to his past life in his diary as well as the broader world view that he brought to his task and that is reflected so eloquently in the diary.

How then did Plaatje's past experiences help to shape his diary?

The starting point for any consideration of Plaatje's diary is that he was, first and foremost, a Morolong, a Setswana speaker, and inheritor of a history that went back many years before the arrival of the first Europeans in southern Africa. This is evident in his diary in his references to Barolong history, in his use of Setswana when describing the words and actions of fellow Barolong, and in his accounts of his encounters with, for example, Wessels Montshiwa, the Barolong chief during the siege.

Plaatje's ancestors were Barolong *ba ga Modiboa*, descendants of a Barolong chief who lost the chiefship to his younger brother. This put them outside the four main Barolong clans which formed after the death of Tau in the 1780s, and probably helped propel them into the orbit of the European missionaries who arrived in the interior of southern Africa in the 1820s and 1830s. Even before Plaatje's father moved to the Mahikeng district in the early 1890s, it is clear that, however attached he was to his Christian faith, he and his family identified with the Tshidi chief Montshiwa, who had been in Mahikeng since the 1850s.[1]

The history of the Tshidi Barolong, in the nineteenth century, was one of conflict with the Boers, and they often appealed to the

British for help. It finally came in 1885 in the form of the Warren expedition, which led to the establishment of the colony of British Bechuanaland and protection for the Barolong, as they saw it, against their long-standing enemies. When war broke out in 1899, there was therefore no doubt where their loyalties would lie. Taking the side of the British, given their recent history, was the natural course of action for the Tshidi Barolong, and for Plaatje too: in his mind the interests of the Barolong in Mahikeng coincided happily with the pro-British outlook adopted by the mission-educated African community in the Cape Colony of which he himself was a part. If all this seems, with the advantage of hindsight, to have been misguided, or even naive, at the time there seemed every reason and justification for their views and actions. Betrayal, as they saw it, would only come later.

Supporting the British cause did not mean that Plaatje agreed with all that the British authorities did during the siege. He was opposed to Colonel Baden-Powell's attempt to depose the Barolong chief, Wessels Montshiwa, and refused to interpret when he sought to do so.[2] He thought the British military authorities negligent in allowing the siege to drag on for so long before, very belatedly, a relief expedition was organised. 'I am inclined to believe,' he wrote on 3 January 1900, 'that the Boers have fully justified their bragging, for we are citizens of a town of subjects of the richest and strongest empire on earth, and the burgers of a small state have successfully besieged us for three months and we are not even able to tell how far off our relief is.'[3]

He was also critical of the way that British officers, given the task of organising food distribution in the *stadt*, went about their task in an inconsiderate and clumsy manner, failing to take account of Barolong sensibilities: 'the young officers,' he said, pointing to the problem, 'know as little about Natives and their mode of living as they know about the man in the moon and his mode of living.'[4] Plaatje, a Morolong himself and part of this community, was in a good position to make such judgements. It did not detract from his overall support for the British against their enemies, the Boers.

If Plaatje's identity as a Morolong permeates his diary, so too do memories of his time on the Pniel mission and the world this represented. His several references to the Christian deity, and to the Bible and prayerbook, are obvious instances of this. But Pniel was where he had acquired his education as well as his religion. He had arrived at the mission in the late 1870s as a small child with his parents, adherents of the Berlin Mission Society, and they came from the Society's main mission at Bethanie in the Orange Free State. It was to prove a highly significant move. In the Orange Free State, had Plaatje remained there, educational provision was minimal and English was not taught. On German missions indigenous languages were usually the medium of instruction.

But at Pniel, located in the Cape Colony, and hence part of the British Empire, educational provision was of a different order. When the Plaatje family joined the mission, it was part of the Crown Colony of Griqualand West but after incorporation into the larger, longer-established Cape Colony the mission school came under the supervision of the Cape's Education Department. This meant that in return for adhering to the Colony's syllabus requirements, the school received a regular grant towards its costs. Most important, English was taught and became the effective medium of instruction, supported by the use of a range of English textbooks. Young Plaatje flourished at this school, gaining a reputation as its best pupil, and towards the end of his time there he became a pupil-teacher, helping in the classroom as well as continuing his own education. One of the missionaries, the Rev. Ernst Westphal, along with his wife Marie, took a particular interest in his progress, providing extra tuition beyond the confines of the classroom.

Among the books used for learning English were the Nelson *Royal Readers*, popular throughout the British Empire. They clearly made an impression upon young Plaatje, and one of the most striking recollections in his diary is of a story in Nelson's *Royal Reader* no. 3. The story was entitled 'The Wonderful Pudding', an instructive tale that impressed upon its readers the many different ingredients required in the pudding, brought together from all over the world, a good part of which consisted of the British Empire, and how this required the labour of over a thousand people. Plaatje was reminded of the story on 30 December 1899 because of the similarity between the tale and what happened that day when his boss, Charles Bell, played a trick on his servants, advising them all to turn up to a grand Christmas dinner – and then failed to provide anything for them.[5]

This may have been a casual reference, but it was also a pointed reminder, and an acknowledgement, of a world that had shaped his being, and without which his diary could not have been contemplated. It spoke, too, of the distance Plaatje had come from the time he read *Royal Reader* no. 3, with its graded vocabulary and limited ambition, to the near-flawless command of English that is evident in the diary.

Plaatje's English must have come on in leaps and bounds after he left the Pniel mission in 1894 to take up a job in the Post Office in Kimberley. Here, living in the Malay Camp, he found himself part of a self-confident group of mission-educated Africans who were determined to take advantage of the opportunities and freedoms that life in Kimberley presented. They made their own musical entertainment, took part in sporting activities like cricket, rugby, football and tennis, and they worked hard to improve their English, an essential skill in the late nineteenth-century Cape Colony.

One organisation played an especially important part in their lives. It was called the South Africans Improvement Society, and it set out its aims as follows: 'firstly, to cultivate the use of the English language, which is foreign to Africans; secondly to help each other by fair and reasonable criticisms in reading, recitation, English composition, etc, etc.' They met fortnightly, and engaged in debates, readings and music. Plaatje, it is clear, was surrounded by like-minded people who left a powerful mark upon his development.

Kimberley, and Plaatje's memories of his time there, often surface in his Mafeking diary. Take his first entry, 29 October 1899, when the sound of rifle and cannon fire brought back musical memories from his time in Kimberley. A fusillade from the armoured train 'was like a member of the Payne family silencing a boisterous crowd with the prelude of a selection she is going to give on the violin'. When that ceased, and the Boers' Maxim gun opened up, 'it was like listening to the Kimberley R.C. choir with their organ, rendering one of their mellifluous carols on Christian eve' – whose charm, he added, 'could be justly compared with that of the Jubilee Singers performing one of their many quaint and classical oratorios'.[6]

He was drawing upon some very specific – and positive – musical memories: the Payne family, a popular musical group from Australia, had been in Kimberley in July 1895 and May 1896, while the famous American Jubilee Singers were in Kimberley in 1889, 1890, 1895 and 1896. They were back again, re-formed, as Macadoo's Minstrels, in April 1898 – inspiring Plaatje's further mention of them in his diary for 6 December 1899. That day an explosion in Mr Gerrans's blacksmith shop had left the owner with 'a face as black as that of a corner man in Macadoo's Vaudevilles'.[7] Musical experiences, it is clear, provided an important cultural repertoire and vocabulary upon which he drew to help convey what he saw going on around him in Mafeking.

Plaatje's memories of Kimberley were also memories of particular people. One was his wife Elizabeth, now no longer with him in Mafeking but safe, or so he hoped, elsewhere in the Colony. He often thought of her – at Christmas, on his birthday or when he remembered 'the long and awful nights in 1897 when the path to the union ... was so rocky'.[8] He didn't elaborate in his diary about why his courtship with Elizabeth was 'so rocky', but we do know – since he wrote about it later in life – what had happened. His parents, and Elizabeth's too, were opposed to their marriage, he being a Morolong and she an Mfengu. Undeterred, they were married by special licence in Kimberley on 25 January 1898. Later he would credit the 'civilised laws' (on civil marriage) of the Cape Colony for making this possible.[9]

Plaatje and Elizabeth had come together through Isaiah Bud-M'belle, Elizabeth's elder brother, who was well known as a High Court interpreter in Kimberley. He is another Kimberley presence in Plaatje's diary and he is mentioned on several occasions. Though he was five years older than Plaatje, the two men had become best of friends, and he had played a leading role in social, sporting and musical associations in Kimberley. When war broke out in 1899 he was on circuit duty, as interpreter, with the Griqualand West High Court, when it was travelling in a remote part of the northern Cape, and Plaatje had no idea what had become of him. Only later did he find out that he had managed to make his way to safety in Cape Town, where he would spend the rest of the war.

Another friend from Kimberley who figured prominently in Plaatje's memory, and that of his friend David Phooko, was Patrick Lenkoane, a member of the South Africans Improvement Society. Lenkoane, of Sotho origin, was well known for his sense of humour. Stories about him were called 'Lenkoaniacs' and in December 1899, when Plaatje was recovering from influenza, David entertained him with tales of Lenkoane's doings in Kimberley, where he had known him too before he moved to Mafeking.[10]

Other friends and acquaintances from Plaatje's time in Kimberley were recalled too. Among them was William Cowen, originally from West Africa, who was vice-president of the South Africans Improvement Society. He once read a paper entitled 'Civilisation and Its Advantages to African Races', but he came to Plaatje's mind on 30 December 1899 when he recalled the words – 'a hell of a smash' – that Cowen used to describe the cause of proceedings in a court case in Kimberley.[11] Another was Joseph Moss, a well-known court interpreter and long-established resident of Kimberley, who once gave a series of 'Lectures on Native Education' in which he argued that 'a classical education is the right and necessary one for the Native people at the present stage'. Plaatje remembered him – on 28 March 1900 – not for his views on education but for having been sued by one Enoch Dingiswayo in a court case in Kimberley in June 1899.[12] Again Plaatje was struck by the similarity in circumstance between this court case and a complicated transaction, in which Plaatje himself was involved in late March 1900, arising from the purchase of a horse captured from the Boers. Past and present, as elsewhere, were often compared and contrasted.

And then there were the Msikinyas, another well-known Kimberley family. The Rev. Davidson Msikinya was the Wesleyan Methodist clergyman who had officiated at the church ceremony that sanctified Plaatje's marriage to Elizabeth in 1897, and he came to mind on 25 March 1900 when Plaatje remembered his fondness for the catchphrase 'nooks and corners'. His son Colbourne Msikinya features too. He is mentioned a couple of weeks earlier when Plaatje described Kolobe Dinku, a teacher at the Wesleyan mission school in Mahikeng, as 'the northern Colbourne Msikinya' – his opposite number at a Wesleyan mission school in Kimberley (which was some 200 miles south of Mafeking, hence the geographical reference).[13]

Kimberley – and Plaatje's memories of his time there in the 1890s – was thus an important reference point. He would often look back to make comparisons with his earlier experiences. The people he mentioned may not have made much of a mark in South Africa's recorded history, but they shared common values and common experiences, they provided a supportive social and cultural network, and they taught him a great deal. They were important in his life and they contributed hugely, it is fair to say, to the making of the person, and the writer, that he became. They were as important a presence in his Mafeking diary as the more immediate surroundings of Mafeking itself. In a way Plaatje's diary was their testament too, for nowhere else were their lives and their foibles recalled so vividly.

One individual contributed more than most to the ideas and perceptions of the young Solomon Plaatje during his time in Kimberley: John Tengo Jabavu, editor of the bilingual (English and isiXhosa) weekly newspaper, *Imvo Zabantsundu*, based in King Williamstown in the eastern Cape.

Imvo was required reading for Kimberley's mission-educated African community – as it was for their counterparts elsewhere in southern Africa. It carried a wide variety of news and comment in both English and Xhosa: of local political and religious developments; of the progress being made by blacks in the United States and West Africa, always a source of inspiration; detailed reports from local correspondents of the social and sporting life of mission-educated communities in the Colony and beyond; and editorials advocating temperance, education, self-help and improvement along the lines pursued by Kimberley's South Africans Improvement Society.[14]

Imvo helped shape the aspirations of a generation of mission-educated Africans. Its influence is evident throughout Plaatje's diary but in a very specific way in his entry for 27 February 1900. On that day Plaatje referred to a letter which Colonel Baden-Powell had written to General Snyman, the Boer commander, threatening to rescind the unspoken agreement that Africans should not be involved in the conflict between Boer and British if Snyman did not release Chief Saane from captivity. If the Tswana chiefs of the Bechuanaland Protectorate then took up the cause of the British, Plaatje thought, they and their men would pour into the Transvaal and cause immense damage and destruction to the Boers and their property. At that point, Plaatje writes, '"Humanity will shudder", to use Jabavu's phrase.'[15] Jabavu's phrase, it turns out on closer investigation, comes from an editorial in *Imvo*, on 23 April 1896, when Jabavu had deployed the phrase in relation to a similar situation. Humanity would shudder, he thought, if Africans in the Transvaal rose up against their oppressors in revenge for the treatment then being meted out to them. Plaatje remembered Jabavu's words and was struck by their relevance to what he saw and heard in February 1900.

Jabavu's influence and advice extended to the conduct of parliamentary politics in the Cape Colony. Here some Africans had the vote and Jabavu advised his readers to exploit this in the most effective ways possible. Africans should become fully involved, he believed, in the political life of the Colony; they should be moderate and cautious in their attitudes and demands, exploit the differences that existed between white politicians in order to extract concessions, and place their trust in various (white) 'friends of the natives' who were sympathetic to their interests. 'Civilised' Africans, Jabavu also believed, had a special responsibility towards their less articulate brethren, and a duty to act as their spokesmen: *Imvo*'s guiding metaphor was the hope that it could serve as 'a rope to tow those stragglers to the desired shore'.[16]

By the time of the Cape Colony's general election in 1898, electoral politics had become distinctly polarised and the two opposing parties, the Progressives and the Afrikaner Bond, competed openly for African support. It proved to be a bitterly fought election, none more so than in the constituency of Barkly West, some twenty miles from Kimberley. This constituency included the Pniel mission where Plaatje had grown up, and where there happened to be significant numbers of African and Coloured voters. The election, as it happens, impinged directly on Plaatje's experience, and his memory of it surfaces in his diary three years later.

In his diary Plaatje recalls the election because he was taken aback by reports, brought into Mafeking by runners, of the behaviour of his former mentor, the Rev. Ernst Westphal, who was alleged to have assisted Boer forces when they occupied the Pniel mission. 'It is marvellous how Rev. Westphal managed to turn traitor, when he sent me that hot letter going for me for having leanings towards the Transvaal and Krugerism, simply because I sympathized with Adv Burton during the last election; and he could not be convinced by my reasons that the young QC earned my sympathies not because he was supported by the Afrikaner Bond, but simply because he was a negrophilist and did a lot for us while I was in Kimberley – directly on the platform, in the press, and at the bar.'[17]

Burton was defeated in the 1898 election by the rival candidate representing the Progressive Party – Cecil Rhodes, who was already the constituency's member of parliament and was seeking re-election. But what is significant is the assumptions underlying Plaatje's memories of the election. He takes it for granted that Africans like him have the vote, that they can play their part in deciding the political future of the Colony, and that it is right for them to judge the candidates on their merits, particularly in relation to their views on African rights.

So it was not surprising that Plaatje preferred Henry Burton to Cecil Rhodes, even if in doing so he incurred the displeasure of Westphal, who was a great supporter of the former prime minister. This was the election, interestingly enough, at which Cecil Rhodes, recognising his need for African and Coloured votes, had come up with his famous slogan, 'Equal rights for all civilised men'. He may not have meant it, and there was ambiguity in the meaning of 'civilised', but the slogan soon took on a life of its own and it proved to be a lasting legacy.

This passage from Plaatje's diary points to another central element in his thinking. When he mentioned what Henry Burton did for Africans 'at the bar', he was thinking of the cases where Burton had acted for them in defence of their legal rights. While the law could be, and often was, an instrument of oppression and control, there was another side to it too. The Colony had a non-racial constitution and the courts were required to dispense justice without regard to race or religion. Even if in practice this did not always happen, the law courts nevertheless provided a forum for the defence of their rights, and enabled black South Africans to challenge, among other things, repressive pass laws which municipalities sought to impose. In Kimberley, in the 1890s, this was the case on several occasions, and the events that followed left a deep impression on Plaatje. He often referred, later in life, to a test case in May 1898, which he must have had in mind when considering what Henry Burton had done for him and his Kimberley contemporaries 'at the bar'.

The case involved a man called Saul Mankazana, a property owner and registered voter, who was arrested for not having a pass when walking down Ross Street in Kimberley in May 1898. When the case was heard in the magistrate's court, he was deemed to have breached pass law regulations and fined five shillings. Believing the regulations were illegal, Saul Mankazana and those who supported him secured the services of Advocate Burton, took the case to the Griqualand West High Court, and won on appeal. Plaatje, and *Imvo*, regarded it as a famous victory, a prime example, as he saw it, of what could be achieved by using the legal and constitutional means open to them.[18]

Plaatje's interest in the law preceded this case – even as a boy he recalled being fascinated by reports of the work of the High Court – and his best friend, Isaiah Bud-M'belle, must have told him all about his work as its interpreter. Once in Mafeking, as clerk and court interpreter himself, albeit working for a magistrate and civil commissioner rather than the Griqualand West High Court, he was immersed in the operation of the law on a daily basis. In his diary he talks about his work in court, invariably in positive terms. Appointed as interpreter to the Court of Summary Jurisdiction, he spoke of officiating here, for example, on 22 November 1899, welcoming the challenge as 'such courts ... transact a lot of business in a very short time as evidence is taken by a shorthand writer, which causes one to extremely enjoy interpreting, as you have to fire away without stoppages'. A few days later, after a temporary replacement was sought when he was absent, 'the fellow being an amateur interpreter ... was completely flabbergasted when it came to cross examinations, and I took his place to immense advantage'.[19]

For Plaatje was well aware of the importance of the role of court interpreter in the administration of justice. Only with knowledgeable and efficient interpreters was there any chance of justice being done in a South African court, and it was all too easy for an incompetent interpreter to cause a serious miscarriage of justice. This was a subject he would write about later and often returned to. His experiences before, during and after the siege only confirmed his views on the subject.[20]

Plaatje's mood as expressed in his diary is mostly one of optimism and self-confidence. Work was interesting, he played an important part in liaising between the Barolong and the military authorities, and he had a chance to make some money on the side through his work for the war correspondents temporarily in Mafeking. He may have felt sorry for himself from time, especially when he was down with influenza, when news from outside was bad or non-existent, or when he worried about the fate of his family. But he had the inner resources to see him through.

His diary gives plenty of clues as to the sources of this inner strength. He draws upon past memories to frame his perception of the present and to keep alive hope for the future, and he does so in a way that distinguishes his diary from the many others which were written during the Siege of Mafeking – whether from soldiers, administrators, medical practitioners, journalists or townspeople. The more you read the diary, the more it reveals the outlook, the personality and the past experiences of its author.

Eleven

The Mafeking Diary of Sol Plaatje and the History of Literary Journalism in South Africa

Lesley Mofokeng

Reading *The Mafeking Diary of Sol T. Plaatje* left me with a riddle.[1] Written between October 1899 and March 1900 during the Siege of Mafeking, one of the most famous episodes of the South African War, it is believed to be the only diary of the war by a black South African to have survived.[2] Its author was a civil servant of the Cape Colony whose job description included court interpreting and typing. He typed the diary of his boss, the magistrate and civil commissioner Charles Bell.[3] But he was also a well-connected man who developed contacts in the media world, working with war correspondents in Mafeking and marshalling dispatch runners and scouts.[4] He effectively positioned himself as the spokesperson of his people, Barolong, who found themselves in the crossfire in the war between Boer and British.

Plaatje was mission-educated up to Standard 3 and was a pupil-teacher at the mission station in Pniel, near Barkly West. He worked for the Post Office in Kimberley as a messenger and, while there, was part of an elite group of educated blacks who strove to improve their command of the English language by forming the South Africans Improvement Society.[5] He was a reader of *Imvo Zabantsundu*, edited by Tengo Jabavu,[6] as well as the Setswana-language journals *Molekoli oa Bechuana*[7] and *Mahoko a Becwana*.[8]

When he sat down to pen his daily experiences of the Mafeking siege, Plaatje may never have guessed that some 120 years later his writing would be reflected upon with interest and its resonance considered as part of the evolving canon of literary journalism.[9] Brian Willan, his biographer, is correct to note that Plaatje had worked hard to improve his written English, and the diary presented an opportunity to practise what he learnt and take it to the next level, free of the formalities of an office such as the magistrate's.[10] Willan further notes that the diary gave expression to a distinctive personality and Plaatje played around with different ways of representing himself as family man, as privileged and conscientious servant of the colonial government, and as loyal British subject.

Willan concludes that Plaatje revelled in creating this literary persona with an ironic and self-deprecating humour.[11] The *Mafeking Diary* is not only rich in detail, colour and experience, it is also well written. The prose, the richly textured self-reflection, sophistication of intimate private expression, and social sensitivity of Plaatje's writing[12] have made the diary an object of interest in literary journalism studies. As John Comaroff notes, 'the diary was rarely, if ever, a literary genre of choice among black South Africans. It belonged, culturally and ideologically, to a European bourgeois sensibility and a modernist one at that, one in which "everyday life", its actions and emotions and thoughts and jottings, becomes the primary frame of relevant social and individual experience.'[13]

Here is the riddle. Now as we read the diary retrospectively, knowing and understanding literary journalism and how it has carved its place as a discipline in recent years,[14] and the amount of effort taken by scholars to trace its roots, could it be that in writing the diary, Plaatje created one of the early ancestor texts of African literary journalism? As a literary journalism scholar, I am presented by the diary with an opportunity to think through how the discipline took root in South Africa and how it can be traced back in history. At this early stage of his writing career, Plaatje captures daily events with the precision of journalistic rigour, yet with a novelistic eye. What role did the diary play ahead of Plaatje's embarking on a journalism career as the editor of *Koranta ea Becoana* in Mafeking after the end of the South African War?

'Literary journalism is as timeless as it is ubiquitous.'[15] With these words, literary journalism scholar and founding president of the International Association for Literary Journalism Studies, John Bak, reminds us that this form of writing has always been with us. It may not always have been identified as such, but a glance at classic texts reveals that literary journalism has been practised for decades. Bak explains this further: 'How one nation sees and understands literary journalism today is thus inextricably tied to that nation's earlier print culture and political development. And given that facticity and aesthetics, the epistemic pillars on which literary journalism firmly rests, are themselves open to historical scrutiny and cultural interpretation, it is perhaps prudent to talk about literary journalisms in their plurality.'[16]

In an earlier work, Bak and his colleague Bill Reynolds wrote that journalists most often turn literary when their nations are at war with others or themselves.[17] They likened literary journalism to a balm that soothes the pain inflicted by the journalistic facts delivered in the written piece or the dispatch, and therefore literary journalism emerges as a by-product.[18] Given that the *Mafeking Diary* was written in wartime and Plaatje may not have intended to publish it, could it have been the balm that soothed his pain of being separated from his family and finding himself in a life-threatening situation?

Reflecting on the complexity of defining literary journalism, Victoria Sgarro questions if literary journalism occupies the space between fiction and journalism.[19] To define literary journalism, she agrees with Bak that it should be approached as a discipline.

John Bak and Monica Martinez argue that literary journalism is in constant construction and that historians have been at work to establish its evolution in time and history.[20] The scholarship has resulted in an increase in the number and visibility of literary journalistic texts around the world. This excavation of 'lost texts for the literary journalism canon' has helped advance the discipline.[21] It is with this approach in mind that, when reading the *Mafeking Diary*, one seeks for 'lost texts'.

Plaatje was not a journalist when he wrote the diary. But he found himself in the intersection of the information superhighway between the dispatch runners, the magistrate, the local court, the war correspondents, the Barolong in the *stadt* and the Boers.[22] He was located in a rare, privileged and powerful position where information bombarded him from all sides.

His relationship with Vere Stent, the Reuters correspondent, was particularly pivotal in his evolution from civil servant to diarist and eventually journalist and editor. In Brian Willan's biography of Plaatje, Stent's recollection of how he met Plaatje is recorded thus:

> One fine morning I became aware of a very smart, sprucely dressed young native standing to attention before me.
> 'Well?' said I.
> 'I hear you need a secretary-typist, sir,' he answered.
> 'Well, so I do. Is your master one?'
> 'I haven't a master,' said Plaatje, with a faint smile, 'but I write shorthand and can use the typewriter.' He spoke perfect English and I engaged him at a ridiculously low wage which he named himself and seemed glad enough to get.[23]

Stent recognised in Plaatje 'an extraordinarily capable assistant'. 'To begin with he could spell, which I can't and never could. He was quick on the machine ... quick-witted and understanding and quick to pick and catch a new expression, ask the meaning and derivation of it and add it to his vocabulary.'[24]

Plaatje became a competent liaison officer between Stent and what he called his 'little corps of native dispatch runners', and Stent reported making in his own diary 'entries of substantial sums of money paid to him for distribution amongst them'. Stent's diary has not survived, but in a letter to H.D. Gwynne, the chief Reuters agent in Cape Town, he said that he had issued a draft in favour of Plaatje 'for £30 for the payment of runners south and for services rendered to the Agency'. Willan says some of the runners were shot or captured though the majority succeeded in bringing the story of the Mafeking siege to the outside world. It was an important task as it impacted on public opinion in the English-speaking world, creating the story of an isolated brave garrison holding out against superior enemy forces. The presence in Mafeking of members of some of England's aristocratic families in town also added to the story's appeal.[25] Plaatje also asked Stent for money to be paid to his wife Elizabeth and to send his own personal messages.

By February 1900, Plaatje was typing the diaries of Charles Bell, William Hayes, the senior medical practitioner in Mafeking, and Herbert Greener, the chief paymaster. All this presented Plaatje with multiple streams of income, typing practice useful for future Civil Service examinations, and the chance to gain some insights into the minds of whites. He was content with the money he made, and it helped him 'keep pace with the hard times'.

Charles Bell allowed him to use the office typewriter so that he could supplement his income. The first correspondent he worked with was E.G. Parslow of the *Daily Chronicle*, who got shot by Lt Murchison in November in a drunken brawl. Plaatje lamented that the death of Parslow deprived him of a good friend and wrecked him financially. 'He paid for my little assistance so liberally that I never felt the prices of foodstuffs that [have] reigned here since the commencement of the siege.'[26]

In his 11 December 1899 entry, Plaatje records that he had received the news that two dispatch runners who were fired at by the Boers while trying to make their way to the *stadt* ended up getting lost and returned to Kanya (present-day Kanye). In the same entry, he talks about how he brought J. Angus Hamilton, the war correspondent for *The Times* and the London illustrated news magazine *Black and White*, to the *stadt* to take photographs for the latter publication. During the tour, Hamilton encountered a Mr Lefenya, who had been wounded in the crossfire. Hamilton washed and dressed the wound.[27]

On Monday, 4 December 1899, Plaatje notes that dispatch runners had arrived bringing news (which turned out to be untrue) of the relief of Kimberley, incidentally on his son St Leger's birthday, 23 November. He also shares information about the Boers capturing cattle, horses, wagons and women, the last-mentioned being returned as they 'are not of any value in war'. Furthermore, he tells of an officer of the Protectorate Regiment whose wife was captured by the Boers and mentions in this regard a prisoner swap offer put on the table.[28]

Some of the court cases Plaatje witnessed are registered in the diary, including one from 5 December 1899 in which a white man was accused of raping an African girl. At the start of the trial Plaatje, a man in demand for his work as an interpreter, was called away by the military authorities, only to return at the end of the court hearing.[29]

Placed in this prime position, Plaatje effectively became a record-keeper, privy to intelligence from the front line of war and through his dealings with the war correspondents. It seems to have been a natural progression for him to pen his thoughts in a diary.

It took two weeks from the start of the war for Plaatje to begin his diary. His biographer Brian Willan argues that it was never intended for publication.[30] It remains a matter of speculation as to whom he wrote the diary for. But what is also interesting is how it was pitched. The register of the language, the beauty of expression and self-reflection contained in the diary point to the fact that Plaatje may have used it to flex his writing muscles. He may have already fancied himself more of a writer than a civil servant.

The image John Comaroff presents of Plaatje as a skilled writer leaves one with the image of a literary journalist. Comaroff notes:

> At the same time, in fashioning the content of his prose, both playful and serious and in experimenting with the genre, Plaatje was self-consciously, even assertively, African, hence for example, his copious use of different languages, of poetic wordplay and in unusual ways, of such devices as onomatopoeia and irony. In this respect, he anticipated the current concern, in cultural studies, with hybridity, hybridity, that is, both as an intrinsic feature of human subjectivity under colonialism and as a characteristic of literary production.[31]

It was fashionable to keep a diary in Victorian times. Writing about this, Anne-Marie Millim argues that the Victorian psychologist Alexander Bain recommended that the diary be used as a vital tool in rational decision-making and self-examination. For Bain, keeping a diary 'was a self-advisatory and therefore self-protective activity of private socialisation that could help the diarist fashion a respectable persona for the public sphere'.[32] There are certainly some traits of the Victorian diary evident in the *Mafeking Diary*, especially the kind of writing committed in solitude.

If *Native Life in South Africa* is a distillation of Plaatje's journalistic career,[33] then the *Mafeking Diary* is its progenitor. It served as a cradle and launch pad in which Plaatje exercised his writing skills. It became a collection of private thoughts, recordings and musings that he probably did not intend to publish, but it sharpened his pen and crafted his skill as a writer.

John Comaroff argues that 'in Plaatje taking up his diary journal, he gave voice to a modernist self-consciousness – cultivated in part by his mission education, in part by having lived among the nascent black bourgeois in Kimberley – which was to come to exquisite maturity in his later work'.[34]

Just as *Native Life* is inseparable from his journalism, with its style and content owing much to the world of the press, I would argue that the diary carries this DNA.³⁵ It is in the fluidity of his writing, the lucid descriptions, irony and melodrama that one notices how much enjoyment the writing must have given him.³⁶

Writing about Daniel Defoe, Jenny McKay calls him the most prolific journalist Britain had ever known until his day.³⁷ She goes on to say that despite this, Defoe has been known more as a fiction writer, even though in 1703 he published a book-length account of a storm that ravaged England. This work is often read by English literature students but is mostly ignored by journalism departments even though it presents an early specimen of reportage. I would like to argue that the same principle applies to Plaatje. The *Mafeking Diary* goes beyond the usual logging of daily events and experiences, presenting journalism of today with an ancestor of early reportage or literary journalism. The diary sits comfortably as a piece of book-length reportage or documentary.

Comaroff makes the point that Plaatje's style and approach were different from those of other accounts of the Siege of Mafeking. Take for example *Petticoat in Mafeking: The Siege Letters of Ada Cock*, edited by John F. Midgley,³⁸ or *Mafeking Memories* by Frederick Saunders.³⁹ Comaroff remarks that most of the other diaries and accounts were long on events, short on analysis and even shorter on richly textured self-reflection. He is correct to say that 'none of them comes close to the sophistication of intimate private expression, let alone social sensitivity, displayed by Plaatje. Nor do they exhibit the same subtlety in playing off biographical recollections of the past with accounts of the historical present.'⁴⁰ The one exception perhaps is *The Siege of Mafeking* (1900) written by J. Angus Hamilton, which exhibits the qualities of what we consider literary journalism today – not surprising, given that he was a professional journalist, exposed to the trends and styles of that period.⁴¹

The stylistic choices made by Plaatje when he wrote the diary provide further clues to his frame of mind, approach and influences. According to Pedro Rosa Mendes, literary journalism involves writing from a novelist's eye with the discipline of a journalist.⁴² However, it must also be said that Plaatje kept an African style of storytelling. Wallace Chuma argues that the hegemonic 5 Ws and an H model of writing – whereby a story is told by prioritising the answers to What, Who, Where, When, Why and How – is inconsistent with African storytelling. He writes: 'it is not the shocking detail that you begin with when you communicate. You prepare the listener before dropping the bombshell. In African folktales or stories, the climax does not come first as is the case with Western ways of communication.'[43]

Take, for example, a few paragraphs from the diary. On Tuesday, 2 January 1900, Plaatje records: 'A shell from "Sanna" hit the east of the stadt, where Ellitson [the butcher] has put up his slaughter-pole since the siege, and amputated an employee in a most piteous manner – both legs and both arms. He died after this.'[44] While the 'breaking news' of this entry is that an employee died from serious injuries, Plaatje delays and drops the bombshell at the end.

The most obvious weapon in the arsenal of non-fiction is verisimilitude, says Nicholas Lemann.[45] It makes the story more powerful when the audience knows that it really happened. For readers of the *Mafeking Diary* and scholars of literary journalism, the writing of Plaatje provides material to sink our teeth into as we figure out its place in journalism and think through what Plaatje set out to achieve.

Lemann says literary journalism ought to be executed in prose that is memorable and stylish, in voice, structure, characterisation and description.[46] The *Mafeking Diary* seems to tick the boxes. Plaatje shows traces of writing techniques that we now, retrospectively, consider as literary journalism; his writing became even more nuanced and vivid in his later works such as *Native Life in South Africa*.

Plaatje's diary belongs to what Lemann calls 'lapidary' work about ordinary life that can be executed in one's own backyard.[47] It didn't take many resources for Plaatje to keep the diary. It was relatively easy work that relied on his skill and talent, keen sense of observation as well as meticulous record-keeping.

Plaatje's writing is accomplished in the literary traditions espoused by Tom Wolfe. Wolfe speaks of scene-by-scene construction, natural dialogue, third-person point of view, and the use of status life details. Scene-by-scene construction 'is a way of telling the story by allowing it to unfold in scenes, like a movie'. The use of colloquial dialogue in the scenes assists authenticity and vital characterisation. Describing scenes from the writer's viewpoint and including dialogue are not far from traditional feature journalism. Status life details are descriptive details that indicate something of the status of the character in society: 'the entire pattern of behaviour and possessions through which people express their position in the world or what they think it is or what they hope it to be.' Referring to the tradition of New Journalism, Wolfe argued that the writer's voice was often lively, inventive and colloquial, a marked departure from the reporterly style of 'serious journalism'.[48]

Let's look at some textual evidence in the diary and its conformity to Wolfe's elements.

On New Year's Day 1900, Sol Plaatje writes in his diary:

> After I went to town and David [Phooko] and Ebie [Plaatje's cousin] were breaking-fast the thing smashed within 50 yards from the house. David cleared helter-skelter with the coffee which had become insipid. Ebie considered his bread too precious and remained chewing as if nothing happened.
>
> In the afternoon David stood watching a train of merry girls, amidst whom were Meko's sisters-in-law in the best of millineries, celebrating the new year with several jolly games. All of a sudden 'Sanna' came round and spoiled the whole fun. Mr Briscoe's garden is an intolerably near spot for 94 pounds of mortar to burst while a train of giggling girls are enjoying the first day in the first year of twentieth century near Bokone – particularly when they were under the impression that it was to town. It sent nearly all the merry maidens in different directions. Some lay flat on the ground – it was for dear life – and 'Sanna' fairly put them in memory that their lives were dearer and more expensive than their new year's dresses.[48]

Plaatje uses characterisation to tell of the terrifying horror of Sanna, the Creusot siege gun, that befell the hapless Barolong in the *stadt*. It is the vivid description, scene creation and voice that make such an entry a subject of interest to literary journalism scholars.

On Wednesday, 10 January 1900, Plaatje writes:

> Things were somewhat quiet today, but Boer fire was somewhat effective. An innocent fellow was taking some water out of a tank when a Mauser bullet entered his body by the neck, coursed through his inside and exited through his left loin. He was stooping down at the time, and stood straight and walked about a little before he fell down. He was taken to the hospital on a stretcher, and died about five hours after.[49]

This entry is typical of Plaatje's descriptions that can best be described as dramatic. It could easily be a scene from a movie about the Wild West. Its graphic – if not grotesque – details lift up the diary to another level. Plaatje goes graphic in the form typical of Hollywood film director Quentin Tarantino in the entry for Saturday, 20 January 1900: 'A big shell struck the abdomen of the town's special constable and fractured his private parts in a most pitiful manner. He is, however, expected to pull through. Sterk [Strong] Morolong.'[50]

On Wednesday, 24 January 1900, Plaatje writes:

> The big gun is still hammering away at us. It was particularly cruel today. One of its shells hit on the Market Square this morning. It bumped right up in the air and singled out old Moshweshwe's hut (one-and-a-half miles away) after its decline it entered the hut from the back, decapitating two women and wounding three brothers severely and one not dangerously. The old boy was not there.[51]

For Sunday, 30 December 1899, he records:

> Turning to our subject, the ruin of the charge office was just as lamentable as many of 'Sanna's' doings, and it was also the occasion of a marvellous escapade. It entered, and shook down, the office. It found about 50 Natives, who took shelter in front of the ill-fated building when the tocsins chimed. The many fragments found their way away from the presence of human beings and only singled out a good young fellow (one of the Maseloas), threw the top of his head away from the body, and left him standing exactly where he was: all this was the work of a second – or a lesser period. Every one of his companions spent a long time reflecting over the narrowness of his (own) escape. Sheets, half sheets and fragments of corrugated iron were scattered all over the street, and they did not notice the occurrence till many minutes after.[52]

The trend continues on Tuesday, 2 January 1900:

> The 7-pounder that fired from the east yesterday had been moved round to Jackal Tree during the night. It sent a number of shells into the stadt early this morning, one of which smashed inside the hut of Mma-Mokoloi and emptied its contents on her head. None of the others were injured. The baby at her breast was not even shaken. A shell from 'Sanna' hit the east of the stadt, where Ellitson has put up his slaughter-pole since the siege, and amputated an employee in a most piteous manner – both legs and both arms. He died after this.[53]

The mournful yet comedic entry for Tuesday, 6 February 1900, is about Whiskey, a horse that was injured from the shelling and was snapped up by Basotho who 'congregated on the spot, and hardly gave him time to die – so much in a hurry were they of getting his meat. They undoubtedly deprived the stadt of its best horse, and put me in a fix, as I doubt if poor Whiskey can easily be replaced – they got salted horse.'[54]

The diary has some rich descriptions; take the entry for Wednesday, 3 January 1900, for example:

> This morning I was trying to go to town. I was just near the two trees when the bells rang. There was a horrible smash all round me and I could see the branches of one of the trees flying in the air in a cloud of dust. From under the tree all the men in the shade were raised from four to seven foot high.[55]

Plaatje devotes time and space to tell the unusual story of an encounter with a precocious seven-year-old spy on Monday, 8 January 1900. He uses tactics and tools such as scene-by-scene construction and dialogue in this diary entry. 'A little boy named Phalaetsile escaped from the Boers yesterday,' he starts.

> A poor chappie of only about seven years old, he found himself accidentally in the hands of the Boers three Sundays ago. Some volunteers are always moved from one end of the camp to the other, and he is one of the youngsters that always carried their blankets for a sixpence and part of their rations.
>
> They were out looking for a similar job about our farthermost redoubts, when he and a companion played into the hands of the Boers. He has since been employed as a herd in the big gun fort. I am afraid we have seldom had so much news from a fellow five times his age. He really has sympathy for Britain in his little heart. He made an earthen plan of the big gun fort – with sand and pieces of wood showing the position of the tents, waggons and horses in it and also the action of the big gun – so cleverly that the Colonel came to study it.
>
> He states that there were two artillery duels lately. After the first, two Boers were killed and one had his left arm broken, after the second he found five dead Boers, but he cannot state if they were wounded. He says the chief gunner was shot during last week and knocks about with the crutch. I asked him why he

[the chief gunner] doesn't lay down when he is wounded. He said, 'Kaitse ke ene ba shupetsang fa toropo e sekgotlho e teng [I knew that he directed them to the town backyard which was there]'.

He tells a whole lot of interesting items. He states that during last week someone rode from the head laager to say that the English wrote to say that they shouldn't fire at the hospital. On hearing this, the gunners fired two shots at the hospital on purpose. Official publication adds that these are the two shots which fell very close to the hospital on the 2nd inst. There is so much about this interesting little boy that I will never forget. The Colonel came round to the residency for the sole purpose of studying his earthen plan of the big gun fort.[56]

In the passages I have quoted above, Plaatje's narration is further evidence of how he was entrenched in the community as a witness of war. No man could have found himself more in the centre of the action than he was. His access to war correspondents, the courts, and the Barolong community and its leaders allowed him to capture the mood, emotions and wonder of the experiences of war.

A diary it might be, but when it takes a different approach from the conventions of literary journalism, it assumes a different veneer and glistens as an exquisite display of the benefits of using literary journalism tools and aids when telling a story.

Reading the diary retrospectively, one gets a sense of a journalistic account that comes from a novelist's desk. It is worth noting that Plaatje went on to have a successful though tumultuous career as a journalist as well as a novelist. The diary transcends many rules and forms, and, viewed from the lens of literary journalism, it provides an insight into Plaatje's mind before he became a spokesman of his people through his journalism and political activism.

In the diary, he delivers a master class in storytelling, taking the mundane work of recording daily occurrences and turning it into a magnificent and well-crafted narrative. Plaatje was bogged down with officialdom as a clerk and interpreter for Charles Bell, the magistrate of Mafeking, compiling reports and translating official documents – hardly an outlet to express creativity or freedom of thought. The diary, with no rules and boundaries of translation, set his soul on fire.

This is where Plaatje finally sat down for an examination of what he learnt from the South Africans Improvement Society in Kimberley years earlier. The reading and writing diet he was put on by Ernst and Marie Westphal, the Berlin Mission Society missionaries who first introduced the written word to Plaatje, finally bore fruit in the *Mafeking Diary*.

The research for this chapter was supported by funding from the National Research Foundation, South Africa, and forms part of a French-South Africa Protea project 'A Centenary of (Post) Colonial Narrative Literary Journalism in South Africa and France' between Wits University and Université de Lorraine.

Twelve

The Heart Goes After Whom It Loves

Sabata-mpho Mokae

In the waiting room at Burghersdorp station, a woman cradled her baby while waiting for the Bloemfontein-bound train. It was in the autumn of the year 1900. As the leaves were beginning to fall from the trees, lining the ground, creating a yellow and orange carpet, temperatures were also beginning to drop.

'Thula thula sana,' she sang a lullaby to calm down her baby boy, who looked just a year old. 'In a couple of days, we'll be with your father.'

She looked at the boy with a smile. 'You're just as handsome as your father, my son. When you grow up, you're going to be as strong as he is. I miss him just as you miss him. I promise you, we'll be with him in a few days from now,' she whispered in his ear as though she was talking to an adult who could understand what she was saying, even hold her to her words. 'Thula thula sana,' she continued to sing softly in his ear. The baby calmed down. In no time his eyes were shut, his face peaceful as the autumn skies. She held him closer to her chest, and smiled. A lone tear trickled down her face. She wiped it off quickly with the back of her hand and looked around to see if anyone had noticed.

The waiting room was teeming with men and women carrying bags and suitcases of varying sizes, depending on how far their destinations were. Some were going as near as Bloemfontein to see their relatives, for one reason or another. Others were going to catch connecting trains in Bloemfontein to proceed to the gold mines in Johannesburg or to the diamond mines in Kimberley.

Each piece of luggage carried the story of the person it belonged to; from the bulging brown suitcase that told the story of a man who was not likely to return home in the next six months or year, to the rucksack that belonged to a young man barely out of his teens who was probably going to seek a job in Johannesburg, the City of Gold, or Kimberley, the City of Diamonds, with hopes for a better life.

In the waiting room there was a cacophony of crying babies and lullabies, men and women having conversations in isiXhosa, Sesotho and other languages. There was excitement in the air, and maybe anxiety and some fear too, especially in those who were venturing into the vast unknown. A long queue of customers stood waiting to buy from the kiosk. An enterprising hawker saw the gap and jumped in to take advantage. 'Sweets, *vetkoek*, snacks, snuff, cigarettes …' he went on and on, as if singing the song of the ape. The only thing he didn't sell was undergarments, at least not in front of people's eyes. He even sold facecloths and bars of soap so small they could be completely enclosed inside one's hand.

Eventually the train arrived: it was chock-a-block. People jumped in while others were kissing each other goodbye. Off it went, leaving Burghersdorp behind.

After what seemed like eternity, the train arrived in Bloemfontein where some people disembarked to board other trains while others remained behind. Tired passengers were woken from sleep by a conductor who was checking that every passenger had a valid ticket to remain on the train and continue with the journey. The woman whose name nobody asked, and her baby boy, were also not disembarking in Bloemfontein. They were to proceed with the train to Kimberley, where they would catch another train to their destination, where their loved ones were waiting for them.

From Bloemfontein, the train faced westwards towards Kimberley in the north of the Cape Colony. It was a short journey in comparison with the one from Burghersdorp to the Free State.

The City of Diamonds looked like a shell of its former self. War is a terrible thing. After the hostilities broke out, Kimberley was besieged by the Boers but had since been relieved. The siege of Kimberley started around the same time as the siege of Mafeking in October 1899. As a result the recently wedded Sol Plaatje could not be with his family for his son's first birthday. The Boer forces closed in on Kimberley and even went on to occupy the nearby town of Barkly West, which they renamed Nieuw Boshof. Relief came after more than a hundred days, in February 1900. Only then could people move freely in and out of Kimberley.

Elizabeth had known Kimberley at its best – as a cosmopolitan town that was full of life. Now she was seeing it on its knees. She had so many questions and almost no answers. Would Kimberley ever be the same again? What about the people she hadn't seen in a while? What about the rugby and cricket clubs in which her brother and his friends had been so involved? Would anybody still have time to play sport? Would the meetings of the South Africans Improvement Society resume? Would her new family ever come back to live in Kimberley, or would Sol say they must settle in Mafeking for good? She felt that the Kimberley she knew was now gone. Would it ever recover its past glory? Stupid war. Why did white people cross the vast seas to come and fight for what was not theirs, disrupting peaceful lives and killing everything and anything on their way? Pitting brother against brother? Leaving children without fathers and wives without husbands? Stupid war.

She regretted her decision to take a walk to the centre of town while waiting for the connecting train to Mafeking. There had been thunderclap after thunderclap. Only the brave ventured out!

At least she was going to be reunited with her husband. Elizabeth's husband was Solomon Tshekisho Plaatje, but everybody called him 'Sol' or 'Sol T', rarely Solomon or Tshekisho or even Mr Plaatje. It was only after the birth of his son, Frederick York St Leger, that he began to be called Rasenti by family and friends. Rasenti was Setswana for 'Sainty's father'. Elizabeth was called Masenti, which meant 'Sainty's mother'. It was customary for parents to be called in this way – by the name of their first child, especially their first son.

Elizabeth looked at the clock on the wall. She had been at Kimberley station for a while and wasn't sure whether she had come too early or the train was just late. She approached a porter.

'How long until the train from Johannesburg to Mafeking arrives, sir?' she asked.

'Another hour, ma'am.'

One hour was not too bad. Sainty was awake and irritable. He needed a nappy change, and maybe he was hungry too. She went to the restroom.

After some time, the train for Mafeking arrived and Elizabeth and her son got on.

During the journey from Kimberley to Mafeking, whenever Sainty wandered in slumberland, his mother would take out Émile Zola's novel *The Ladies' Paradise* and read. Elizabeth was an avid reader, just like her husband. He was a real bookworm; even strangers could read books on his forehead! Maybe the love for reading was the magnet that drew Elizabeth and Sol to each other when they first met in Kimberley, on the occasion when Elizabeth had come to visit her brother, Isaiah Budlwana M'belle. Bud, as Budlwana was fondly called, was a man of many tongues, a court interpreter. Just like Sol, he was a man in search of words too. He read everything and anything. Being a teacher by profession, one of the things Elizabeth liked about visiting her brother during the school holiday was his large collection of books, which she devoured with unremitting passion.

Every unoccupied moment she had, Elizabeth used to read; from novels to old newspapers that her husband liked collecting and stored at home. Being a multilingual speaker and reader, Elizabeth read Tengo Jabavu's newspaper *Imvo Zabantsundu* as well as the Setswana newsletter published by the London Missionary Society in Kuruman, *Mahoko a Becwana*. Time flies when one's head is buried in a novel, particularly if it is a good one. *The Ladies' Paradise* held Elizabeth's attention.

By this time *stimela*, the steam train, was making its way towards Mafeking, having long since left behind the friends and families who had come to see the passengers off. Elizabeth couldn't believe that after not seeing her husband for such a long time, she and her son were finally on the train to Mafeking, the town where her husband had gone in search of a better life, only for it to swallow him at the time of war.

The train pulled in at another busy centre, Vryburg, which was unusually quiet. Vryburg looked as war-hit as Kimberley and deserted like a dried pan of water. There were very few people waiting on the platform. Even the nameboard looked incomplete with a 'V' missing, and only the letters 'RYBURG' left on it.

Between Vryburg and Stella, a kudu, an antelope with a torso as large as that of a cow, called *tholo* in Setswana, jumped over the tracks. The train missed it by a few inches. What a relief! Elizabeth couldn't help thinking how her husband would have felt hurt had the train killed the *tholo*, his people's totem animal. Members of Barolong, the nation of which Sol was part, called each other Tholo, interchangeably with 'Morolong'. They always displayed the spiral horns of the *tholo* in their *kgotla*, the royal seat. 'Enkosi Thixo,' she silently thanked God that the *tholo* had survived the heavy iron of the train.

On the seat behind Elizabeth's was an elderly woman who had boarded the train in Taung. She had been singing a bittersweet hymn, 'Tumelo ke thebe' (Faith is my shield), since she got on. Elizabeth thanked the heavens that the woman was singing in a low voice and that, instead of disturbing the peace, her singing was rather soothing. Fortunately, she got off in Setlagole, before others who were sitting very close to her had had enough of her singing.

Elizabeth asked another elderly woman who had been sitting next to her why she thought the woman had sung that one song for so long.

'We'll never know, my child. Maybe that song is all she is left with after the war. Who knows? People lost their cattle. Some lost their homes. Some lost their families. Some are dead people walking,' said the elderly woman to Elizabeth. She took out a handkerchief and wiped her eyes. 'That hymn, my child, may just be all she has left after the storm.' She took off her spectacles and wiped her eyes again.

'Where is the father?' the elderly woman asked, pointing at the sleeping baby.

'He is in Mafeking. We last saw him before the war.'

The elderly woman told Elizabeth she needed to count herself lucky, for many were not as fortunate. 'Are you saying that your husband is an interpreter at the magistrate's court? That is quite respectable work, my child. You are still young. You have a bright future ahead of yourselves. Rona re tšohetse, re setse re le melora,' she said. *We are old. We're just spent ashes that are ready for the grave.*

The elderly woman looked at Sainty and, turning her eyes at Elizabeth, smiled. 'Love is a beautiful thing, my child. Just look at you.'

Elizabeth nodded with some shyness. 'Ee, mma.'

'Pelo e ja serati ngwanake,' the elderly woman said with a slightly loud laugh. *The heart goes after whom it loves.* Other passengers turned to look at her.

Indeed, Elizabeth's husband's people would say 'o ya boratwaepelo', *she was going to a place where the heart loved.*

The train continued to snake through the farmlands, villages and small towns, its throat warning whoever might be in its way to steer clear of the tracks lest they be crushed to death. By the time it arrived in Mafeking, the elderly woman was asleep and snoring.

'Mma, mma! Tšoga re itlhile,' Elizabeth woke her up, informing her that they had reached their destination.

The elderly woman replied that her station was the next one. 'Tsamayang le Modimo ngwanake,' she said. *May God be with you.*

'Re a leboga, mma.'

'Go didimetse jaanong, ngwanake. Dipheho di hitile,' the elderly woman said. *It is quiet now; the storm has passed.*

Elizabeth looked at her with a smile, her face full of contentment. Indeed, it was quiet after the storm. The war had ended, and it was time to reconnect with loved ones, to rekindle burnt-out lamps.

By the time the train entered the town of Mafeking from the south, Sol had been waiting for his wife and son at the station for an hour. Sol, a handsome young man in his early twenties; was dressed in perfectly ironed grey trousers and a white shirt. He had a broad chest, his hair thick like a bush. His black and penetrating eyes were full of wisdom. He had with him a notepad, a pen and a book to read, his permanent companions. The train had been running slightly late and some of the people who were waiting for their loved ones were becoming impatient.

All that time, Sol's head was buried in a book, Rider Haggard's *King Solomon's Mines*. The train then arrived and the long wait was over. Sol took a piece of grass and marked the page where he had paused. He made his way through the throng who were waiting for their loved ones to disembark.

Elizabeth spotted her husband from a distance. With a baby on her back, a huge suitcase in one hand and a clutch bag in the other, she headed straight towards him.

'Ngwetsi ya Barolong,' Sol said about his wife in a voice so loud that he even attracted attention. *Daughter-in-law of Barolong.*

He pushed his way through the crowds until he reached his wife and son and embraced them. He held them closely for a long while. Then he helped Elizabeth to get Sainty from her back. The moment he held his son in his hands, the boy opened his eyes.

'Mosimane! Son of Barolong! Daddy missed you, my son. I'm so sorry we couldn't be together to celebrate your birthday, but Autata

Thelesho Molema and I slaughtered a sheep and celebrated your birthday,' Sol said, looking him in the eye, all the while directing his talk at Elizabeth.

Indeed, when Sainty turned a year old on Thursday, 23 November 1899, he and his mother were in Burghersdorp and were separated from Sol by the raging war. On that spring day of soft rains, Sol and old man Silas Thelesho Molema bought a sheep to celebrate the birthday of Sol's first child.

Now it was time for the newlyweds to go back to the *stadt* and start catching up after their long separation by war.

'Mogatsake, ke bogologolo re sa bonane,' Sol said to his wife. *It's been a long time since we last saw each other.* 'Our conversation will fill up a pot until it overflows.'

Elizabeth remarked how her husband had lost weight.

'Mogatsake, working in the court at the time of war is no child's play, especially interpreting in the Court of Summary Jurisdiction. People are arrested and brought to court in such a short space of time; before you can blink, they have already been found guilty and a sentence handed out,' Sol said.

He told his wife about a case of one old man called Albert who was found in the premises of a young widow called Masethaisho at midnight one Saturday. Masethaisho lived with her young child in a hut and, upon realising there was a man in her premises, she got a fright. The following day she went to report him.

Albert was arrested and brought before the magistrate on a charge of attempted rape. In his defence the old man said he was just taking a stroll. At that time of the night! He was found guilty and sentenced to 36 lashes with a cat-o'-nine-tails.

'Just imagine, mogatsake! An old man whipped on his rear in front of the whole community! He cried so much, he even called on his mother whose body has long been the culinary delight of worms and her bones peeled and white, six feet under the ground. In front of children! In my whole life I have never heard an old man cry like that.

He cried like a boy!'

Sol told his wife that even though people received a fair trial, being the bearer of the sad news was taking a toll on him. 'Sometimes I dream about children who are crying for their fathers who are sent to jail. Some people steal food because they are hungry. Hunger makes a thief out of an honest man,' he said.

Elizabeth told her husband about the shell that Kimberley had become after the siege. 'We took a walk outside the station, towards the Post Office and the Town Hall. The centre of town is as silent as the graveyard, ke a go bolelela mogatsake. It's not like the Kimberley you know, the city where you went to the theatre to watch *Hamlet* or where my brother played rugby and cricket. Kimberley is dead quiet.'

But the storm was over, or maybe the pot was simmering under the lid. However, it all looked quiet after the storm. It was time to pick up the pieces, to mop up after the big storm. It was time, too, to clean and salve the wounds. The storm had left colossal destruction, the tremors of which were to be felt for decades later. But Kimberley and Mafeking had been relieved, and Solomon Plaatje, Elizabeth and their little boy were together again.

Acknowledgements

The illustrations in the plate section are drawn from the following sources:

p. 1 Portrait of Sol Plaatje: Molema/Plaatje Papers, Wits University Historical Papers, UW A979-Fca2

p. 2 First pages of diary: UW A2550

p. 3 Pniel church and buildings: University of South Africa Archives, Hesse collection, Acc.27, Baumbach Collection

p. 3 Scene in *stadt*: *Black and White Budget*, 16 February 1900

p. 4 Elizabeth Plaatje: UW A979

p. 4 Charles Bell: *South African Law Journal*, 26, 1909

p. 4 Barolong chiefs and headmen: Edward Ross, *Mafeking Siege Views* (London, 1900)

p. 5 Boer artillerymen: R.S.S. Baden-Powell, *Sketches in Mafeking and East Africa* (London, 1907)

p. 5 War correspondents: D. Taylor, *Souvenir of the Siege of Mafeking* (London, 1900)

p. 6 Family portrait: UW A979-Fcb5

p. 7 Court of Summary Jurisdiction: Ross, *Mafeking Siege Views*

p. 7 Shell explosion in Market Square: Brenthurst Library, Johannesburg, MS147/9/1/218

p. 8 Interpreting for Bell and Goold-Adams: *Black and White Budget*, 9 June 1900

p. 8 Armed guard: UW, A979-Fa2

p. 9 African raiding party: Western Cape Archives, image no. L1164

p. 9 Issuing rations in *stadt*: Ross, *Mafeking Siege Views*

p. 10 Page from diary: UW A2550

p. 11 Captured horses and rifles: Lord Baden Powell Papers, Scout Association Heritage Collection, Frank Whiteley Collection

p. 11 Shell damage to *Mafeking Mail* office: Ross, *Mafeking Siege Views*

p. 12 Marie and Ernst Westphal: Unisa Archives, Hesse Collection, Acc.21, Ernst Gotthilf Westphal

p. 12 Silas Molema: S.T. Plaatje, *Sechuana Proverbs* (London, 1916)

p. 12 1898 Barkly West election: Western Cape Archives, CSC 2/1/1/355, no. 14 Illiquid case

p. 13 Boer rebels captured in siege: Africana Library, Kimberley, P3247.3

p. 13 Presenting Lord Roberts' in the *stadt*: Brenthurst Library, Johannesburg, MS.147/9/1/274

p. 14 Tiyo Soga: Public domain (Wikipedia)

p. 14 John Tengo Jabavu: D.D.T. Jabavu, *The Life of John Tengo Jabavu, Editor of* Imvo Zabantsundu, *1884–1921* (Lovedale, 1921), frontispiece

p. 14 *Koranta ea Becoana* staff 1903: UW A979-Fcb1

p. 15 Page from *Koranta ea Becoana: Koranta ea Becoana*, 15 June 1901, National Library of South Africa, Cape Town

p. 16 Covers: author's collection

The author and publishers are grateful to the copyright holders indicated for permission to reproduce the images in this book.

Notes

INTRODUCTION

1 Sol T. Plaatje, 'Thirty Years Ago: Siege Memories and Others', *Diamond Fields Advertiser*, 16 May 1930.
2 The following paragraphs draw upon Brian Willan, 'Revisiting Sol Plaatje's Mafeking Diary', *Journal of the African Literature Association*, 2022, DOI: 10.1080/21674736.2021.2016252.
3 John Comaroff and Brian Willan, with Solomon Molema and Andrew Reid (eds.), *The Mafeking Diary of Sol T. Plaatje* (Oxford: James Currey, Cape Town: David Philip, 1999), Preface, 4.
4 The following paragraphs draw upon *Mafeking Diary*, 'Introduction', 8–16 and Brian Willan, *Sol Plaatje: A Life of Solomon Tshekisho Plaatje, 1876–1932* (Auckland Park: Jacana, 2018), chapters 1–4.
5 'The South Africans Improvement Society', *Diamond Fields Advertiser*, 23 August 1895.
6 *Mafeking Diary*, 8 February 1900.

CHAPTER 1

1 Jean Comaroff and John L. Comaroff, *Theory from the South: or, How Euro-America Is Evolving Toward Africa* (Boulder, CO: Paradigm Publishers, 2012), 133ff.
2 Silas Modiri Molema, *The Bantu, Past and Present* (Edinburgh: W. Green and

Son, 1920).

3 Njabulo S. Ndebele, *Rediscovery of the Ordinary: Essays on South African Literature and Culture* (Johannesburg: Congress of South African Writers, 1991).

4 Peter Limb, 'Sol Plaatje Reconsidered: Rethinking Plaatje's Attitudes to Class, Nation, Gender, and Empire', *African Studies* 62, no. 1 (2003): 33–52.

5 Some of those critics are quick to dismiss Plaatje in highly pejorative terms. Andile Mngxitama, for example, has allegedly referred to him as a 'good house N—'. See Sean O'Toole, 'In the Lost Land', *Sunday Times*, 15 May 2016; https://www.pressreader.com/south-africa/sunday-times-1107/20160515/282815010466247.

6 Wits University Research Archives, Historical Papers, File De3, Obituaries by Prof. C.M. Doke, Rev. Bernard Huss and Rev. John L. Dube; http://historicalpapers-atom.wits.ac.za/uploads/r/historical-papers-research-archive-library-university-of-witwatersrand/f/3/a/f3ac46509e60a6865bd7947341567accfe1787057f020a22a4db7da71f2e4f31/A979-De3-01-jpeg.pdf.

7 Wits University Research Archives, Historical Papers, File De2, Edison Malebe Bokako, 'To Sol Plaatje', eulogy, Healdtown; http://historicalpapers-atom.wits.ac.za/bokako-edison-malebe-to-sol-plaatje-eulogy-healdtown.

8 Wits University Research Archives, Historical Papers, File De3, Obituaries by Prof. C.M. Doke, Rev. Bernard Huss and Rev. John L. Dube; http://historicalpapers-atom.wits.ac.za/uploads/r/historical-papers-research-archive-library-university-of-witwatersrand/f/3/a/f3ac46509e60a6865bd7947341567accfe1787057f020a22a4db7da71f2e4f31/A979-De3-01-jpeg.pdf.

9 Paul B. Rich, 'Bernard Huss and the Experiment in African Cooperatives in South Africa, 1926–1948', *International Journal of African Historical Studies* 26, no. 2 (1993): 297–317.

10 Brian Willan, *Sol Plaatje: A Biography* (Johannesburg: Ravan Press, 1984), 389–90.

11 See https://www.flatinternational.org/template_volume.php?volume_id=267 on the history of the recording; for the YouTube clip, see https://www.youtube.com/watch?v=4kxoYeVdDrI.

12 This odyssey on a bicycle, now the stuff of legend, has been questioned by Sean O'Toole, who refers to it as a 'myth'. O'Toole, 'In the Lost Land'.

13 See Sol Plaatje Museum, 'Commemoration and Recognition of Plaatje in the Public Domain'; http://solplaatjemuseumandlibrary.co.za/commemoration.htm.

14 Brian Willan, 'Revisiting Sol Plaatje's *Mafeking Diary*', *Journal of the African Literature Association* 16, no. 1 (2022): 9–22.

15 John Comaroff and Brian Willan, with Solomon Molema and Andrew Reid (eds.), *The Mafeking Diary of Sol T. Plaatje* (Oxford: James Currey; Cape Town: David Philip, 1999).

16 Jane Starfield, 'Re-thinking Sol Plaatje's *Mafeking Diary*', *Journal of Southern African Studies* 27, no. 4 (2001): 855, 867.

17 Jane Taylor, 'Sol Plaatje under Lockdown', *Daily Maverick*, 6 July 2021; https://www.dailymaverick.co.za/article/2021-06-07-sol-plaatje-under-lockdown/.

18 Kevin Davie, 'The Mafeking Diary of Sol T. Plaatje, 120 Years Later', News24, 10 September 2021; https://www.news24.com/channel/arts/the-mafeking-diary-of-sol-t-plaatje-120-years-later-20210910. Davie is a former convener of the Financial Journalism Programme at the University of the Witwatersrand.

19 Willan, 'Revisiting Sol Plaatje's *Mafeking Diary*'. The quotation in the following sentence is to be found on p. 10.

20 Willan, 'Revisiting Sol Plaatje's *Mafeking Diary*', 13.

21 Willan, 'Revisiting Sol Plaatje's *Mafeking Diary*', 18–19.

22 Karin Barber (ed.), *Africa's Hidden Histories: Everyday Literacy and Making the Self* (Bloomington, IN: Indiana University Press, 2006), 8, quoted in Willan, 'Revisiting Sol Plaatje's *Mafeking Diary*', 16.

23 V.S. Naipaul, *The Mimic Men* (London: André Deutsch, 1967).

24 I take the liberty here of expanding beyond Willan's insightful discussion of the question of identity in the *Diary*.

25 See John L. Comaroff and Jean Comaroff, 'On Personhood: An Anthropological Perspective from Africa', *Social Identities* 7, no. 2 (2001): 267–283, reprinted in Comaroff and Comaroff, *Theory from the South*.

CHAPTER 2

1 Gary Mead, *Odyssey Illustrated Guide to South Africa* (Hong Kong: The Guide Book Company, 1997), 203.

2 Rayne Kruger, *Goodbye Dolly Gray: The Story of the Boer War* (London: Cassell, 1957).

3 Herman Charles Bosman, *Mafeking Road: And Other Stories* (Johannesburg: Dassie Books/Central News Agency, 1947). For the famous 'Mafeking Road' story itself, see Michael Rice, *From Dolly Gray to Sarie Marais: The Boer War in Popular Memory* (Noordhoek: Fischer Press, 2004), 94–5.

4 The classic reading was (and remains) Richard Price, *An Imperial War and the British Working Class: Working Class Attitudes and Reactions to the Boer War, 1899–1902* (London: Routledge, 1972).

5 C.W. de Kiewiet, *A History of South Africa: Social and Economic* (Oxford: Oxford University Press, 1941).

6 John L. Comaroff (ed.), *The Boer War Diary of Sol T. Plaatje* (London: Macmillan, 1973) and subsequently republished in paperback (London: Cardinal, 1976). All following text references are to the 1976 edition.

7 Comaroff, *Diary*, 8.

8 'The English Flag', *St James's Gazette*, 4 April 1891, 8.

9 Donald Denoon, 'Participation in the "Boer War": People's War, People's Non-War or Non-People's War?', in Bethwell A. Ogot (ed.), *War and Society in Africa* (London: Frank Cass, 1972), 109–23.

10 Fransjohan Pretorius, *The A to Z of the Anglo-Boer War* (Lanham, MD: Scarecrow Press, 2009), 331.

11 J.F.C. Fuller, *The Last of the Gentlemen's Wars* (London: Faber, 1937).

12 F.L. Rothmann, *Oorlogsdagboek van 'n Transvaalse burgher te velde, 1900–1901* (Cape Town: Nasionale Pers, 1947).

13 J.G. Farrell, *The Siege of Krishnapur* (London: Weidenfeld and Nicolson, 1973).

14 Peter Warwick, *Black People and the South African War 1899–1902* (Cambridge: Cambridge University Press, 1983).

15 Warwick, *Black People*, 31, 37.

16 Comaroff, *Diary*, 150. See also Jabulani Maphalala, 'The African People and the Anglo-Boer War', in *A Century Is a Short Time: New Perspectives on the*

Anglo-Boer War (Pretoria: Nexus, 2005), 192.

17 Bill Nasson, *Abraham Esau's War: A Black South African War in the Cape, 1899–1902* (Cambridge: Cambridge University Press, 1991).

18 Nasson, *Abraham Esau's War*, 3. Aside from the obvious Sol Plaatje *Boer War Diary* itself, notable literature at the time encompassed Brian Willan, 'The Siege of Mafeking', in Peter Warwick (ed.), *The South African War: The Anglo-Boer War, 1899–1902* (London: Longman, 1980), esp. 150–60; Willan, *Sol Plaatje: A Biography, 1876–1932* (Johannesburg: Ravan, 1984), 77–103; Warwick, *Black People*, 30–8. Although Plaatje's *Diary* did not feature prominently in his more military-minded Mafeking chapter, the siege provided the basis of Thomas Pakenham's 'The White Man's War' perspective in his *The Boer War* (London: Weidenfeld and Nicolson, 1979), 396–418.

19 Willan, *Sol Plaatje: A Life of Solomon Tshekisho Plaatje 1876–1932* (Johannesburg: Jacana, 2018), 130.

20 Willan, *Sol Plaatje*, 131.

21 John Boje, *An Imperfect Occupation: Enduring the South African War* (Urbana: University of Illinois Press, 2015), 154–5. The quotation is from Solomon Plaatje, *Mafeking Diary: A Black Man's View of a White Man's Conflict*, ed. John Comaroff (Johannesburg: Southern, 1989), 23. See also Nasson, 'The War for South Africa', in Hermann Giliomee, Bernard Mbenga and Bill Nasson (eds.), *New History of South Africa* (Cape Town: Tafelberg, 2022), 303.

22 Published in English translation as Martin Bossenbroek, *The Boer War* (Johannesburg: Jacana, 2015).

23 Greg Cuthbertson, Albert Grundlingh and Mary-Lynn Suttie (eds.), *Writing a Wider War: Rethinking Gender, Race, and Identity in the South African War, 1899–1902* (Athens, OH: Ohio University Press, 2002).

24 Oorlogsmuseum van die Boererepublieke, *Die Anglo-Boereoorlog in 100 objekte* (Johannesburg: Jonathan Ball, 2017), 36.

25 Johan van Zyl, Rodney Constantine and Tokkie Pretorius, *An Illustrated History of Black South Africans in the Anglo-Boer War, 1899–1902* (Bloemfontein: The War Museum of the Boer Republics, 2012), 141.

26 Sol Ventner as told to Hugh Gault, *Beleaguered and Besieged: A Year in a Place of Rocks* (Cambridge: Gretton Books, 2021).

27 *Beleaguered and Besieged*, 1.

28 *Beleaguered and Besieged*, 3.
29 *Beleaguered and Besieged*, 12.
30 *Beleaguered and Besieged*, 108.
31 *Beleaguered and Besieged*, 78.
32 Maggie Jooste, *Maggie: My lewe in die kamp; Die aangrypende verhaal van 'n jong meisie in die Anglo-Boereoorlog* (Cape Town: Tafelberg, 2020), 116. Author's translation.
33 Denis Judd and Keith Surridge, *The Boer War* (London: John Murray, 2002), 117.
34 Edmund Blunden, *Undertones of War* (London: Cobden-Sanderson, 1928).
35 Paul Fussell, *The Great War and Modern Memory* (Oxford: Oxford University Press, 1975), 339.
36 Comaroff, *Diary*, 143.

CHAPTER 3

1 John Comaroff and Brian Willan, with Solomon Molema and Andrew Reid (eds.), *The Mafeking Diary of Sol T. Plaatje* (Oxford: James Currey; Cape Town: David Philip, 1999).
2 Brian Willan, *Sol Plaatje: A Life of Solomon Tshekisho Plaatje, 1876–1932* (Johannesburg: Jacana, 2018).
3 Thomas Pakenham, *The Boer War* (London: Random House, 1973).
4 Tom Wolfe, *The New Journalism* (London: Picador, 1975).
5 Andrew Griffiths, 'Literary Journalism and Empire: George Warrington Steevens in Africa, 1898–1900', *Literary Journalism Studies* 9 (2017).
6 George Steevens, *From Cape Town to Ladysmith* (Edinburgh: William Blackwood and Sons, 1900)

CHAPTER 5

1 https://www.etymonline.com/word/perspective.
2 William Robertson Fuller, *The Siege of Mafeking*, ed. John William Fuller (1998), n.p. http://www.usscouts.org/usscouts/history/siegediary.asp.
3 F.D. Baillie, *Mafeking: A Diary of the Siege* (Westminster: Archibald Constable, 1900), https://www.gutenberg.org/cache/epub/41511.
4 Emily Hobhouse, *Report of a Visit to the Camps of Women and Children in the Cape and Orange River Colonies* (London: Friars Printing Associates, 1901), 11.

5 Susarha Nel, 'The Diary of Susarha Nel and Her Ordeal in the "Death Camp" at Mafeking, July 1901 to August 1902', ed. John Bottomley and Carla Luijks, *New Contree* 43 & 44 (1998): 41. (With warm appreciation to Hein Viljoen of North-West University for expert help with translation.)

6 Sol T. Plaatje, *The Mafeking Diary of Sol T. Plaatje*, Centenary Edition, ed. John Comaroff, Brian Willan, Solomon Molema and Andrew Reed (Cape Town: David Philip; Oxford: James Currey, 1999), 28.

7 Plaatje, *Mafeking Diary*, 28, n2. Willan's footnote 3, for November 1899, in his edition of Edward Ross's siege diary lists 'Aunt Sally', 'Black Maria' and 'Her Ladyship' as among other nicknames this gun attracted. See Edward Ross, *Diary of the Siege of Mafeking, October 1899 to May 1900*, ed. Brian P. Willan (Cape Town: Van Riebeeck Society, 1980), 9.

8 David Phooko was a friend of Plaatje's, an Mfengu, and a distant relative of his wife.

9 Plaatje, *Mafeking Diary*, 28.

10 Ross, *Diary of the Siege of Mafeking*, 199.

11 Plaatje, *Mafeking Diary*, 170, n5.

12 G.W. Steevens, *From Capetown to Ladysmith*, ed. Vernon Blackburn (New York: Dod, Mead and Company, 1900), 102.

13 Agatha Ijeoma Onwuekwe, 'The Sociological Implications of African Music and Dance', *Creative Artist: A Journal of Theatre and Media Studies* 3, no. 1 (2009): 171; A.F. Odunuga and D.O.A. Ogunrinade, 'Bequests and Veracities of African Indigenous Knowledge System as a Means of Improving Music Education', *International Journal of African Society, Cultures and Traditions* 3, no. 4 (2015), 11; Meki Nzewi, *A Contemporary Study of Musical Arts Informed by African Indigenous Knowledge Systems*, vol. 4: *Illuminations, Reflections and Explorations* (Pretoria: Centre for Indigenous Instrumental African Music and Dance, 2007).

14 Nzewi, *A Contemporary Study of Musical Arts*, 10.

15 Ernst Cassirer, *The Philosophy of Symbolic Forms*, vol. 2: *Mythical Thought* (New Haven and London: Yale University Press, 1955), 24.

16 Immanuel Kant, *Critique of Pure Reason*, trans. and ed. Paul Guyer and Allen W. Wood (Cambridge: Cambridge University Press, 1999 [1781, 1787]).

17 Arthur Schopenhauer, *The World as Will and Representation*, trans. E.F.J. Payne, 2 vols. (New York: Dover Publications, 1969), vol. 1, 112–13.

18 This is hardly surprising. Artists from every clime and culture find

themselves exploring humanity's place *in the same universe*, both noumenal and phenomenal, even if the articulations which emerge differ strikingly. Disparate epistemic beliefs embodied in these articulations cannot logically subtend disparate universes, a realisation which underlines the importance of intercultural discourse. Today's trend towards intercultural appreciation is one of the period's more endearing and hopeful aspects, enhancing the scope of human cultural identity and dissolving to a degree many excluding barriers.

19 R.L. Brett and A.L. Jones (eds.), *Lyrical Ballads: Wordsworth and Coleridge* (London and New York: Routledge, 1991), 251; William Wordsworth, *The Prelude*, ed. Jonathan Wordsworth (London: Penguin, 1995 [1799 text]), 288–94.

20 Plaatje, *Mafeking Diary*, 29.

21 Plaatje, *Mafeking Diary*, 28.

22 Shakespeare, *Othello*, The Norton Shakespeare, ed. Stephen Greenblatt (New York: Norton and Company, 1997), 1.3.135.

23 Plaatje, *Mafeking Diary*, 27.

24 Plaatje, *Mafeking Diary*, 29.

25 Plaatje, *Mafeking Diary*, 29–30.

26 Plaatje, *Mafeking Diary*, 27.

27 Plaatje, *Mafeking Diary*, 27.

28 *Mhudi: An Epic of South African Native Life a Hundred Years Ago* (Alice: Lovedale Press, 1930); e.g. *Mabolelo a ga Tsikinya-Chaka: Diphosho-phosho* (Morija: Morija Press, 1930); *Sechuana Proverbs, with Literal Translations and Their European Equivalents* (London: Kegan Paul, Trench, Trübner and Co., 1916); Daniel Jones and Plaatje, *A Sechuana Reader in International Phonetic Orthography (with English Translations)* (London: The University of London Press, 1916); *Native Life in South Africa, before and since the European War and the Boer Rebellion* (London: P.S. King and Son, 1916).

CHAPTER 6

1 Brian Willan, 'Revisiting Sol Plaatje's *Mafeking Diary*', *Journal of the African Literature Association* 16, no. 1 (2022): 9–22.

2 Willan, 'Revisiting Sol Plaatje's *Mafeking Diary*'. The online version consulted is unpaginated.

3 Vivian Bickford-Smith, 'The Betrayal of Creole Elites, 1880–1920', in Philip D. Morgan and Sean Hawkins (eds.), *Black Experience and the Empire* (Oxford: Oxford University Press, 2006), 197. For much more on Plaatje in this regard see Brian Willan, *Sol Plaatje: A Life of Solomon Tshekisho Plaatje, 1876–1932* (Johannesburg: Jacana, 2018).
4 Willan, 'Revisiting Sol Plaatje's *Mafeking Diary*', gives the example of Plaatje's use of the word 'funambulism', the art of tightrope walking.
5 John Comaroff and Brian Willan (eds.), *The Mafeking Diary of Sol T. Plaatje* (Cape Town: David Philip, 1999), 37–9, 140.
6 Comaroff and Willan, *The Mafeking Diary*, passim.
7 For a discussion of the rise and decline of black British loyalism and accompanying cultural hybridity in both South and West Africa, see Bickford-Smith, 'The Betrayal of Creole Elites', 194–227.
8 Rebecca Steinitz, citing a number of others who have wrestled with the question of whether there is necessarily any difference between the terms diary and journal, concludes that they have historically been used interchangeably. See Rebecca Steinitz, *Time, Space and Gender in the Nineteenth-Century British Diary* (New York: Palgrave Macmillan, 2011), 8.
9 Formerly the Van Riebeeck Society. Their full list of publications including and beyond diaries can be found on their website: https://hipsa.org.za.
10 A rare exception would seem to be Andre Alaszewski, *Using Diaries for Social Research* (Thousand Oaks, CA: Sage, 2006). Steinitz, *Time, Space and Gender* provides a degree of overview of the genre as a whole with important insights here.
11 The biographical information that follows is drawn in large part from existing biographies. The first of these was written by his friend John Chalmers; see John A. Chalmers, *Tiyo Soga: A Page of South African Missionary Work* (Edinburgh, London, Glasgow and Cape Town: Andrew Elliot, Hodder and Stoughton, David Bryce and Sons, and James Hay, 1878). Most subsequent biographies have drawn extensively from Chalmers, notably H.T. Cousins, *From Kaffir Kraal to Pulpit: The Story of Tiyo Soga* (London: S.W. Partridge, 1899). Exactly a century after Chalmers's biography, and marking the centenary of its publication, came Donovan Williams, *Umfundisi: A Biography of Tiyo Soga, 1829–1871* (Lovedale: Lovedale Press, 1978).

Much subsequent academic work on Soga draws on or reacts to Chalmers and Williams. It includes: M. Gideon Khabela, *Tiyo Soga: The Struggle of the Gods; A Study in Christianity and the African Culture* (Alice: Lovedale Press, 1996); Malinge McLaren, "*Subversive Subservience*": *A Comparative Study of the Responses of Tiyo Soga and Mpambani Mzimba to the Scottish Missionary Enterprise,* unpublished PhD, University of Cape Town, 2000; and Mcebisi Ndletyana, 'Tiyo Soga', in Mcebisi Ndletyana (ed.), *African Intellectuals in 19th and 20th Century South Africa* (Pretoria: HSRC Press, 2008), 17–30. The short biographical sketch also draws on two previous pieces I have written on Soga. Vivian Bickford-Smith, 'African Nationalist or British Loyalist? The Complicated Case of Tiyo Soga', *History Workshop Journal* 71, no. 1 (2011): 74–97; Vivian Bickford-Smith, 'Tiyo Soga: The Object of Wonder', in Vivian Bickford-Smith and Bill Nasson (eds.), *Illuminating Lives: Biographies of Fascinating People in South African History* (Cape Town: Penguin Random House, 2018), 9–29.

12 Tiyo Soga, Letter to Foreign Mission of the United Presbyterian Church (FMUPC), 3 July 1857, cited in Chalmers, *Tiyo Soga*, 131–2.

13 Chalmers, *Soga*, 438. See also Clifton Crais, *White Supremacy and Black Resistance in the Pre-industrial South Africa: The Making of the Colonial Order in the Eastern Cape, 1770–1865* (Cambridge: Cambridge University Press, 1992).

14 On the Xhosa–British encounter see Richard Price, *Making Empire: Colonial Encounters and the Creation of Imperial Rule in Nineteenth-Century Africa* (Cambridge: Cambridge University Press, 2008), especially 267–90, 316–17, 330–1, 336–7. The Cattle-Killing began as a logical 'veterinary' response to the appearance of lung disease before developing into a religiously syncretic millenarian movement, as is frequently associated with indigenous reactions to colonial encounter. In this case, the killing of cattle was seen as a means to resurrect warrior ancestors and drive the British into the sea. An estimated 400,000 cattle were slain by followers of Sandile, and grain stocks destroyed. The population of what was then British 'Kaffraria' was consequently reduced from around 105,000 to about 37,000 by starvation and diseases associated with malnutrition. Still the fullest and most readable account of the Cattle-Killing is Jeff B. Peires, *The Dead Will Arise: Nongqawuse and the*

Great Xhosa Cattle-Killing Movement of 1856–7 (Bloomington IN: Indiana University Press, 1989) though it has generated considerable academic debate.

15 Like Plaatje's, which having been handed by his grandson Barolong Victor Molema to the young South African academic John Comaroff in 1969, was lodged with the Cullen Library at the University of the Witwatersrand, Soga's journal remained in Soga family possession for some seven decades until given by a family member to an academic institution. In Soga's journal's case, preservation and subsequent accessibility were provided by its being lodged by his son, the Rev. John Henderson Soga, in the Howard Pim Library of Fort Hare University in 1936. Together with Tiyo's considerable correspondence, some newspaper articles and a lecture, the journal was published in 1983, ten years after Plaatje's. In a further parallel of a kind, the published edition was introduced and edited by another North American academic, the Canadian Donovan Williams, who had taught at Fort Hare in the 1950s. Donovan Williams (ed.), *The Journal and Selected Writings of the Reverend Tiyo Soga* (Cape Town: A.A. Balkema, 1983), 9–11.

16 Alaszewski, *Using Diaries for Social Research*, 7.

17 Steinitz, *Time, Space and Gender*, 2; Max Weber, *The Protestant Ethic and the Spirit of Capitalism* (London: Unwin University Books, 1930).

18 Willan, 'Revisiting Sol Plaatje's *Mafeking Diary*', mentions several other diary writers in Mafeking known to Plaatje.

19 Steinitz, *Time, Space and Gender*, 2.

20 Reading the two diaries in quick succession makes this abundantly clear.

21 Comaroff and Willan, *The Mafeking Diary*, 73.

22 Tiyo Soga, 'The Journal', in Williams, *The Journal*, 37.

23 Soga, 'The Journal', in Williams, *The Journal*, 11–12. Mr J. was the Rev. Robert Johnston, UPC missionary, who worked with Soga at Mgwali, 1857–9.

24 Soga, 'The Journal', in Williams, *The Journal*, 12–13.

25 Soga, 'The Journal', in Williams, *The Journal*, 13.

26 Steinitz, *Time, Space and Gender*, 4–7.

27 Comaroff and Willan, *The Mafeking Diary*, 68.

28 Soga, 'The Journal', in Williams, *The Journal*, 25.

29 Soga, 'The Journal', in Williams, *The Journal*, 27–9, 36–7.
30 According to Alaszewski, *Using Diaries for Social Research* and Steinitz, *Time, Space and Gender*.
31 Soga, 'The Journal', in Williams, *The Journal*, 22. The translation is by Williams.
32 A suggestion made for Plaatje in this respect in Willan, 'Revisiting Sol Plaatje's *Mafeking Diary*'.
33 Soga, 'The Journal', in Williams, *The Journal*, 23.
34 Soga, 'The Journal', in Williams, *The Journal*, 24.
35 Steinitz, *Time, Space and Gender*, 4–7.
36 See Bickford-Smith, 'The Betrayal of Creole Elites, 1880-1920'.
37 Comaroff and Willan, *The Mafeking Diary*, 50.
38 *The Boy's Own Paper* was first published in 1878 by the Religious Tract Society in Britain and in early decades promoted a muscular Christian form of unquestioning patriotism to young boys around the Empire, including many in colonial South Africa.
39 Comaroff and Willan, *The Mafeking Diary*, 88.
40 Comaroff and Willan, *The Mafeking Diary*, 121.
41 Comaroff and Willan, *The Mafeking Diary*, 132.
42 Tiyo Soga, Letter to FUMPC, 4 June 1864, cited (in full) in Chalmers, *Soga*, 306–9.
43 For far more extensive discussion on Soga's British loyalism, and how some academics have questioned this or asserted Soga's credentials as a pioneering African nationalist, or pan-Africanist, or even Black Consciousness advocate, see Bickford-Smith, 'African Nationalist or British Loyalist?'; also, Bickford-Smith, 'Tiyo Soga: The Object of Wonder'.
44 From Tiyo Soga, Letter to Rev. Anderson, FMUPC, 10 May 1871, published in the *Missionary Record of the Presbyterian Church*, 2 October 1871, 650–4.
45 Comaroff and Willan, *The Mafeking Diary*, 59.
46 Tiyo Soga, 'The Inheritance of My Children', cited in Chalmers, *Soga*, 431.
47 Soga, 'The Journal', in Williams, *The Journal*, 39; Comaroff and Willan, *The Mafeking Diary*, 106.
48 Soga, 'The Journal', in Williams, *The Journal*, 22; Comaroff and Willan, *The*

Mafeking Diary, 59, 76.

49 Comaroff and Willan, *The Mafeking Diary*, 96.

50 Comaroff and Willan, *The Mafeking Diary*, 69.

51 Comaroff and Willan, *The Mafeking Diary*, 91, 141.

52 Soga, 'The Journal', in Williams, *The Journal*, 30.

53 Comaroff and Willan, *The Mafeking Diary*, 29, 73–4, 77–8, 92, 100.

54 Kwame Anthony Appiah, *The Lies That Bind: Rethinking Identity* (London: Profile Books, 2018).

55 Comaroff and Willan, *The Mafeking Diary*, 32, 120, 196.

CHAPTER 7

1 B. Willan, *Sol Plaatje: A Life of Solomon Plaatje, 1876–1932* (Auckland Park: Jacana, 2018), 139.

2 See A. Manson, 'Conflict in the Western Highveld/Southern Kalahari, 1750–1820', in C. Hamilton (ed.), *The Mfecane Aftermath: Reconstructive Debates in Southern African History* (Johannesburg and Pietermaritzburg: Wits and Natal University Press, 1995), 356–8.

3 Another pioneer of Barolong history was Z.K Mathews. See 'A Short History of the Barolong' in *Fort Hare Papers* 1, no. 5 (1945).

4 Margie Kinsman has written of these events in M. Kinsman, '"Hungry Wolves": The Impact of Violence on Rolong Life, 1923–1836', in Hamilton, *The Mfecane Aftermath*, 363–94.

5 S. Molema, *Montshiwa, 1815–1896: Barolong Chief and Patriot* (Cape Town: Struik, 1966), 79.

6 Molema, *Montshiwa*, 87.

7 Molema, *Montshiwa*, 86.

8 K. Shillington, *The Colonisation of the Southern Tswana, 1870–1900* (Johannesburg: Ravan Press, 1985), 129.

9 A. Manson, *'The Valiant Englishman': Christopher Bethell, Montshiwa's Barolong and the Bechuanaland Wars, 1878, 1886* (Pretoria: Unisa Press, 2023), 24.

10 Manson, *The Valiant Englishman*, 24.

11 British Parliamentary Papers (BPP), C. 3381, Correspondence re Affairs of Transvaal and Adjacent Territories, Enclosure in no. 31, Capt. H. Nourse to Sir Hercules Robinson, 6 February 1882.

12 BPP, C. 3381, Enclosure in no. 31, Capt. H. Nourse to Sir Hercules Robinson, 6 February 1882.
13 Cited in Molema, *Montshiwa*, 111.
14 C. van Onselen, *The Cowboy Capitalist: John Hayes Hammond, the American West and the Jameson Raid* (Johannesburg: Jonathan Ball, 2017), 56.
15 BPP, C. 3686, Enclosure in no. 26, H. Campbell Johnson to Sir Hercules Robinson (High Commissioner), 4 February 1883.
16 Molema, *Montshiwa*, 118–120; and BPP, C. 3419, Correspondence re Affairs of Transvaal and Adjacent Territories.
17 Manson, *The Valiant Englishman*, 27–9.
18 Molema, *Montshiwa*, 120.
19 Manson, *The Valiant Englishman*, 34.
20 These events are described and analysed in Shillington, *Colonisation of the Southern Tswana* and in J.A.I. Agar-Hamilton, *The Road to the North* (London: Longman, 1937) as well as several other books.
21 J. Comaroff (ed.), *Mafeking Diary: A Black Man's View of a White Man's War* (London: James Currey; Athens, OH: Ohio University Press, 1990), 17.
22 This occurred when General Charles Warren visited the Ratlou capital. J. Mackenzie, *Austral Africa: Losing It or Ruling It*, vol. 1 (London, 1887), 223.
23 Willan, *Plaatje*, 116.
24 Willan, *Plaatje*, 139.
25 Willan, *Plaatje*, 128.
26 A. Manson and B. Mbenga, *Land, Chiefs, Mining: The North-West Province since 1840* (Johannesburg: Wits University Press, 2014), 95. See also Silas T. Molema and Solomon T. Plaatje Papers, A979, housed in the William Cullen Library, Historical and Literary Papers, University of the Witwatersrand. Even after Bell's decision was reversed, it had little effect in practice: the Ratshidi continued to maintain a close presence at Lotlhakane.
27 Molema, *Montshiwa*, 79–80.
28 Manson, *The Valiant Englishman*, 48.
29 BPP, C. 3486, Enclosure in no. 55, item D, R. Rutherfoord to W. Bok, quoting declaration of Silas Molema. Montshiwa was essentially tricked into signing the treaty, much as the Ndebele king Lobengula was deceived into signing the Rudd Concession to agents of Cecil Rhodes, by which he signed

away mineral rights in Matabeleland in 1881.
30 The details are laid out in Molema, *Montshiwa*, 123–7.
31 Comaroff, *Mafeking Diary*, 81, 5 January 1900.
32 Comaroff, *Mafeking Diary*, 55, 10 October 1899.
33 Comaroff, *Mafeking Diary*, 61, 19 December 1899.
34 Manson, *The Valiant Englishman*, 45, 75.
35 See Willan, *Plaatje*, 117.
36 Manson, *The Valiant Englishman*, 32–3.
37 Willan, *Plaatje*, 118.
38 Comaroff, *Mafeking Diary*, 31.
39 Willan, *Plaatje*, 126.

CHAPTER 9

1 Sol T. Plaatje, 18 Feb. 1900, in John Comaroff (ed.), *Mafeking Diary: A Black Man's View of a White Man's War* (Cambridge: Meridor Books, 1990), 103–4.
2 V. Bickford-Smith, 'The Betrayal of Creole Elites, 1880–1920', in P. Morgan and S. Hawkins (eds.), *Black Experience and the Empire* (New York: Oxford University Press, 2004), 194–227.
3 For a recent study on the role of violence in British imperialism, see Caroline Elkins, *Legacy of Violence: A History of the British Empire* (New York: Knopf, 2022).
4 Frederick Cooper, 'Conflict and Connection: Rethinking Colonial African History', *American Historical Review* 99, no. 5 (1994): 1516–45.
5 See for example Ntongela Masilela, 'African Intellectual and Literary Responses to Colonial Modernity in South Africa', in P. Limb, N. Etherington and P. Midgley (eds.), *Grappling with the Beast: Indigenous Southern African Responses to Colonialism, 1840–1930* (Leiden: Brill, 2010), 245–75; Roger Levine, *A Living Man from Africa: Jan Tzatsoe, Xhosa Chief and Missionary, and the Making of Nineteenth-Century South Africa* (New Haven: Yale University Press, 2011); Vivian Bickford-Smith, 'African Nationalist or British Loyalist? The Complicated Case of Tiyo Soga', *History Workshop Journal* 71, no. 1 (2011): 74–97.
6 Khwezi Mkhize, '"To See Us as We See Ourselves": John Tengo Jabavu and the Politics of the Black Periodical', *Journal of Southern African Studies* 44,

no. 3 (2018): 423–30; Siyasanga Tyali, 'Ambiguities of a Decolonising Press Culture: On South Africa's *Imvo Zabantstundu* (*Native Opinion*)', *South African Journal of African Languages* 38, no. 3 (2018): 303–9.

7 Kevin Shillington, *The Colonisation of the Southern Tswana, 1870–1910* (Johannesburg: Ravan Press, 1985); Neil Parsons, *King Khama, Emperor Joe and the Great White Queen* (Chicago: University of Chicago Press, 1998).

8 Part Mgadla and Stephen Volz (eds.), *Words of Batswana: Letters to the Editor of Mahoko a Becwana, 1883–1896* (Cape Town: Van Riebeeck Society, 2006). Plaatje mentions reading the newspaper aloud for groups of elderly men in *Sechuana Proverbs* (London: Keegan Paul, 1916), 5.

9 Brian Willan, 'An African in Kimberley: Sol T. Plaatje, 1894–1898', in Shula Marks and Richard Rathbone (eds.), *Industrialisation and Social Change in South Africa* (London: Longman, 1982), 238–58. See also Khumisho Moguerane, 'A History of the Molemas, African Notables in South Africa, 1880s to 1920s', DPhil thesis, Oxford University, 2014.

10 Leo Spitzer, 'The Sierra Leone Creoles', in Philip Curtin (ed.), *Africa and the West: Intellectual Responses to European Culture* (Madison: University of Wisconsin Press, 1972), 99–138. For a study of non-Creole involvement in the history of Sierra Leone's colonial towns, see Joseph Bangura, *The Temne of Sierra Leone: African Agency in the Making of a British Colony* (Cambridge: Cambridge University Press, 2017).

11 Jean Herskovits, 'The Sierra Leoneans of Yorubaland', in Curtin, *Africa and the West*, 75–98.

12 Esperanza Brizuela-Garcia, 'Cosmopolitanism: Why Nineteenth Century Gold Coast Thinkers Matter in the Twenty-First Century', *Ghana Studies* 17 (2014): 203–21.

13 For a study of the journals, see J.D.Y. Peel, *Religious Encounter and the Making of the Yoruba* (Bloomington, IN: Indiana University Press, 2000), and for a study of later personal writings in West Africa and elsewhere, see Karin Barber (ed.), *Africa's Hidden Histories: Everyday Literacy and Making the Self* (Bloomington, IN: Indiana University Press, 2006).

14 Stephanie Newell, 'Articulating Empire: Newspaper Readerships in Colonial West Africa', *New Formations* 73 (2011): 27.

15 'Significance of British Rule in Africa', *Sierra Leone Weekly News*, 6 Jan.

1894, 7–8. The Latin phrase is from the Roman historian Tacitus, meaning that 'we must take refuge in the government'.

16 'The African and European Civilization', *Lagos Weekly Record*, 18 April 1896, 4.

17 29 Oct. 1899 and 19 Dec. 1899, in Comaroff, *Mafeking Diary*, 23 and 61.

18 12 Nov. 1899, in Comaroff, *Mafeking Diary*, 32.

19 28 Dec. 1899 and 3 Jan. 1900, in Comaroff, *Mafeking Diary*, 68 and 78.

20 13 Jan. 1900, in Comaroff, *Mafeking Diary*, 85.

21 Plaatje, 27 Feb. 1900, in Comaroff, *Mafeking Diary*, 107. See also Peter Warwick, *Black People and the South African War, 1899–1902* (Cambridge: Cambridge University Press, 1983).

22 9 Dec. 1899, in Comaroff, *Mafeking Diary*, 52.

23 11 Mar. 1900, in Comaroff, *Mafeking Diary*, 115.

24 21 Mar. 1900, in Comaroff, *Mafeking Diary*, 125.

25 L.D. Ngcongco, 'Jabavu and the Anglo-Boer War', *Kleio* 2, no. 2 (1970): 6–18.

26 'Imvo', *Koranta ea Becoana*, 14 Sept. 1901, 2.

27 Christopher Saunders, 'African Attitudes to Britain and the Empire before and after the South African War', in Donal Lowry (ed.), *The South African War Reappraised* (Manchester: Manchester University Press, 2000), 145.

28 For discussions of Boer identity, see for example *Gold Coast Chronicle*, 15 and 22 July 1899, 2; and 15 and 22 July 1899, 3; and *Sierra Leone Times*, 28 Oct. 1899, 3.

29 *Gold Coast Aborigines*, 7 Feb. 1900, 4.

30 *Sierra Leone Weekly News*, 11 Nov. 1899, 4–5.

31 The siege of Kumasi is mentioned in *Gold Coast Chronicle*, 22 Sept. 1900, 3; and Kipling's poem is critiqued in *Sierra Leone Weekly News*, 25 Nov. 1899, 4–5.

32 *Lagos Weekly Record*, 18 April 1896, 4–5; 7 Oct. 1899, 6–7; 4 Nov. 1899, 6.

33 *Lagos Weekly Record*, 11 Nov. 1899, 6.

34 *Lagos Weekly Record*, 18 Nov. 1899, 5.

35 *Gold Coast Aborigines*, 11 Nov. 1899, 2; 30 Mar. 1900, 3–4.

36 *Gold Coast Aborigines*, 31 Aug. 1900, 3–4.

37 *Lagos Weekly Record*, 26 May 1900, 3; and *Sierra Leone Times*, 26 May 1900, 2.

38 An article on 26 May 1900, 6 asks for assistance to improve Freetown's water supply, and a letter to the editor on 4 Aug. 1900, 5 asks if loyal British subjects in Sierra Leone will receive the same compensation for their losses from warfare as those in Natal and the Cape.

39 *Sierra Leone Weekly News*, 28 June 1902, 4.

40 Philip Zachernuk, *Colonial Subjects: An African Intelligentsia and Atlantic Ideas* (Charlottesville: University Press of Virginia, 2000), 70.

41 See for example Robin Law, 'Constructing "A Real National History": A Comparison of Edward Blyden and Samuel Johnson'; and Michael Doortmont, 'The Invention of the Yorubas: Regional and Pan-African Nationalism versus Ethnic Provincialism', in P.F. de Moraes Farias and Karin Barber (eds.), *Self-Assertion and Brokerage* (Birmingham: Birmingham University Centre of West African Studies, 1990), 78–100, 101–8.

42 Ali Mazrui, 'Africa's Identity: The Western Aftermath', in *The Africans: A Triple Heritage* (Boston: Little, Brown, 1986), 99–113.

43 *Lagos Weekly Record*, 1 April 1905, 5.

44 *Koranta*, 27 April 1901.

45 See for example *Koranta*, 1 June 1904, 2.

46 *Koranta*, 20 July 1904, 3.

47 Sean Hawkins and Philip D. Morgan, describing analysis by Winston James, in 'Blacks and the British Empire: An Introduction', in Philip D. Morgan and Sean Hawkins (eds.), *Black Experience and the Empire* (New York: Oxford University Press, 2004), 4.

CHAPTER 10

1 For further details on Plaatje's family history, see B.P. Willan, *Sol Plaatje: A Life of Solomon Tshekisho Plaatje, 1876–1932* (Auckland Park: Jacana, 2018), 1–37.

2 S.M. Molema, *Lover of His People: A Biography of Sol Plaatje* (Johannesburg: Wits University Press, 2012), 36.

3 *Mafeking Diary*, 88.

4 *Mafeking Diary*, 90.

5 *Nelson's Royal Reader*, III (London, 1872), 26–8.

6 *Mafeking Diary*, 28.

7 *Mafeking Diary*, 53.

8 *Mafeking Diary*, 76
9 'A South African's Homage', in I. Gollancz (ed.), *Tercentenary Homage to Shakespeare* (Oxford: Oxford University Press), 336; Willan, *Sol Plaatje: A Life*, 69–72.
10 *Mafeking Diary*, 77.
11 *Mafeking Diary*, 80 and 186; Willan, *Sol Plaatje: A Life*, 52.
12 Willan, *Sol Plaatje: A Life*, 50; *Mafeking Diary*, 149–50.
13 *Mafeking Diary*, 146, 136.
14 Willan, *Sol Plaatje: A Life*, 63–4.
15 *Mafeking Diary*, 122; Willan, *Sol Plaatje: A Life*, 64.
16 Willan, *Sol Plaatje: A Life*, and L.D. Ngcongco, 'John Tengo Jabavu 1859–1921', in C. Saunders (ed.), *Black Leaders in South African History* (London: Heinemann Educational, 1979), 146.
17 *Mafeking Diary*, 141 and 201. 'Krugerism' meant the ideas and policies of Paul Kruger, president of the South African Republic from 1883 to 1900. In a court case in 1903 Westphal was subsequently convicted of high treason (second class) and disfranchised for five years.
18 Willan, *Sol Plaatje: A Life*, 66–7.
19 *Mafeking Diary*, 43 and 44.
20 See particularly his 'The Essential Interpreter', in Brian Willan (ed.), *Sol Plaatje: Selected Writings* (Johannesburg: Witwatersrand University Press), 50–60.

Chapter 11

1 The research for this chapter was supported by funding from the National Research Foundation, South Africa, and forms part of a French–South Africa Protea project 'A Centenary of (Post) Colonial Narrative Literary Journalism in South Africa and France'. An earlier version of the chapter was presented at Rhodes University at a regional meeting of the annual conference of the International Association of Literary Journalism Studies (IALJS), 12–14 May 2022. Thanks are due to colleagues who contributed to my thinking about Plaatje as a journalist, in particular my supervisor Professor Lesley Cowling, Kevin Davie, Professor Brian Willan and Sabata-mpho Mokae.
2 John Comaroff and Brian Willan (eds.), *The Mafeking Diary of Sol T. Plaatje* (Cape Town: David Philip, 1999). Until Comaroff discovered the diary, the

narrative around the Boer War was that it was a 'white man's war'. The diary lifted the lid on the role Barolong of Mahikeng played and critiques the conduct of the warring white populations.

3 Brian Willan, *Sol Plaatje: A Life of Solomon Tshekisho Plaatje, 1876–1932* (Johannesburg: Jacana Media, 2018), 109.

4 Comaroff and Willan, *The Mafeking Diary*, 32.

5 Willan, *Sol Plaatje*, 49.

6 Willan, *Sol Plaatje*, 63, 127.

7 Tim Couzens, *The Struggle to Be Independent: A History of the Black Press in South Africa 1836–1960* (Johannesburg: Wits University Press, 1990). Couzens notes that *Molekoli oa Bechuana* (The Bechuana Visitor) was described by Plaatje as 'the first newspaper published in the Sechuana language, from 1856 to 1857'; and he wrote in *Sechuana Proverbs* (1916) that he had a file of its issues which were one of his most valued treasures.

8 Peter Limb, 'The Print World of the Press and *Native Life in South Africa*', in Janet Remmington, Brian Willan and Bhekizizwe Peterson (eds.), *Sol Plaatje's Native Life in South Africa: Past and Present* (Johannesburg: Wits University Press, 2016), 42. Limb writes that the press was often present in Plaatje's early life when he read aloud *Mahoko a Becwana*.

9 See, for example, Jane L. Chapman, 'Gandhi as Literary Journalist in Hind Swaraj', in Richard Lance Keeble and John Tulloch (eds.), *Global Literary Journalism: Exploring the Journalistic Imagination*, vol. 2 (New York: Peter Lang Publishing, 2014), 35. Chapman expands the influence of Mahatma Gandhi, the political icon and editor of *Indian Opinion*, into literary journalism. She argues that the classic texts Gandhi produced in Hind Swaraj deserve a place in the 'evolving canon of literary journalism'.

10 Willan, *Sol Plaatje*, 110.

11 Willan, *Sol Plaatje*, 131.

12 Comaroff and Willan, *The Mafeking Diary*, 4.

13 John S. Bak and Bill Reynolds (eds.), *The Routledge Companion to World Literary Journalism* (London: Routledge, 2023), 1.

14 John S. Bak and Bill Reynolds, *Literary Journalism across the Globe: Journalistic Traditions and Transnational Influences* (Amherst: University of Massachusetts, 2011), 18. Bak argues that literary journalism should not be

referred to as a genre or form, instead it must be called a discipline. Doing so would 'institute a moratorium on the barrage of definitions and defences that have hindered the advancement of literary journalism studies'.

15 Bak and Reynolds, *The Routledge Companion to World Literary Journalism*, 1.
16 Bak and Reynolds, *World Literary Journalism*, 1.
17 Bak and Reynolds, *Literary Journalism across the Globe*, 14.
18 Bak and Reynolds, *Literary Journalism across the Globe*, 14.
19 Victoria R. Sgarro, 'Defining International Literary Journalism: Case Studies from South Africa, the U.S. and China', *Inquiries Journal/Student Pulse*, 2015, 2. Sgarro raises questions about the understanding of the origins of literary journalism and uses John Bak's 2011 argument that 'a European, African or Asian literary journalism is not like an American literary journalism' and also Tom Wolfe's New Journalism manifesto popularised in the 1960s and 1970s, to advance our understanding and appreciation of the form.
20 John S. Bak and Monica Martinez, 'Introduction: Literary Journalism as a Discipline', *Brazilian Journalism Research* 14, no. 3 (2018): 621. Bak and Martinez argue that literary journalism continues to evolve and advance. They further say that to determine its pedigree and moments of institutional crisis it needs historians to track it, and they name Norman Sims, John C. Hartsock, Edvaldo Pereira Lima, Paul Aron, Myriam Boucharenc and Isabel Soares among others 'who have established the main periods of literary journalism's development over the centuries … which scholars have been fleshing out'.
21 Bak and Martinez, 'Literary Journalism as a Discipline', 621.
22 Willan, *Sol Plaatje*, 118, 119, 126, 129.
23 Willan, *Sol Plaatje*, 118–19.
24 Willan, *Sol Plaatje*, 119.
25 Willan, *Sol Plaatje*, 119.
26 Willan, *Sol Plaatje*, 118. This fact is also reported in Comaroff and Willan, *The Mafeking Diary*, 32.
27 Comaroff and Willan, *The Mafeking Diary*, 62–3.
28 Comaroff and Willan, *The Mafeking Diary*, 51.
29 Comaroff and Willan, *The Mafeking Diary*, 52.

30 Willan, *Sol Plaatje*, 129.

31 Comaroff and Willan, *The Mafeking Diary*, 4.

32 Anne-Marie Millim, *The Victorian Diary: Authorship and Emotional Labour* (London: Routledge, 2019).

33 Limb, *Sol Plaatje's Native Life*, 47. Limb describes *Native Life* as a 'distillation' of Plaatje's journalistic career.

34 Comaroff and Willan, *The Mafeking Diary*, 4.

35 Limb, 'The Print World of the Press and *Native Life in South Africa*', 37. Limb notes that *Native Life* is inseparable from Plaatje's journalism and its style and content owed much to the press.

36 Bak and Reynolds, *Literary Journalism across the Globe*, 52.

37 Bak and Reynolds, *Literary Journalism across the Globe*, 52.

38 John Midgley, *Petticoat in Mafeking: The Letters of Ada Cock* (Cape Town, self-published, 1974). This is an account based on 57 letters by Ada Cock, who took refuge in Mafeking with her husband and four small children.

39 Frederick Saunders, *Mafeking Memories* (London: Associated University Presses, 1996). Written by the 16-year-old Saunders, a white volunteer defending Mafeking against the Boers, the memoir retells the story of the siege from his perspective as a common soldier.

40 Comaroff and Willan, *The Mafeking Diary*, 4.

41 J. Angus Hamilton, *The Siege of Mafeking* (London: Methuen, 1900) is a collection of letters and dispatches that constitute insights into the goings-on of the siege.

42 Pedro Rosa Mendes, The Lettre Ulysses Award for the Art of Reportage (www.lettre-ulysses-award.org).

43 Wallace Chuma, 'Western Paradigms: African Media Experiences', *Rhodes Journalism Review*, 2010, 15–17. Chuma says that in Shona culture, it is not the shocking detail that one begins with when Shona communicate; instead one prepares the listener before dropping the bombshell. The climax does not come first.

44 Comaroff and Willan, *The Mafeking Diary*, 86.

45 Nicholas Lemann, 'The Journalism in Literary Journalism', *Literary Journalism Studies* 7, no. 2 (2015): 53. Lemann uses the word 'verisimilitude' as a synonym for realism. This is a further argument for realism as a quality

of literary journalism.

46 Lemann, 'The Journalism in Literary Journalism', 54.

47 Lemann, 'The Journalism in Literary Journalism', 54.

48 Tom Wolfe and E.W. Johnson (eds.), *The New Journalism* (New York: Harper and Row, 1973).

48 Comaroff and Willan, *The Mafeking Diary*, 85.

49 Comaroff and Willan, *The Mafeking Diary*, 95.

50 Comaroff and Willan, *The Mafeking Diary*, 99.

51 Comaroff and Willan, *The Mafeking Diary*, 101.

52 Comaroff and Willan, *The Mafeking Diary*, 81.

53 Comaroff and Willan, *The Mafeking Diary*, 86.

54 Comaroff and Willan, *The Mafeking Diary*, 104.

55 Comaroff and Willan, *The Mafeking Diary*, 86.

56 Comaroff and Willan, *The Mafeking Diary*, 93.

Index

A

African National Congress (ANC) 21, 24, 44
African Renaissance 21
Afrikaner Bond 154
Alfred, Prince 91
Anglo-Boer War 10, 31, 34, 35, 38, 39, 67, 71, 105, 112 (see also 'South African War')
apartheid 17, 20, 23, 24, 31, 100
Au Sanna (Old Susanna) (aka Sanna) 47, 48, 49, 50, 51, 52, 74, 76, 77, 88, 113, 167, 168, 169, 170

B

Baden-Powell, Colonel Robert 2, 9, 27, 31, 36, 41, 47, 55, 96, 142, 147, 153
Baillie, Major F.D. 68, 69
Bain, Alexander 165
Bak, John 161, 162
bantustan 17
Barber, Karin 28
Africa's Hidden Histories: Everyday Literacy and Making the Self 28
Barolong 4, 8, 12, 20, 28, 29, 36, 38, 41, 45, 46, 54, 55, 61, 63, 65, 66, 71, 72, 86, 88, 98, 101, 102, 103, 110, 111, 112, 113, 114, 115, 139, 140, 143, 146, 147, 156, 159, 162, 169, 172, 179, 181
Bechuanaland 45, 109, 111, 115, 136, 147, 153
Bell, Charles 6, 7, 9, 14, 100, 111, 149, 159, 163, 173
Berlin Mission Society 4, 148, 173
Bethell, Christopher 107, 109, 114
Black Consciousness 97
Blackburn, Vernon 54
Blunden, Edmund 42
Undertones of War 42
Blyden, Edward W. 137
Boer(s) 1, 2, 7, 8, 9, 10, 12, 31, 32, 35,

211

41, 44, 45, 46, 47, 48, 49, 50, 51,
53, 55, 58, 59, 60, 62, 64, 65, 67,
68, 69, 74, 77, 82, 88, 96, 99, 103,
104, 105, 106, 107, 110, 111, 112,
113, 114, 133, 138, 139, 140, 141,
142, 143, 144, 146, 147, 152, 153,
154, 159, 162, 164, 169, 171, 177
(see also 'South African War')
Boer republics 39, 44, 45, 68, 109, 143
Boer War (see 'Anglo-Boer War' and
'South African War')
Boje, John 39
Bokako, Edison Malebe 23
Bosman, Herman Charles 32
  Mafeking Road 32
Bud-M'belle, Isaiah 6, 72, 150, 156,
  178
Burgers, President Thomas 105
Burnside, Janet 90, 91 (see also 'Soga,
  Rev. Tiyo')
Burton, Adv. Henry 154, 155

C
Cannon Kopje (aka Makane) 49
Cape Colony 4, 5, 6, 13, 27, 28, 31,
  37, 39, 45, 72, 145, 147, 148, 149,
  150, 153, 154, 155, 159, 177
capitalism 92, 142
Casely Hayford, J.E. 137
Cassirer, Ernst 80
  The Philosophy of Symbolic Forms
  80
Centre for Southern African Studies
  (University of York) 35
Chamberlain, Joseph 143

Chuma, Wallace 167
colonial(ism) 3, 9, 21, 22, 23, 25, 27,
  28, 29, 30, 35, 65, 87, 89, 97, 109,
  134, 135, 137, 140, 143, 160, 165
Comaroff, Jean 17, 18
Comaroff, John 2, 3, 33, 44, 45, 109,
  160, 164, 165, 166
Conrad, Joseph 93
  Heart of Darkness 93
Court of Summary Jurisdiction 8, 38,
  88, 118, 129, 156, 182
Couzens, Tim 2
Cowen, William 151
Cronje, General Piet 48, 55, 62, 74,
  96, 112, 113
Crossthwaite, Rev. Herbert 4, 5

D
Davie, Kevin 26, 27
De Wet, General Christiaan 40
decolonisation 18, 19, 22, 24, 25
Denoon, Donald 34
Du Bois, W.E.B. 21
Dube, Rev. John Langalibalele 22

E
eastern Cape region 5, 72, 89, 90, 93,
  98, 135, 140, 152
Eloff, General Sarel 63, 64
Ernest Oppenheimer Memorial
  Gardens 25

F
Farrell, J.G. 35, 40
First World War 4, 11, 96

franchise 5, 72
freebooters 107, 108, 109, 110, 112, 113
Fuller, Major-General J.F.C. 35
Fuller, Trooper William Robertson, 68

G
Garvey, Marcus 21
Gaseitsiwe, Chief 104
Gault, Hugh 40, 41
  Beleaguered and Besieged: A Year in a Place of Rocks 40
Geyer, F. 7
Glasgow Missionary Society 94
Glasgow University 90
Global North 18
Global South 18
Great Trek 74
Greener, Herbert 163
Griffiths, Andrew 46, 55
Gwynne, H.D. 163

H
Hamilton, J. Angus 13, 164, 166
  The Siege of Mafeking 166
Hayes, William 163
Historical Publications Southern Africa 89
Hobhouse, Emily 69
Honey, James 113
Hudson, George 106
Huss, Father Bernard 23

I
imperial(ism) 5, 9, 19, 31, 32, 35, 39, 54, 56, 91, 93, 97, 98, 107, 109, 110, 121, 128, 133, 134, 135, 137, 139, 141, 142, 143
Indian Rebellion (1857) 35
International Association for Literary Journalism Studies 161

J
Jabavu, John Tengo 136, 137, 140, 152, 153, 154, 160, 179
Jackal Scouts 124
Jameson Raid 109
Jones, Daniel 86
Jooste, Margaretha 41
Joubert, Commandant-General Piet 106
Jubilee Singers 75, 76, 150

K
Kant, Immanuel 80
Keate Award (1871) 105
Kenyon, J.P. 37
Kimberley 4, 5, 6, 7, 13, 23, 24, 31, 44, 46, 57, 59, 63, 71, 72, 75, 76, 84, 85, 96, 99, 106, 113, 114, 149, 150, 151, 152, 153, 154, 155, 160, 164, 165, 176, 177, 178, 179, 183
Kimberley, Earl of 108
Kreli, Chief 91

L
Lemann, Nicholas 167
Lenkoane, Patrick 151

Lennox, George 113
Levin, Bernard 33
Limb, Peter 22
literary journalism 11, 26, 46, 47, 159, 160, 161, 162, 166, 167, 169, 172
London Missionary Society 179

M

Macadoo's Minstrels 150
Mackenzie, Rev. John 109
Mafeking 2, 6, 7, 8, 9, 11, 13, 14, 20, 21, 27–28, 31–32, 34–36, 38–41, 44–47, 53, 55–59, 67, 69, 71, 74, 76–78, 82–83, 88–89, 93, 95, 109, 111–114, 138–140, 142–144, 150–152, 154, 156, 159, 161, 163, 173, 177, 179–181, 183 (see also 'Mahikeng')
Mafeking Diary (see 'Plaatje, Sol(omon) Tshekisho')
Mafeking siege (1882) 12, 102, 106, 107, 108, 109, 112, 113, 114
Mafeking siege (1899–1900) 1, 3, 7, 8, 11–14, 20, 25, 26, 28, 30, 32, 36–40, 42, 43, 45–49, 51, 54, 58–59, 62–64, 67–68, 71–74, 76–77, 81, 84, 87–89, 93, 96, 99, 109, 110, 111, 113–115, 117, 121, 126, 131, 133, 138–139, 141–142, 144–147, 156–157, 159, 160, 163, 166–167, 177, 183
Mahikeng 1, 2, 8, 11, 12, 14, 17, 20, 24, 29, 45, 104, 105, 106, 108, 111, 146, 147 (see also 'Mafeking')
Mahumapelo, Supra 45

Makgetla (Barolong) 102
Mankazana, Saul 155
Marsham, Hon. Captain 49, 100
Martinez, Monica 162
Masibi, Chief Jan 114
Matlaba, Chief 105, 106, 107, 111, 112
Matuba, Chief Abraham 110, 111
M'belle, Elizabeth 6, 72, 150 (see also 'Plaatje, Elizabeth')
Mead, Gary 31
Mfengu 6, 8, 47, 72, 82, 83, 132, 150
Midgley, John F. 166
Petticoat in Mafeking: The Siege Letters of Ada Cock 166
Millim, Anne-Marie 165
Moagi, Moses 58, 59, 60, 64
Mokae, Sabata 46
Molema, Barolong, 2
Molema, Galefele 51
Molema, Rex 2
Molema, Silas Modiri 6, 18, 45, 102, 105, 108, 111, 112, 143, 182
The Bantu, Past and Present 18
Molema, Solomon 2
Molema, Victor 44
Montshiwa, Chief (d. 1896) 102, 104, 105, 106, 107, 108, 109, 110, 112, 113, 114, 146
Montshiwa, Chief Wessels (d. 1903) 147
Moshete, Chief 105, 106, 107, 108, 109, 110
Moss, Joseph 151
Motswalle, Mafura 119, 120, 126

Msikinya, Colbourne 152
Msikinya, Rev. Davidson 152
Mzilikazi, Chief 102, 103

N
Nasson, Bill 37
  Abraham Esau's War 37
National Heritage Museum 25
nationalism 3, 35, 89, 97, 100, 135
Natives Land Act of 1913 13, 86
Ndebele 102, 103
Nel, Mrs Susarha 69
New Journalism 46 (see also 'Wolfe, Tom')
northern Cape region 24, 31, 151
Nourse, Captain H. 106
Nzewi, Meki 79

O
Orange Free State 4, 39, 69, 71, 103, 148, 177

P
Pakenham, Thomas 45
  The Boer War 45
Pan-African 21, 97
Parslow, E.G. 163
pass laws 155
Pax Britannica 12, 133, 134, 135, 137, 138, 143, 144
Payne family 76, 85, 150
Phooko, David 8, 9, 57, 75, 100, 151, 168
Plaatje, Elizabeth 8, 14, 88, 92, 150, 152, 163, 177, 178, 179, 180, 181, 182, 183 (see also 'M'belle, Elizabeth')
Plaatje, Frederick St Leger ('Sainty') 8, 164, 178, 180, 181, 182
Plaatje, Gabriel 113
Plaatje, Sol(omon) Tshekisho 1–14, 18–30, 34–40, 42–53, 55–61, 64–65, 67, 71–78, 81–99, 101–102, 111–113, 115, 132–136, 138–140, 143–156, 159–169, 171–173, 177–179, 181–183
  The Boer War Diary of Sol T. Plaatje 33, 34, 35, 36, 38, 39, 41, 42
  The Mafeking Diary of Sol T. Plaatje 1, 2, 3, 4, 10, 13, 19, 20, 23, 24, 25, 26, 27, 28, 29, 30, 87, 88, 89, 92, 145, 149, 152, 159, 161, 162, 164, 165, 166, 167, 173
  Mhudi 2, 3, 21, 22, 23, 25, 36, 44, 46, 86, 102
  Native Life in South Africa 1, 3, 13, 21, 25, 36, 44, 86, 165, 167
Plaatje, Violet 1, 2
Potgieter, Hendrik 103
Pretoria Convention (1881) 107, 108
Progressives 154
Protestantism 22, 92

R
racial capitalism 22
Rapulana (Barolong) 4, 101, 102, 103, 104, 105, 106, 107, 110, 111
Ratlou (Barolong) 4, 101, 102, 103, 104, 105, 106, 107, 108, 109, 110

Ratshidi (Barolong) 20, 101, 102, 103, 104, 105, 106, 107, 108, 110, 111, 112, 114 (see also 'Tshidi (Barolong)')
Reed, Andrew 2
Reynolds, Bill 161
Rhodes, Cecil 154, 155
Rosa Mendes, Pedro 166
Ross, Edward 75
Rothmann, F.L. 35
  Oorlogsdagboek 35

S
Saane, Chief 110, 153
Samson, Barnabas 82
Sand River Convention 104
Sandile, Chief 90, 91, 94, 99
Saunders, Frederick 166
  Mafeking Memories 166
Schopenhauer, Arthur 80
Schreiner, Cronwright 5
Schreiner, Olive 5
Seleka (Barolong) 4, 102
Siege of Kimberley 37, 77, 177
Siege of Ladysmith 46, 52, 53, 54, 77
Siege of Mafeking (see 'Mafeking siege (1899–1900)')
Sgarro, Victoria 161
Smith, Scotty (see 'George Lennox')
Smith, Sir Harry 57
Snyman, General Jacobus 41, 48, 96, 110, 112, 113, 153
Snyman Treaty 112
Soga, Jotello 90
Soga, Nosuthu 90

Soga, Rev. Tiyo 12, 87, 88, 89, 90, 91, 92, 93, 94, 95, 96, 97, 98, 99, 100
Sol Plaatje (see 'Plaatje, Sol(omon) Tshekisho')
Sol Plaatje Educational Trust and Museum 24
Sol Plaatje University 13, 46
South Africans Improvement Society 5, 72, 149, 151, 153, 160, 173, 177
South African Native National Congress (SANNC) 3, 4, 21, 22, 24, 44 (see also 'African National Congress')
South African Republic (SAR) 104, 105, 106
South African War (1899–1902) 1, 2, 4, 8, 10, 11, 12, 14, 25, 27, 31, 34, 36, 37, 39, 40, 41, 44, 46, 109, 115, 133, 134, 140, 141, 143, 145, 146, 147, 151, 159, 161
southern Africa 5, 6, 20, 134, 135, 138, 146, 152
Starfield, Jane 26
Steevens, George Warrington 11, 27, 46, 52, 53, 54, 55, 56, 77
  From Capetown to Ladysmith 52, 54
Steinitz, Rebecca 92, 94, 95
Stent, Vere 13, 162, 163
Stuart, Sergeant 47

T
Tau, Chief 102, 146
Taylor, Jane 26
Tshidi (Barolong) 4, 12, 36, 41, 101,

102, 105, 107, 114, 144, 146, 147 (see also 'Ratshidi (Barolong)')
Transvaal 9, 36, 45, 68, 105, 106, 107, 108, 109, 110, 112, 113, 114, 153, 154

U
University of Bophuthatswana (aka Unibo) 17, 18
University of Cape Town 24
University of Hull 32, 37
University of Johannesburg 13
University of London 38
University of South Africa 13
University of the North-West 17
University of the Witwatersrand 44
University of York 36

V
Ventner, Sol 40, 41 (see also 'Gault, Hugh')

W
War Museum of the Boer Republics 40
War of Mlanjeni (1850–1853) 90
War of the Axe (1846–1847) 90
Warren, Charles 109, 147
Warwick, Peter 36
   Black People and the South African War 36, 37

Weber, Max 92
Webers, Commandant Carl Hendrick 106
West Africa 12, 134, 135, 136, 137, 138, 140, 141, 142, 143, 144, 151, 153
Westphal, Marie 5, 72, 148, 173
Westphal, Rev. Ernst 4, 5, 7, 72, 148, 154, 155, 173
white man's war 2, 25, 38, 39, 55, 65, 66, 110
Willan, Brian 2, 18, 20, 23, 25, 26, 27, 28, 37, 44, 46, 55, 87, 88, 89, 92, 100, 101, 102, 111, 160, 162, 163, 164
   Sol Plaatje: A Biography 20, 23, 162
   Sol Plaatje: A Life of Solomon Tshekisho Plaatje, 1876–1932 20, 44
Wolfe, Tom 46, 167, 168 (see also 'New Journalism')

X
Xhosa Cattle-Killing 91

Z
Zachernuk, Philip 143
Zola, Émile 178
   The Ladies' Paradise 178, 179